Effective STL

Addison-Wesley Professional Computing Series

Brian W. Kernighan, Consulting Editor

Ken Arnold/John Peyton, *A C User's Guide to ANSI C*

Matthew H. Austern, *Generic Programming and the STL: Using and Extending the C++ Standard Template Library*

David R. Butenhof, *Programming with POSIX® Threads*

Brent Callaghan, *NFS Illustrated*

Tom Cargill, *C++ Programming Style*

William R. Cheswick/Steven M. Bellovin, *Firewalls and Internet Security: Repelling the Wily Hacker*

David A. Curry, *UNIX® System Security: A Guide for Users and System Administrators*

Erich Gamma/Richard Helm/Ralph Johnson/John Vlissides, *Design Patterns: Elements of Reusable Object-Oriented Software*

Erich Gamma/Richard Helm/Ralph Johnson/John Vlissides, *Design Patterns CD: Elements of Reusable Object-Oriented Software*

Peter Haggar, *Practical Java™ Programming Language Guide*

David R. Hanson, *C Interfaces and Implementations: Techniques for Creating Reusable Software*

Mark Harrison/Michael McLennan, *Effective Tcl/Tk Programming: Writing Better Programs with Tcl and Tk*

Michi Henning/Steve Vinoski, *Advanced CORBA® Programming with C++*

Brian W. Kernighan/Rob Pike, *The Practice of Programming*

S. Keshav, *An Engineering Approach to Computer Networking: ATM Networks, the Internet, and the Telephone Network*

John Lakos, *Large-Scale C++ Software Design*

Scott Meyers, *Effective C++ CD: 85 Specific Ways to Improve Your Programs and Designs*

Scott Meyers, *Effective C++, Second Edition: 50 Specific Ways to Improve Your Programs and Designs*

Scott Meyers, *More Effective C++: 35 New Ways to Improve Your Programs and Designs*

Scott Meyers, *Effective STL: 50 Specific Ways to Improve Your Use of the Standard Template Library*

Robert B. Murray, *C++ Strategies and Tactics*

David R. Musser/Gillmer J. Derge/Atul Saini, *STL Tutorial and Reference Guide, Second Edition: C++ Programming with the Standard Template Library*

John K. Ousterhout, *Tcl and the Tk Toolkit*

Craig Partridge, *Gigabit Networking*

J. Stephen Pendergrast Jr., *Desktop KornShell Graphical Programming*

Radia Perlman, *Interconnections, Second Edition: Bridges, Routers, Switches, and Internetworking Protocols*

Stephen A. Rago, *UNIX® System V Network Programming*

Curt Schimmel, *UNIX® Systems for Modern Architectures: Symmetric Multiprocessing and Caching for Kernel Programmers*

W. Richard Stevens, *Advanced Programming in the UNIX® Environment*

W. Richard Stevens, *TCP/IP Illustrated, Volume 1: The Protocols*

W. Richard Stevens, *TCP/IP Illustrated, Volume 3: TCP for Transactions, HTTP, NNTP, and the UNIX® Domain Protocols*

Gary R. Wright/W. Richard Stevens, *TCP/IP Illustrated, Volume 2: The Implementation*

Ruixi Yuan/ W. Timothy Strayer, *Virtual Private Networks: Technologies and Solutions*

Please see our web site (http://www.awl.com/cseng/series/professionalcomputing) for more information on these titles.

Effective STL

50 Specific Ways to Improve Your Use of the Standard Template Library

Scott Meyers

ADDISON–WESLEY

Boston • San Francisco • New York • Toronto • Montreal
London • Munich • Paris • Madrid
Capetown • Sydney • Tokyo • Singapore • Mexico City

Many of the designations used by manufacturers and sellers to distinguish their products are claimed as trademarks. Where those designations appear in this book, and we were aware of a trademark claim, the designations have been printed in initial capital letters or in all capitals.

The author and publisher have taken care in the preparation of this book, but make no expressed or implied warranty of any kind and assume no responsibility for errors or omissions. No liability is assumed for incidental or consequential damages in connection with or arising out of the use of the information or programs contained herein.

The excerpt from *How the Grinch Stole Christmas!* by Dr. Suess is trademarked and copyright © Dr. Suess Enterprises, L.P., 1957 (renewed 1985). Used by permission of Random House Children's Books, a division of Random House, Inc.

The publisher offers discounts on this book when ordered in quantity for special sales. For more information, please contact:

Pearson Education Corporate Sales Division
201 W. 103rd Street
Indianapolis, IN 46290
(800) 428-5331
corpsales@pearsoned.com

Visit AW on the Web: www.awl.com/cseng/

Library of Congress Cataloging-in-Publication Data
Meyer, Scott (Scott Douglas)
  Effective STL: 50 specific ways to improve your use of the standard template library/
  Scott Meyers.
    p. cm.— (Addison-Wesley professional computing series)
  Includes bibliographical references and index.
  ISBN: 0-201-74962-9
  1. C++ (Computer program language) 2. Standard template library. I. Title. II. Series.

  QA76.73.C153.M49 2001
  005.13'3—dc21

                                                    2001022851
                                                    CIP

ISBN 0-201-74962-9
Text printed on recycled paper
2 3 4 5 6 7 8 9 10—CRW—0504030201
Second printing, July 2001

For Woofieland.

Contents

Preface

It came without ribbons! It came without tags!
It came without packages, boxes or bags!

— Dr. Seuss, *How the Grinch Stole Christmas!*, Random House, 1957

I first wrote about the Standard Template Library in 1995, when I concluded the final Item of *More Effective C++* with a brief STL overview. I should have known better. Shortly thereafter, I began receiving mail asking when I'd write *Effective STL*.

I resisted the idea for several years. At first, I wasn't familiar enough with the STL to offer advice on it, but as time went on and my experience with it grew, this concern gave way to other reservations. There was never any question that the library represented a breakthrough in efficient and extensible design, but when it came to *using* the STL, there were practical problems I couldn't overlook. Porting all but the simplest STL programs was a challenge, not only because library implementations varied, but also because template support in the underlying compilers ranged from good to awful. STL tutorials were hard to come by, so learning "the STL way of programming" was difficult, and once that hurdle was overcome, finding comprehensible and accurate reference documentation was a challenge. Perhaps most daunting, even the smallest STL usage error often led to a blizzard of compiler diagnostics, each thousands of characters long, most referring to classes, functions, or templates not mentioned in the offending source code, almost all incomprehensible. Though I had great admiration for the STL and for the people behind it, I felt uncomfortable recommending it to practicing programmers. I wasn't sure it was *possible* to use the STL effectively.

Then I began to notice something that took me by surprise. Despite the portability problems, despite the dismal documentation, despite the compiler diagnostics resembling transmission line noise, many of my consulting clients were using the STL anyway. Furthermore, they weren't just playing with it, they were using it in production code! That was a revelation. I knew that the STL featured an elegant design, but any library for which programmers are willing to endure portability headaches, poor documentation, and incomprehensible error messages has a lot more going for it than just good design. For an increasingly large number of professional programmers, I realized, even a bad implementation of the STL was preferable to no implementation at all.

Furthermore, I knew that the situation regarding the STL would only get better. Libraries and compilers would grow more conformant with the Standard (they have), better documentation would become available (it has — consult the bibliography beginning on page 225), and compiler diagnostics would improve (for the most part, we're still waiting, but Item 49 offers suggestions for how to cope while we wait). I therefore decided to chip in and do my part for the STL movement. This book is the result: 50 specific ways to improve your use of C++'s Standard Template Library.

My original plan was to write the book in the second half of 1999, and with that thought in mind, I put together an outline. But then I changed course. I suspended work on the book and developed an introductory training course on the STL, which I then taught several times to groups of programmers. About a year later, I returned to the book, significantly revising the outline based on my experiences with the training course. In the same way that my *Effective C++* has been successful by being grounded in the problems faced by real programmers, it's my hope that *Effective STL* similarly addresses the practical aspects of STL programming — the aspects most important to professional developers.

I am always on the lookout for ways to improve my understanding of C++. If you have suggestions for new guidelines for STL programming or if you have comments on the guidelines in this book, please let me know. In addition, it is my continuing goal to make this book as accurate as possible, so for each error in this book that is reported to me — be it technical, grammatical, typographical, or otherwise — I will, in future printings, gladly add to the acknowledgments the name of the first person to bring that error to my attention. Send your suggested guidelines, your comments, and your criticisms to estl@aristeia.com.

I maintain a list of changes to this book since its first printing, including bug-fixes, clarifications, and technical updates. The list is available at the *Effective STL Errata* web site, http://www.aristeia.com/BookErrata/estl1e-errata.html.

If you'd like to be notified when I make changes to this book, I encourage you to join my mailing list. I use the list to make announcements likely to be of interest to people who follow my work on C++. For details, consult http://www.aristeia.com/MailingList/.

SCOTT DOUGLAS MEYERS   STAFFORD, OREGON
http://www.aristeia.com/   APRIL 2001

Acknowledgments

I had an enormous amount of help during the roughly two years it took me to make some sense of the STL, create a training course on it, and write this book. Of all my sources of assistance, two were particularly important. The first is Mark Rodgers. Mark generously volunteered to review my training materials as I created them, and I learned more about the STL from him than from anybody else. He also acted as a technical reviewer for this book, again providing observations and insights that improved virtually every Item.

The other outstanding source of information was several C++-related Usenet newsgroups, especially comp.lang.c++.moderated ("clcm"), comp.std.c++, and microsoft.public.vc.stl. For well over a decade, I've depended on the participants in newsgroups like these to answer my questions and challenge my thinking, and it's difficult to imagine what I'd do without them. I am deeply grateful to the Usenet community for their help with both this book and my prior publications on C++.

My understanding of the STL was shaped by a variety of publications, the most important of which are listed in the Bibliography. I leaned especially heavily on Josuttis' *The C++ Standard Library* [3].

This book is fundamentally a summary of insights and observations made by others, though a few of the ideas are my own. I've tried to keep track of where I learned what, but the task is hopeless, because a typical Item contains information garnered from many sources over a long period of time. What follows is incomplete, but it's the best I can do. Please note that my goal here is to summarize where *I* first learned of an idea or technique, not where the idea or technique was originally developed or who came up with it.

In Item 1, my observation that node-based containers offer better support for transactional semantics is based on section 5.11.2 of Josuttis' *The C++ Standard Library* [3]. Item 2 includes an example from Mark Rodgers on how typedefs help when allocator types are changed.

Item 5 was motivated by Reeves' *C++ Report* column, "STL Gotchas" [17]. Item 8 sprang from Item 37 in Sutter's *Exceptional C++* [8], and Kevlin Henney provided important details on how containers of auto_ptrs fail in practice. In Usenet postings, Matt Austern provided examples of when allocators are useful, and I include his examples in Item 11. Item 12 is based on the discussion of thread safety at the SGI STL web site [21]. The material in Item 13 on the performance implications of reference counting in a multithreaded environment is drawn from Sutter's writings on this topic [20]. The idea for Item 15 came from Reeves' *C++ Report* column, "Using Standard string in the Real World, Part 2," [18]. In Item 16, Mark Rodgers came up with the technique I show for having a C API write data directly into a vector. Item 17 includes information from Usenet postings by Siemel Naran and Carl Barron. I stole Item 18 from Sutter's *C++ Report* column, "When Is a Container Not a Container?" [12]. In Item 20, Mark Rodgers contributed the idea of transforming a pointer into an object via a dereferencing functor, and Scott Lewandowski came up with the version of DereferenceLess I present. Item 21 originated in a Doug Harrison posting to microsoft.public.vc.stl, but the decision to restrict the focus of that Item to equality was mine. I based Item 22 on Sutter's *C++ Report* column, "Standard Library News: sets and maps" [13]; Matt Austern helped me understand the status of the Standardization Committee's Library Issue #103. Item 23 was inspired by Austern's *C++ Report* article, "Why You Shouldn't Use set — and What to Use Instead" [15]; David Smallberg provided a neat refinement for my implementation of DataCompare. My description of Dinkumware's hashed containers is based on Plauger's *C/C++ Users Journal* column, "Hash Tables" [16]. Mark Rodgers doesn't agree with the overall advice of Item 26, but an early motivation for that Item was his observation that some container member functions accept only arguments of type iterator. My treatment of Item 29 was motivated and informed by Usenet discussions involving Matt Austern and James Kanze; I was also influenced by Kreft and Langer's *C++ Report* article, "A Sophisticated Implementation of User-Defined Inserters and Extractors" [25]. Item 30 is due to a discussion in section 5.4.2 of Josuttis' *The C++ Standard Library* [3]. In Item 31, Marco Dalla Gasperina contributed the example use of nth_element to calculate medians, and use of that algorithm for finding percentiles comes straight out of section 18.7.1 of Stroustrup's *The C++ Programming Language* [7]. Item 32 was influenced by the material in section 5.6.1 of Josuttis' *The C++ Standard Library* [3]. Item 35 originated in Austern's *C++ Report* column "How to Do Case-Insensitive String Comparison" [11], and James Kanze's and John Potter's clcm postings helped me refine my understanding of the issues involved. Stroustrup's implementation for copy_if, which I show in Item 36, is from section 18.6.1 of his *The C++ Programming Language* [7]. Item 39 was largely motivated by the publications of Josuttis, who has written about "stateful predicates" in his *The C++ Standard Library* [3], in Standard Library Issue #92, and in his *C++ Report* article, "Predicates vs. Function Objects" [14]. In my treatment, I use his example and recommend a solution he has proposed, though the use of the term "pure function" is my own. Matt Austern confirmed my suspicion in Item 41 about the history of the terms mem_fun and mem_fun_ref. Item 42 can be traced to a lecture I got from Mark Rodgers when I considered violating that guideline. Mark Rodgers is also responsible for the insight in Item 44 that non-member searches over maps and multimaps examine both components of each pair, while member searches examine only the first (key) component. Item 45 contains information from various clcm contributors, including John Potter, Marcin Kasperski, Pete Becker, Dennis Yelle, and David Abrahams. David Smallberg alerted me to the utility of equal_range in performing equivalence-based searches and counts over sorted sequence containers. Andrei Alexandrescu helped me understand the conditions under which "the reference-to-reference problem" I describe in Item 50 arises, and I modeled my example of the problem on a similar example provided by Mark Rodgers at the Boost Web Site [22].

Credit for the material in Appendix A goes to Matt Austern, of course. I'm grateful that he not only gave me permission to include it in this book, he also tweaked it to make it even better than the original.

Good technical books require a thorough pre-publication vetting, and I was fortunate to benefit from the insights of an unusually talented group of technical reviewers. Brian Kernighan and Cliff Green offered early comments on a partial draft, and complete versions of the manuscript were scrutinized by Doug Harrison, Brian Kernighan, Tim Johnson, Francis Glassborow, Andrei Alexandrescu, David Smallberg, Aaron Campbell, Jared Manning, Herb Sutter, Stephen Dewhurst, Matt Austern, Gillmer Derge, Aaron Moore, Thomas Becker, Victor Von, and, of course, Mark Rodgers. Katrina Avery did the copyediting.

One of the most challenging parts of preparing a book is finding good technical reviewers. I thank John Potter for introducing me to Jared Manning and Aaron Campbell.

Herb Sutter kindly agreed to act as my surrogate in compiling, running, and reporting on the behavior of some STL test programs under a beta version of Microsoft's Visual Studio .NET, while Leor Zolman undertook the herculean task of testing all the code in this book. Any errors that remain are my fault, of course, not Herb's or Leor's.

Angelika Langer opened my eyes to the indeterminate status of some aspects of STL function objects. This book has less to say about function objects than it otherwise might, but what it does say is more likely to remain true. At least I hope it is.

This printing of the book is better than earlier printings, because I was able to address problems identified by the following sharp-eyed readers: Jon Webb, Michael Hawkins, Derek Price, and Jim Scheller. I'm grateful for their help in improving *Effective STL*.

My collaborators at Addison-Wesley included John Wait (my editor and now a senior VP), Alicia Carey and Susannah Buzard (his assistants n and $n+1$), John Fuller (the production coordinator), Karin Hansen (the cover designer), Jason Jones (all-around technical guru, especially with respect to the demonic software spewed forth by Adobe), Marty Rabinowitz (their boss, but he works, too), and Curt Johnson, Chanda Leary-Coutu, and Robin Bruce (all marketing people, but still very nice).

Abbi Staley made Sunday lunches a routinely pleasurable experience.

As she has for the six books and one CD that came before it, my wife, Nancy, tolerated the demands of my research and writing with her usual forbearance and offered me encouragement and support when I needed it most. She never fails to remind me that there's more to life than C++ and software.

And then there's our dog, Persephone. As I write this, it is her sixth birthday. Tonight, she and Nancy and I will visit Baskin-Robbins for ice cream. Persephone will have vanilla. One scoop. In a cup. To go.

Introduction

You're already familiar with the STL. You know how to create containers, iterate over their contents, add and remove elements, and apply common algorithms, such as find and sort. But you're not satisfied. You can't shake the sensation that the STL offers more than you're taking advantage of. Tasks that should be simple aren't. Operations that should be straightforward leak resources or behave erratically. Procedures that should be efficient demand more time or memory than you're willing to give them. Yes, you know how to use the STL, but you're not sure you're using it *effectively*.

I wrote this book for you.

In *Effective STL*, I explain how to combine STL components to take full advantage of the library's design. Such information allows you to develop simple, straightforward solutions to simple, straightforward problems, and it also helps you design elegant approaches to more complicated problems. I describe common STL usage errors, and I show you how to avoid them. That helps you dodge resource leaks, code that won't port, and behavior that is undefined. I discuss ways to optimize your code, so you can make the STL perform like the fast, sleek machine it is intended to be.

The information in this book will make you a better STL programmer. It will make you a more productive programmer. And it will make you a happier programmer. Using the STL is fun, but using it effectively is outrageous fun, the kind of fun where they have to drag you away from the keyboard, because you just can't believe the good time you're having. Even a cursory glance at the STL reveals that it is a wondrously cool library, but the coolness runs broader and deeper than you probably imagine. One of my primary goals in this book is to convey to you just how amazing the library is, because in the nearly 30 years I've been programming, I've never seen anything like the STL. You probably haven't either.

Defining, Using, and Extending the STL

There is no official definition of "the STL," and different people mean different things when they use the term. In this book, "the STL" means the parts of C++'s Standard Library that work with iterators. That includes the standard containers (including string), parts of the iostream library, function objects, and algorithms. It excludes the standard container adapters (stack, queue, and priority_queue) as well as the containers bitset and valarray, because they lack iterator support. It doesn't include arrays, either. True, arrays support iterators in the form of pointers, but arrays are part of the C++ *language*, not the library.

Technically, my definition of the STL excludes extensions of the standard C++ library, notably hashed containers, singly linked lists, ropes, and a variety of nonstandard function objects. Even so, an effective STL programmer needs to be aware of such extensions, so I mention them where it's appropriate. Indeed, Item 25 is devoted to an overview of nonstandard hashed containers. They're not in the STL now, but something similar to them is almost certain to make it into the next version of the standard C++ library, and there's value in glimpsing the future.

One of the reasons for the existence of STL extensions is that the STL is a library designed to be extended. In this book, however, I focus on *using* the STL, not on adding new components to it. You'll find, for example, that I have little to say about writing your own algorithms, and I offer no guidance at all on writing new containers and iterators. I believe that it's important to master what the STL already provides before you embark on increasing its capabilities, so that's what I focus on in *Effective STL*. When you decide to create your own STLesque components, you'll find advice on how to do it in books like Josuttis' *The C++ Standard Library* [3] and Austern's *Generic Programming and the STL* [4]. One aspect of STL extension I *do* discuss in this book is writing your own function objects. You can't use the STL effectively without knowing how to do that, so I've devoted an entire chapter to the topic (Chapter 6).

Citations

The references to the books by Josuttis and Austern in the preceding paragraph demonstrate how I handle bibliographic citations. In general, I try to mention enough of a cited work to identify it for people who are already familiar with it. If you already know about these authors' books, for example, you don't have to turn to the Bibliography to find out that [3] and [4] refer to books you already know. If you're not familiar with a publication, of course, the Bibliography (which begins on page 225) gives you a full citation.

I cite three works often enough that I generally leave off the citation number. The first of these is the International Standard for C++ [5], which I usually refer to as simply "the Standard." The other two are my earlier books on C++, *Effective C++* [1] and *More Effective C++* [2].

The STL and Standards

I refer to the C++ Standard frequently, because *Effective STL* focuses on portable, standard-conformant C++. In theory, everything I show in this book will work with every C++ implementation. In practice, that isn't true. Shortcomings in compiler and STL implementations conspire to prevent some valid code from compiling or from behaving the way it's supposed to. Where that is commonly the case, I describe the problems, and I explain how you can work around them.

Sometimes, the easiest workaround is to use a different STL implementation. Appendix B gives an example of when this is the case. In fact, the more you work with the STL, the more important it becomes to distinguish between your *compilers* and your *library implementations*. When programmers run into difficulties trying to get legitimate code to compile, it's customary for them to blame their compilers, but with the STL, compilers can be fine, while STL implementations are faulty. To emphasize the fact that you are dependent on both your compilers and your library implementations, I refer to your *STL platforms*. An STL platform is the combination of a particular compiler and a particular STL implementation. In this book, if I mention a compiler problem, you can be sure that I mean it's the compiler that's the culprit. However, if I refer to a problem with your STL platform, you should interpret that as "maybe a compiler bug, maybe a library bug, possibly both."

I generally refer to your "compilers" — *plural*. That's an outgrowth of my longstanding belief that you improve the quality (especially the portability) of your code if you ensure that it works with more than one compiler. Furthermore, using multiple compilers generally makes it easier to unravel the Gordian nature of error messages arising from improper use of the STL. (Item 49 is devoted to approaches to decoding such messages.)

Another aspect of my emphasis on standard-conforming code is my concern that you avoid constructs with undefined behavior. Such constructs may do anything at runtime. Unfortunately, this means they may do precisely what you want them to, and that can lead to a false sense of security. Too many programmers assume that undefined behavior always leads to an obvious problem, e.g., a segmentation fault or other catastrophic failure. The results of undefined behavior can actually be much more subtle, e.g., corruption of rarely-referenced data. They can also vary across program runs. I find that a good working definition of undefined behavior is "works for me, works for you, works during development and QA, but blows up in your most important customer's face." It's important to avoid undefined behavior, so I point out common situations where it can arise. You should train yourself to be alert for such situations.

Reference Counting

It's close to impossible to discuss the STL without mentioning reference counting. As you'll see in Items 7 and 33, designs based on containers of pointers almost invariably lead to reference counting. In addition, many string implementations are internally reference counted, and, as Item 15 explains, this may be an implementation detail you can't afford to ignore. In this book, I assume that you are familiar with the basics of reference counting. If you're not, most intermediate and advanced C++ texts cover the topic. In *More Effective C++*, for example, the relevant material is in Items 28 and 29. If you don't know what reference counting is and you have no inclination to learn, don't worry. You'll get through this book just fine, though there may be a few sentences here and there that won't make as much sense as they otherwise would.

string and wstring

Whatever I say about string applies equally well to its wide-character counterpart, wstring. Similarly, any time I refer to the relationship between string and char or char*, the same is true of the relationship between wstring and wchar_t or wchar_t*. In other words, just because I don't explicitly mention wide-character strings in this book, don't assume that the STL fails to support them. It supports them as well as char-based strings. It has to. Both string and wstring are instantiations of the same template, basic_string.

Terms, Terms, Terms

This is not an introductory book on the STL, so I assume you know the fundamentals. Still, the following terms are sufficiently important that I feel compelled to review them:

- vector, string, deque, and list are known as the *standard sequence containers*. The *standard associative containers* are set, multiset, map, and multimap.

- Iterators are divided into five categories, based on the operations they support. Very briefly, *input iterators* are read-only iterators where each iterated location may be read only once. *Output iterators* are write-only iterators where each iterated location may be written only once. Input and output iterators are modeled on reading and writing input and output streams (e.g., files). It's thus unsurprising that the most common manifestations of input and output iterators are istream_iterators and ostream_iterators, respectively.

  Forward iterators have the capabilities of both input and output iterators, but they can read or write a single location repeatedly. They don't support operator--, so they can move only forward with any degree of efficiency. All standard STL containers support iterators that are more powerful than forward iterators, but, as you'll see in Item 25, one design for hashed containers yields forward iterators. Containers for singly linked lists (considered in Item 50) also offer forward iterators.

  Bidirectional iterators are just like forward iterators, except they can go backward as easily as they go forward. The standard associative containers all offer bidirectional iterators. So does list.

  Random access iterators do everything bidirectional iterators do, but they also offer "iterator arithmetic," i.e., the ability to jump forward or backward in a single step. vector, string, and deque each provide random access iterators. Pointers into arrays act as random access iterators for the arrays.

- Any class that overloads the function call operator (i.e., operator()) is a *functor class*. Objects created from such classes are known as *function objects* or *functors*. Most places in the STL that work with function objects work equally well with real functions, so I often use the term "function objects" to mean both C++ functions as well as true function objects.

- The functions bind1st and bind2nd are known as *binders*.

A revolutionary aspect of the STL is its complexity guarantees. These guarantees bound the amount of work any STL operation is allowed to perform. This is wonderful, because it can help you determine the relative efficiency of different approaches to the same problem, regardless of the STL platform you're using. Unfortunately, the terminology behind the complexity guarantees can be confusing if you haven't been formally introduced to the jargon of computer science. Here's a quick primer on the complexity terms I use in this book. Each refers to how long it takes to do something as a function of n, the number of elements in a container or range.

- An operation that runs in *constant time* has performance that is unaffected by changes in n. For example, inserting an element into a list is a constant-time operation. Regardless of whether the list has one element or one million, the insertion takes about the same amount of time.

  Don't take the term "constant time" too literally. It doesn't mean that the amount of time it takes to do something is literally constant, it just means that it's unaffected by n. For example, two STL platforms might take dramatically different amounts of time to perform the same "constant-time" operation. This could happen if one library has a much more sophisticated implementation than another or if one compiler performs substantially more aggressive optimization.

- An operation that runs in *logarithmic time* needs more time to run as n gets larger, but the time it requires grows at a rate proportional to the logarithm of n. For example, an operation on a million items would be expected to take only about three times as long as on a hundred items, because $\log n^3 = 3 \log n$. Most search operations on associative containers (e.g., set::find) are logarithmic-time operations.

- The time needed to perform an operation that runs in *linear time* increases at a rate proportional to increases in n. The standard algorithm count runs in linear time, because it has to look at every element of the range it's given. If the range triples in size, it has to do three times as much work, and we'd expect it to take about three times as long to do it.

As a general rule, a constant-time operation runs faster than one requiring logarithmic time, and a logarithmic-time operation runs faster than one whose performance is linear. This is always true when n gets big enough, but for relatively small values of n, it's sometimes possible for an operation with a worse theoretical complexity to outperform an operation with a better theoretical complexity. If you'd like to know more about STL complexity guarantees, turn to Josuttis' *The C++ Standard Library* [3].

As a final note on terminology, recall that each element in a map or multimap has two components. I generally call the first component the *key* and the second component the *value*. Given

```
map<string, double> m;
```

for example, the string is the key and the double is the value.

Code Examples

This book is filled with example code, and I explain each example when I introduce it. Still, it's worth knowing a few things in advance.

You can see from the map example above that I routinely omit #includes and ignore the fact that STL components are in namespace std. When defining the map m, I could have written this,

```
#include <map>
#include <string>

using std::map;
using std::string;

map<string, double> m;
```

but I prefer to save us both the noise.

When I declare a formal type parameter for a template, I use typename instead of class. That is, instead of writing this,

```
template<class T>
class Widget { ... };
```

I write this:

```
template<typename T>
class Widget { ... };
```

In this context, class and typename mean exactly the same thing, but I find that typename more clearly expresses what I usually want to say: that *any* type will do; T need not be a class. If you prefer to use class to declare type parameters, go right ahead. Whether to use typename or class in this context is purely a matter of style.

It is not a matter of style in a different context. To avoid potential parsing ambiguities (the details of which I'll spare you), you are required to use typename to precede type names that are dependent on formal type parameters. Such types are known as *dependent types*, and an example will help clarify what I'm talking about. Suppose you'd like to write a template for a function that, given an STL container, returns whether the last element in the container is greater than the first element. Here's one way to do it:

```
template<typename C>
bool lastGreaterThanFirst(const C& container)
{
   if (container.empty()) return false;

   typename C::const_iterator begin(container.begin());
   typename C::const_iterator end(container.end());

   return *--end > *begin;
}
```

In this example, the local variables begin and end are of type
C::const_iterator. const_iterator is a type that is dependent on the formal
type parameter C. Because C::const_iterator is a dependent type, you
are required to precede it with the word typename. (Some compilers incorrectly accept the code without the typenames, but such code isn't
portable.)

I hope you've noticed my use of color in the examples above. It's there
to focus your attention on parts of the code that are particularly important. Often, I highlight the differences between related examples,
such as when I showed the two possible ways to declare the parameter T in the Widget example. This use of color to call out especially
noteworthy parts of examples carries over to diagrams, too. For instance, this diagram from Item 5 uses color to identify the two pointers that are affected when a new element is inserted into a list:

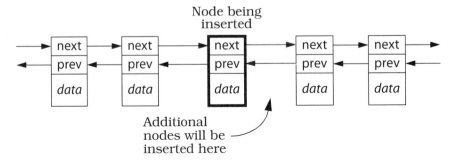

I also use color for chapter numbers, but such use is purely gratuitous. This being my first two-color book, I hope you'll forgive me a little chromatic exuberance.

Two of my favorite parameter names are lhs and rhs. They stand for
"left-hand side" and "right-hand side," respectively, and I find them
especially useful when declaring operators. Here's an example from
Item 19:

```
class Widget { ... };

bool operator==(const Widget& lhs, const Widget& rhs);
```

When this function is called in a context like this,

```
if (x == y) ...                              // assume x and y are Widgets
```

x, which is on the left-hand side of the "==", is known as lhs inside operator==, and y is known as rhs.

As for the class name Widget, that has nothing to do with GUIs or toolkits. It's just the name I use for "some class that does something." Sometimes, as on page 7, Widget is a class template instead of a class. In such cases, you may find that I still refer to Widget as a class, even though it's really a template. Such sloppiness about the difference between classes and class templates, structs and struct templates, and functions and function templates hurts no one as long as there is no ambiguity about what is being discussed. In cases where it could be confusing, I do distinguish between templates and the classes, structs, and functions they generate.

Efficiency Items

I considered including a chapter on efficiency in *Effective STL*, but I ultimately decided that the current organization was preferable. Still, a number of Items focus on minimizing space and runtime demands. For your performance-enhancing convenience, here is the table of contents for the virtual chapter on efficiency:

The Guidelines in *Effective STL*

The guidelines that make up the 50 Items in this book are based on the insights and advice of the world's most experienced STL programmers. These guidelines summarize things you should almost always do — or almost always avoid doing — to get the most out of the Standard Template Library. At the same time, they're just guidelines. Under some conditions, it makes sense to violate them. For example, the title of Item 7 tells you to invoke delete on newed pointers in a container before the container is destroyed, but the text of that Item makes clear that this applies only when the objects pointed to by those pointers should go away when the container does. This is often the case, but it's not universally true. Similarly, the title of Item 35 beseeches you to use STL algorithms to perform simple case-insensitive string comparisons, but the text of the Item points out that in some cases, you'll be better off using a function that's not only outside the STL, it's not even part of standard C++!

Only you know enough about the software you're writing, the environment in which it will run, and the context in which it's being created to determine whether it's reasonable to violate the guidelines I present. Most of the time, it won't be, and the discussions that accompany each Item explain why. In a few cases, it will. Slavish devotion to the guidelines isn't appropriate, but neither is cavalier disregard. Before venturing off on your own, you should make sure you have a good reason.

1

Containers

Sure, the STL has iterators, algorithms, and function objects, but for most C++ programmers, it's the containers that stand out. More powerful and flexible than arrays, they grow (and often shrink) dynamically, manage their own memory, keep track of how many objects they hold, bound the algorithmic complexity of the operations they support, and much, much more. Their popularity is easy to understand. They're simply better than their competition, regardless of whether that competition comes from containers in other libraries or is a container type you'd write yourself. STL containers aren't just good. They're *really* good.

This chapter is devoted to guidelines applicable to all the STL containers. Later chapters focus on specific container types. The topics addressed here include selecting the appropriate container given the constraints you face; avoiding the delusion that code written for one container type is likely to work with other container types; the significance of copying operations for objects in containers; difficulties that arise when pointers of auto_ptrs are stored in containers; the ins and outs of erasing; what you can and cannot accomplish with custom allocators; tips on how to maximize efficiency; and considerations for using containers in a threaded environment.

That's a lot of ground to cover, but don't worry. The Items break it down into bite-sized chunks, and along the way, you're almost sure to pick up several ideas you can apply to your code *now*.

Item 1:   Choose your containers with care.

You know that C++ puts a variety of containers at your disposal, but do you realize just how varied that variety is? To make sure you haven't overlooked any of your options, here's a quick review.

- The **standard STL sequence containers**, vector, string, deque, and list.

- The **standard STL associative containers**, set, multiset, map, and multimap.

- The **nonstandard sequence containers** slist and rope. slist is a singly linked list, and rope is essentially a heavy-duty string. (A "rope" is a heavy-duty "string." Get it?) You'll find a brief overview of these nonstandard (but commonly available) containers in Item 50.

- The **nonstandard associative containers** hash_set, hash_multiset, hash_map, and hash_multimap. I examine these widely available hash-table-based variants on the standard associative containers in Item 25.

- **vector<char> as a replacement for string**. Item 13 describes the conditions under which such a replacement might make sense.

- **vector as a replacement for the standard associative containers**. As Item 23 makes clear, there are times when vector can outperform the standard associative containers in both time and space.

- Several **standard non-STL containers**, including arrays, bitset, valarray, stack, queue, and priority_queue. Because these are non-STL containers, I have little to say about them in this book, though Item 16 mentions a case where arrays are preferable to STL containers and Item 18 explains why bitset may be better than vector<bool>. It's also worth bearing in mind that arrays can be used with STL algorithms, because pointers can be used as array iterators.

That's a panoply of options, and it's matched in richness by the range of considerations that should go into choosing among them. Unfortunately, most discussions of the STL take a fairly narrow view of the world of containers, ignoring many issues relevant to selecting the one that is most appropriate. Even the Standard gets into this act, offering the following guidance for choosing among vector, deque, and list:

> vector, list, and deque offer the programmer different complexity trade-offs and should be used accordingly. vector is the type of sequence that should be used by default. list should be used when there are frequent insertions and deletions from the middle of the sequence. deque is the data structure of choice when most insertions and deletions take place at the beginning or at the end of the sequence.

If your primary concern is algorithmic complexity, I suppose this constitutes reasonable advice, but there is so much more to be concerned with.

In a moment, we'll examine some of the important container-related issues that complement algorithmic complexity, but first I need to introduce a way of categorizing the STL containers that isn't discussed as often as it should be. That is the distinction between contiguous-memory containers and node-based containers.

Contiguous-memory containers (also known as *array-based containers*) store their elements in one or more (dynamically allocated) chunks of memory, each chunk holding more than one container element. If a new element is inserted or an existing element is erased, other elements in the same memory chunk have to be shifted up or down to make room for the new element or to fill the space formerly occupied by the erased element. This kind of movement affects both performance (see Items 5 and 14) and exception safety (as we'll soon see). The standard contiguous-memory containers are vector, string, and deque. The nonstandard rope is also a contiguous-memory container.

Node-based containers store only a single element per chunk of (dynamically allocated) memory. Insertion or erasure of a container element affects only pointers to nodes, not the contents of the nodes themselves, so element values need not be moved when something is inserted or erased. Containers representing linked lists, such as list and slist, are node-based, as are all the standard associative containers. (They're typically implemented as balanced trees.) The nonstandard hashed containers use varying node-based implementations, as you'll see in Item 25.

With this terminology out of the way, we're ready to sketch some of the questions most relevant when choosing among containers. In this discussion, I omit consideration of non-STL-like containers (e.g., arrays, bitsets, etc.), because this is, after all, a book on the STL.

- *Do you need to be able to insert a new element at an arbitrary position in the container?* If so, you need a sequence container; associative containers won't do.

- *Do you care how elements are ordered in the container?* If not, a hashed container becomes a viable choice. Otherwise, you'll want to avoid hashed containers.

- *Must the container be part of standard C++?* If so, that eliminates hashed containers, slist, and rope.

- *What category of iterators do you require?* If they must be random access iterators, you're technically limited to vector, deque, and string, but you'd probably want to consider rope, too. (See Item 50 for information on rope.) If bidirectional iterators are required, you must avoid slist (see Item 50) as well as one common implementation of the hashed containers (see Item 25).

- *Is it important to avoid movement of existing container elements when insertions or erasures take place?* If so, you'll need to stay away from contiguous-memory containers (see Item 5).

- *Does the data in the container need to be layout-compatible with C?* If so, you're limited to vectors (see Item 16).

- *Is lookup speed a critical consideration?* If so, you'll want to look at hashed containers (see Item 25), sorted vectors (see Item 23), and the standard associative containers — probably in that order.

- *Do you mind if the underlying container uses reference counting?* If so, you'll want to steer clear of string, because many string implementations are reference-counted (see Item 13). You'll need to avoid rope, too, because the definitive rope implementation is based on reference counting (see Item 50). You have to represent your strings somehow, of course, so you'll want to consider vector<char>.

- *Do you need transactional semantics for insertions and erasures?* That is, do you require the ability to reliably roll back insertions and erasures? If so, you'll want to use a node-based container. If you need transactional semantics for multiple-element insertions (e.g., the range form — see Item 5), you'll want to choose list, because list is the only standard container that offers transactional semantics for multiple-element insertions. Transactional semantics are particularly important for programmers interested in writing exception-safe code. (Transactional semantics can be achieved with contiguous-memory containers, too, but there is a performance cost, and the code is not as straightforward. To learn more about this, consult Item 17 of Sutter's *Exceptional C++* [8].)

- *Do you need to minimize iterator, pointer, and reference invalidation?* If so, you'll want to use node-based containers, because insertions and erasures on such containers never invalidate iterators, pointers, or references (unless they point to an element you are erasing). In general, insertions or erasures on contiguous-memory containers may invalidate all iterators, pointers, and references into the container.

- *Would it be helpful to have a sequence container with random ac-cess iterators where pointers and references to the data are not in-validated as long as nothing is erased and insertions take place only at the ends of the container?* This is a very special case, but if it's *your* case, deque is the container of your dreams. (Interest-ingly, deque's iterators *may* be invalidated when insertions are made only at the ends of the container. deque is the only standard STL container whose iterators may be invalidated without also in-validating its pointers and references.)

These questions are hardly the end of the matter. For example, they don't take into account the varying memory allocation strategies employed by the different container types. (Items 10 and 14 discuss some aspects of such strategies.) Still, they should be enough to con-vince you that, unless you have no interest in element ordering, stan-dards conformance, iterator capabilities, layout compatibility with C, lookup speed, behavioral anomalies due to reference counting, the ease of implementing transactional semantics, or the conditions under which iterators are invalidated, you have more to think about than simply the algorithmic complexity of container operations. Such complexity is important, of course, but it's far from the entire story.

The STL gives you lots of options when it comes to containers. If you look beyond the bounds of the STL, there are even more options. Before choosing a container, be sure to consider *all* your options. A "default container"? I don't think so.

Item 2: Beware the illusion of container-independent code.

The STL is based on generalization. Arrays are generalized into con-tainers and parameterized on the types of objects they contain. Func-tions are generalized into algorithms and parameterized on the types of iterators they use. Pointers are generalized into iterators and parameterized on the type of objects they point to.

That's just the beginning. Individual container types are generalized into sequence and associative containers, and similar containers are given similar functionality. Standard contiguous-memory containers (see Item 1) offer random-access iterators, while standard node-based containers (again, see Item 1) provide bidirectional iterators. Sequence containers support push_front and/or push_back, while associative containers don't. Associative containers offer logarithmic-time lower_bound, upper_bound, and equal_range member functions, but sequence containers don't.

With all this generalization going on, it's natural to want to join the movement. This sentiment is laudable, and when you write your own containers, iterators, and algorithms, you'll certainly want to pursue it. Alas, many programmers try to pursue it in a different manner. Instead of committing to particular types of containers in their software, they try to generalize the notion of a container so that they can use, say, a vector, but still preserve the option of replacing it with something like a deque or a list later — all without changing the code that uses it. That is, they strive to write *container-independent code*. This kind of generalization, well-intentioned though it is, is almost always misguided.

Even the most ardent advocate of container-independent code soon realizes that it makes little sense to try to write software that will work with both sequence and associative containers. Many member functions exist for only one category of container, e.g., only sequence containers support push_front or push_back, and only associative containers support count and lower_bound, etc. Even such basics as insert and erase have signatures and semantics that vary from category to category. For example, when you insert an object into a sequence container, it stays where you put it, but if you insert an object into an associative container, the container moves the object to where it belongs in the container's sort order. For another example, the form of erase taking an iterator returns a new iterator when invoked on a sequence container, but it returns nothing when invoked on an associative container. (Item 9 gives an example of how this can affect the code you write.)

Suppose, then, you aspire to write code that can be used with the most common sequence containers: vector, deque, and list. Clearly, you must program to the intersection of their capabilities, and that means no uses of reserve or capacity (see Item 14), because deque and list don't offer them. The presence of list also means you give up operator[], and you limit yourself to the capabilities of bidirectional iterators. That, in turn, means you must stay away from algorithms that demand random access iterators, including sort, stable_sort, partial_sort, and nth_element (see Item 31).

On the other hand, your desire to support vector rules out use of push_front and pop_front, and both vector and deque put the kibosh on splice and the member form of sort. In conjunction with the constraints above, this latter prohibition means that there is no form of sort you can call on your "generalized sequence container."

That's the obvious stuff. If you violate any of those restrictions, your code will fail to compile with at least one of the containers you want to be able to use. The code that *will* compile is more insidious.

The main culprit is the different rules for invalidation of iterators, pointers, and references that apply to different sequence containers. To write code that will work correctly with vector, deque, and list, you must assume that any operation invalidating iterators, pointers, or references in any of those containers invalidates them in the container you're using. Thus, you must assume that every call to insert invalidates everything, because deque::insert invalidates all iterators and, lacking the ability to call capacity, vector::insert must be assumed to invalidate all pointers and references. (Item 1 explains that deque is unique in sometimes invalidating its iterators without invalidating its pointers and references.) Similar reasoning leads to the conclusion that every call to erase must be assumed to invalidate everything.

Want more? You can't pass the data in the container to a C interface, because only vector supports that (see Item 16). You can't instantiate your container with bool as the type of objects to be stored, because, as Item 18 explains, vector<bool> doesn't always behave like a vector, and it never actually stores bools. You can't assume list's constant-time insertions and erasures, because vector and deque take linear time to perform those operations.

When all is said and done, you're left with a "generalized sequence container" where you can't call reserve, capacity, operator[], push_front, pop_front, splice, or any algorithm requiring random access iterators; a container where every call to insert and erase takes linear time and invalidates all iterators, pointers, and references; and a container incompatible with C where bools can't be stored. Is that really the kind of container you want to use in your applications? I suspect not.

If you rein in your ambition and decide you're willing to drop support for list, you still give up reserve, capacity, push_front, and pop_front; you still must assume that all calls to insert and erase take linear time and invalidate everything; you still lose layout compatibility with C; and you still can't store bools.

If you abandon the sequence containers and shoot instead for code that can work with different associative containers, the situation isn't much better. Writing for both set and map is close to impossible, because sets store single objects while maps store pairs of objects. Even writing for both set and multiset (or map and multimap) is tough. The insert member function taking only a value has different return types for sets/maps than for their multi cousins, and you must religiously avoid making any assumptions about how many copies of a value are stored in a container. With map and multimap, you must avoid using operator[], because that member function exists only for map.

Face the truth: it's not worth it. The different containers are *different*, and they have strengths and weaknesses that vary in significant ways. They're not designed to be interchangeable, and there's little you can do to paper that over. If you try, you're merely tempting fate, and fate doesn't like to be tempted.

Still, the day will dawn when you'll realize that a container choice you made was, er, suboptimal, and you'll need to use a different container type. You now know that when you change container types, you'll not only need to fix whatever problems your compilers diagnose, you'll also need to examine all the code using the container to see what needs to be changed in light of the new container's performance characteristics and rules for invalidation of iterators, pointers, and references. If you switch from a vector to something else, you'll also have to make sure you're no longer relying on vector's C-compatible memory layout, and if you switch to a vector, you'll have to ensure that you're not using it to store bools.

Given the inevitability of having to change container types from time to time, you can facilitate such changes in the usual manner: by encapsulating, encapsulating, encapsulating. One of the easiest ways to do this is through the liberal use of typedefs for container and iterator types. Hence, instead of writing this,

```
class Widget { ... };

vector<Widget> vw;

Widget bestWidget;

...                                           // give bestWidget a value

vector<Widget>::iterator i =                  // find a Widget with the
    find(vw.begin(), vw.end(), bestWidget);   // same value as bestWidget
```

write this:

```
class Widget { ... };

typedef vector<Widget> WidgetContainer;
typedef WidgetContainer::iterator WCIterator;

WidgetContainer vw;

Widget bestWidget;

...

WCIterator i = find(vw.begin(), vw.end(), bestWidget);
```

This makes it a lot easier to change container types, something that's especially convenient if the change in question is simply to add a custom allocator. (Such a change doesn't affect the rules for iterator/pointer/reference invalidation.)

```
class Widget { ... };

template<typename T>                       // see Item 10 for why this
SpecialAllocator { ... };                  // needs to be a template

typedef vector<Widget,  SpecialAllocator<Widget>> WidgetContainer;
typedef WidgetContainer::iterator WCIterator;

WidgetContainer vw;                                        // still works

Widget bestWidget;

...

WCIterator i = find(vw.begin(), vw.end(), bestWidget);      // still works
```

If the encapsulating aspects of typedefs mean nothing to you, you're still likely to appreciate the work they can save. For example, if you have an object of type

```
map< string,
     vector<Widget>::iterator,
     ClStringCompare>            // ClStringCompare is "case-
                                 // insensitive string compare;"
                                 // Item 19 describes it
```

and you want to walk through the map using const_iterators, do you really want to spell out

```
map<string, vector<Widget>::iterator, ClStringCompare>::const_iterator
```

more than once? Once you've used the STL a little while, you'll realize that typedefs are your friends.

A typedef is just a synonym for some other type, so the encapsulation it affords is purely lexical. A typedef doesn't prevent a client from doing (or depending on) anything they couldn't already do (or depend on). You need bigger ammunition if you want to limit client exposure to the container choices you've made. You need classes.

To limit the code that may require modification if you replace one container type with another, hide the container in a class, and limit the amount of container-specific information visible through the class interface. For example, if you need to create a customer list, don't use a list directly. Instead, create a CustomerList class, and hide a list in its private section:

```
class CustomerList {
private:
   typedef list<Customer> CustomerContainer;
   typedef CustomerContainer::iterator CCIterator;

   CustomerContainer customers;

public:                            // limit the amount of list-specific
   ...                             // information visible through
};                                 // this interface
```

At first, this may seem silly. After all a customer list is a *list*, right? Well, maybe. Later you may discover that you don't need to insert or erase customers from the middle of the list as often as you'd anticipated, but you do need to quickly identify the top 20% of your customers — a task tailor-made for the nth_element algorithm (see Item 31). But nth_element requires random access iterators. It won't work with a list. In that case, your customer "list" might be better implemented as a vector or a deque.

When you consider this kind of change, you still have to check every CustomerList member function and every friend to see how they'll be affected (in terms of performance and iterator/pointer/reference invalidation, etc.), but if you've done a good job of encapsulating CustomerList's implementation details, the impact on CustomerList clients should be small. *You* can't write container-independent code, but *they* might be able to.

Item 3:   Make copying cheap and correct for objects in containers.

Containers hold objects, but not the ones you give them. Furthermore, when you get an object from a container, the object you get is not the one that was in the container. Instead, when you add an object to a container (via, e.g., insert or push_back, etc.), what goes into the container is a *copy* of the object you specify. When you get an object from a container (via, e.g., front or back), what you get is a *copy* of what was contained. Copy in, copy out. That's the STL way.

Once an object is in a container, it's not uncommon for it to be copied further. If you insert something into or erase something from a vector, string, or deque, existing container elements are typically moved (copied) around (see Items 5 and 14). If you use any of the sorting algorithms (see Item 31); next_permutation or previous_permutation; remove, unique, or their ilk (see Item 32); rotate or reverse, etc., objects will be moved (copied) around. Yes, copying objects is the STL way.

It may interest you to know how all this copying is accomplished. That's easy. An object is copied by using its copying member functions, in particular, its *copy* constructor and its *copy* assignment operator. (Clever names, no?) For a user-defined class like Widget, these functions are traditionally declared like this:

```
class Widget {
public:
  ...
  Widget(const Widget&);               // copy constructor
  Widget& operator=(const Widget&);    // copy assignment operator
  ...
};
```

As always, if you don't declare these functions yourself, your compilers will declare them for you. Also as always, the copying of built-in types (e.g., ints, pointers, etc.) is accomplished by simply copying the underlying bits. (For details on copy constructors and assignment operators, consult any introductory book on C++. In *Effective C++*, Items 11 and 27 focus on the behavior of these functions.)

With all this copying taking place, the motivation for this Item should now be clear. If you fill a container with objects where copying is expensive, the simple act of putting the objects into the container could prove to be a performance bottleneck. The more things get moved around in the container, the more memory and cycles you'll blow on making copies. Furthermore, if you have objects where "copying" has an unconventional meaning, putting such objects into a container will invariably lead to grief. (For an example of the kind of grief it can lead to, see Item 8.)

In the presence of inheritance, of course, copying leads to slicing. That is, if you create a container of base class objects and you try to insert derived class objects into it, the derivedness of the objects will be removed as the objects are copied (via the base class copy constructor) into the container:

```
vector<Widget> vw;

class SpecialWidget:           // SpecialWidget inherits from
  public Widget { ... };       // Widget above

SpecialWidget sw;

vw.push_back(sw);              // sw is copied as a base class
                              // object into vw. Its specialness
                              // is lost during the copying
```

The slicing problem suggests that inserting a derived class object into a container of base class objects is almost always an error. If you want the resulting object to *act* like a derived class object, e.g., invoke derived class virtual functions, etc., it *is* always an error. (For more background on the slicing problem, consult *Effective C++*, Item 22. For another example of where it arises in the STL, see Item 38.)

An easy way to make copying efficient, correct, and immune to the slicing problem is to create containers of *pointers* instead of containers of objects. That is, instead of creating a container of Widget, create a container of Widget*. Copying pointers is fast, it always does exactly what you expect (it copies the bits making up the pointer), and nothing gets sliced when a pointer is copied. Unfortunately, containers of pointers have their own STL-related headaches. You can read about them in Items 7 and 33. As you seek to avoid those headaches while still dodging efficiency, correctness, and slicing concerns, you'll probably discover that containers of *smart pointers* are an attractive option. To learn more about this option, turn to Item 7.

If all this makes it sound like the STL is copy-crazy, think again. Yes, the STL makes lots of copies, but it's generally designed to avoid copying objects *unnecessarily*. In fact, it's generally designed to avoid *creating* objects unnecessarily. Contrast this with the behavior of C's and C++'s only built-in container, the lowly array:

```
Widget w[maxNumWidgets];   // create an array of maxNumWidgets
                           // Widgets, default-constructing each one
```

This constructs maxNumWidgets Widget objects, even if we normally expect to use only a few of them or we expect to immediately overwrite each default-constructed value with values we get from someplace else (e.g., a file). Using the STL instead of an array, we can use a vector that grows when it needs to:

```
vector<Widget> vw;              // create a vector with zero Widget
                                // objects that will expand as needed
```

We can also create an empty vector that contains enough space for maxNumWidgets Widgets, but where zero Widgets have been constructed:

```
vector<Widget> vw;

vw.reserve(maxNumWidgets);      // see Item 14 for details on reserve
```

Compared to arrays, STL containers are much more civilized. They create (by copying) only as many objects as you ask for, they do it only when you direct them to, and they use a default constructor only when you say they should. Yes, STL containers make copies, and yes, you need to understand that, but don't lose sight of the fact that they're still a big step up from arrays.

Item 4: Call empty instead of checking size() against zero.

For any container c, writing

```
if (c.size() == 0) ...
```

is essentially equivalent to writing

```
if (c.empty()) ...
```

That being the case, you might wonder why one construct should be preferred to the other, especially in view of the fact that empty is typically implemented as an inline function that simply returns whether size returns 0.

You should prefer the construct using empty, and the reason is simple: empty is a constant-time operation for all standard containers, but for some list implementations, size takes linear time.

But what makes list so troublesome? Why can't it, too, offer a constant-time size? The answer has much to do with list's unique splicing functions. Consider this code:

```
list<int> list1;
list<int> list2;

...

list1.splice(                                // move all nodes in list2
    list1.end(), list2,                      // from the first occurrence
    find(list2.begin(), list2.end(), 5),     // of 5 through the last
    find(list2.rbegin(), list2.rend(), 10).base()  // occurrence of 10 to the
);                                           // end of list1. See Item 28
                                             // for info on the "base()" call
```

This code won't work unless list2 contains a 10 somewhere beyond a 5, but let's assume that's not a problem. Instead, let's focus on this question: how many elements are in list1 after the splice? Clearly, list1 after the splice has as many elements as it did before the splice plus however many elements were spliced into it. But how many elements were spliced into it? As many as were in the range defined by find(list2.begin(), list2.end(), 5) and find(list2.rbegin(), list2.rend(), 10).base(). Okay, how many is that? Without traversing the range and counting them, there's no way to know. And therein lies the problem.

Suppose you're responsible for implementing list. list isn't just any container, it's a *standard* container, so you know your class will be widely used. You naturally want your implementation to be as efficient as possible. You figure that clients will commonly want to find out how many elements are in a list, so you'd like to make size a constant-time operation. You'd thus like to design list so it always knows how many elements it contains.

At the same time, you know that of all the standard containers, only list offers the ability to splice elements from one place to another without copying any data. You reason that many list clients will choose list specifically because it offers high-efficiency splicing. They know that splicing a range from one list to another can be accomplished in constant time, and you know that they know it, so you certainly want to meet their expectation that splice is a constant-time member function.

This puts you in a quandary. If size is to be a constant-time operation, each list member function must update the sizes of the lists on which it operates. That includes splice. But the only way for splice to update the sizes of the lists it modifies is for it to count the number of elements being spliced, and doing that would prevent splice from achieving the constant-time performance you want for *it*. If you eliminate the requirement that splice update the sizes of the lists it's modifying, splice can be made constant-time, but then size becomes a linear-time operation. In general, it will have to traverse its entire data structure to see how many elements it contains. No matter how you look at it, something — size or splice — has to give. One or the other can be a constant-time operation, but not both.

Different list implementations resolve this conflict in different ways, depending on whether their authors choose to maximize the efficiency of size or splice. If you happen to be using a list implementation where a constant-time splice was given higher priority than a constant-time size, you'll be better off calling empty than size, because empty is always a constant-time operation. Even if you're not using such an implementation, you might find yourself using such an implementation in the future. For example, you might port your code to a different platform where a different implementation of the STL is available, or you might just decide to switch to a different STL implementation for your current platform.

No matter what happens, you can't go wrong if you call empty instead of checking to see if size() == 0. So call empty whenever you need to know whether a container has zero elements.

Item 5: Prefer range member functions to their single-element counterparts.

Quick! Given two vectors, v1 and v2, what's the easiest way to make v1's contents be the same as the second half of v2's? Don't agonize over the definition of "half" when v2 has an odd number of elements, just do something reasonable.

Time's up! If your answer was

```
v1.assign(v2.begin() + v2.size() / 2, v2.end());
```

or something quite similar, you get full credit and a gold star. If your answer involved more than one function call, but didn't use any kind of loop, you get nearly full credit, but no gold star. If your answer involved a loop, you've got some room for improvement, and if your answer involved multiple loops, well, let's just say that you really need this book.

By the way, if your response to the *answer* to the question included "Huh?", pay close attention, because you're going to learn something really useful.

This quiz is designed to do two things. First, it affords me an opportunity to remind you of the existence of the assign member function, a convenient beast that too many programmers overlook. It's available for all the standard sequence containers (vector, string, deque, and list). Whenever you have to completely replace the contents of a container, you should think of assignment. If you're just copying one container to another of the same type, operator= is the assignment function of choice, but as this example demonstrates, assign is available for the times when you want to give a container a completely new set of values, but operator= won't do what you want.

The second reason for the quiz is to demonstrate why range member functions are superior to their single-element alternatives. A *range member function* is a member function that, like STL algorithms, uses two iterator parameters to specify a range of elements over which something should be done. Without using a range member function to solve this Item's opening problem, you'd have to write an explicit loop, probably something like this:

```
vector<Widget> v1, v2;              // assume v1 and v2 are vectors
                                    // of Widgets
...
v1.clear();
for (vector<Widget>::const_iterator ci = v2.begin() + v2.size() / 2;
    ci != v2.end();
    ++ci)
  v1.push_back(*ci);
```

Item 43 examines in detail why you should try to avoid writing explicit loops, but you don't need to read that Item to recognize that writing this code is a lot more work than is writing the call to assign. As we'll see shortly, the loop also happens to impose an efficiency penalty, but we'll deal with that in a moment.

One way to avoid the loop is to follow the advice of Item 43 and employ an algorithm instead:

```
v1.clear();
copy(v2.begin() + v2.size() / 2, v2.end(), back_inserter(v1));
```

Writing this is still more work than writing the call to assign. Furthermore, though no loop is present in this code, one certainly exists inside copy (see Item 43). As a result, the efficiency penalty remains. Again, I'll discuss that below. At this point, I want to digress briefly to observe that almost all uses of copy where the destination range is specified using an insert iterator (i.e., via inserter, back_inserter, or front_inserter) can be — *should* be — replaced with calls to range member functions. Here, for example, the call to copy can be replaced with a range version of insert:

```
v1.insert(v1.end(), v2.begin() + v2.size() / 2, v2.end());
```

This involves slightly less typing than the call to copy, but it also says more directly what is happening: data is being inserted into v1. The call to copy expresses that, too, but less directly. It puts the emphasis in the wrong place. The interesting aspect of what is happening is not that elements are being copied, it's that v1 is having new data added to it. The insert member function makes that clear. The use of copy obscures it. There's nothing interesting about the fact that things are being copied, because the STL is *built* on the assumption that things will be copied. Copying is so fundamental to the STL, it's the topic of Item 3 in this book!

Too many STL programmers overuse copy, so the advice I just gave bears repeating: Almost all uses of copy where the destination range is specified using an insert iterator should be replaced with calls to range member functions.

Returning to our assign example, we've already identified two reasons to prefer range member functions to their single-element counterparts:

- It's generally less work to write the code using the range member functions.

- Range member functions tend to lead to code that is clearer and more straightforward.

In short, range member functions yield code that is easier to write and easier to understand. What's not to like?

Alas, some will dismiss these arguments as matters of programming style, and developers enjoy arguing about style issues almost as much as they enjoy arguing about which is the One True Editor. (As if there's any doubt. It's Emacs.) It would be helpful to have a more universally agreed-upon criterion for establishing the superiority of range member functions to their single-element counterparts. For the standard sequence containers, we have one: efficiency. When dealing with the standard sequence containers, application of single-element member functions makes more demands on memory allocators, copies objects more frequently, and/or performs redundant operations compared to range member functions that achieve the same end.

For example, suppose you'd like to copy an array of ints into the front of a vector. (The data might be in an array instead of a vector in the first place, because the data came from a legacy C API. For a discussion of the issues that arise when mixing STL containers and C APIs, see Item 16.) Using the vector range insert function, it's honestly trivial:

```
int data[numValues];                            // assume numValues is
                                                // defined elsewhere
vector<int> v;

...

v.insert(v.begin(), data, data + numValues);    // insert the ints in data
                                                // into v at the front
```

Using iterative calls to insert in an explicit loop, it would probably look more or less like this:

```
vector<int>::iterator insertLoc(v.begin());
for (int i = 0; i < numValues; ++i) {
   insertLoc = v.insert(insertLoc, data[i]);
}
```

Notice how we have to be careful to save the return value of insert for the next loop iteration. If we didn't update insertLoc after each insertion, we'd have two problems. First, all loop iterations after the first would yield undefined behavior, because each insert call would invalidate insertLoc. Second, even if insertLoc remained valid, we'd always insert at the front of the vector (i.e., at v.begin()), and the result would be that the ints copied into v would end up in reverse order.

If we follow the lead of Item 43 and replace the loop with a call to copy, we get something like this:

```
copy(data, data + numValues, inserter(v, v.begin()));
```

By the time the copy template has been instantiated, the code based on copy and the code using the explicit loop will be almost identical, so for purposes of an efficiency analysis, we'll focus on the explicit loop, keeping in mind that the analysis is equally valid for the code employing copy. Looking at the explicit loop just makes it easier to understand where the efficiency hits come from. Yes, that's "hits," plural, because the code using the single-element version of insert levies up to three different performance taxes on you, none of which you pay if you use the range version of insert.

The first tax consists of unnecessary function calls. Inserting numValues elements into v one at a time naturally costs you numValues calls to insert. Using the range form of insert, you pay for only one function call, a savings of numValues-1 calls. Of course, it's possible that inlining will save you from this tax, but then again, it's possible that it won't. Only one thing is sure. With the range form of insert, you definitely won't pay it.

Inlining won't save you from the second tax, which is the cost of inefficiently moving the existing elements in v to their final post-insertion positions. Each time insert is called to add a new value to v, every element above the insertion point must be moved up one position to make room for the new element. So the element at position p must be moved up to position $p+1$, etc. In our example, we're inserting numValues elements at the front of v. That means that each element in v prior to the insertions will have to be shifted up a total of numValues positions. But each will be shifted up only one position each time insert is called, so each element will be moved a total of numValues times. If v has n elements prior to the insertions, a total of n*numValues moves will take place. In this example, v holds ints, so each move will probably boil down to an invocation of memmove, but if v held a user-defined type like Widget, each move would incur a call to that type's assignment operator or copy constructor. (Most calls would be to the assignment operator, but each time the last element in the vector was moved, that move would be accomplished by calling the element's copy constructor.) In the general case, then, inserting numValues new objects one at a time into the front of a vector<Widget> holding n elements exacts a cost of n*numValues function calls: $(n-1)$*numValues calls to the Widget assignment operator and numValues calls to the Widget copy constructor. Even if these calls are inlined, you're still doing the work to move the elements in v numValues times.

In contrast, the Standard requires that range insert functions move existing container elements directly into their final positions, i.e., at a cost of one move per element. The total cost is n moves, numValues to the copy constructor for the type of objects in the container, the remainder to that type's assignment operator. Compared to the single-element insert strategy, the range insert performs $n*(numValues-1)$ fewer moves. Think about that for a minute. It means that if numValues is 100, the range form of insert would do 99% fewer moves than the code making repeated calls to the single-element form of insert!

Before I move on to the third efficiency cost of single-element member functions vis-à-vis their range counterparts, I have a minor correction. What I wrote in the previous paragraph is the truth and nothing but the truth, but it's not quite the whole truth. A range insert function can move an element into its final position in a single move only if it can determine the distance between two iterators without losing its place. This is almost always possible, because all forward iterators offer this functionality, and forward iterators are nearly ubiquitous. All iterators for the standard containers offer forward iterator functionality. So do the iterators for the nonstandard hashed containers (see Item 25). Pointers acting as iterators into arrays offer such functionality, too. In fact, the only standard iterators that don't offer forward iterator capabilities are input and output iterators. Thus, everything I wrote above is true except when the iterators passed to the range form of insert are input iterators (e.g. istream_iterators — see Item 6). In that case only, range insert must move elements into their final positions one place at a time, too, and its advantage in that regard ceases to exist. (For output iterators, this issue fails to arise, because output iterators can't be used to specify a range for insert.)

The final performance tax levied on those so foolish as to use repeated single-element insertions instead of a single range insertion has to do with memory allocation, though it has a nasty copying side to it, too. As Item 14 explains, when you try to insert an element into a vector whose memory is full, the vector allocates new memory with more capacity, copies its elements from the old memory to the new memory, destroys the elements in the old memory, and deallocates the old memory. Then it adds the element that is being inserted. Item 14 also explains that most vector implementations double their capacity each time they run out of memory, so inserting numValues new elements could result in new memory being allocated up to $\log_2 numValues$ times. Item 14 notes that implementations exist that exhibit this behavior, so inserting 1000 elements one at a time can result in 10 new allocations (including their incumbent copying of elements). In contrast (and, by now, predictably), a range insertion can figure out how much new memory it needs before it starts inserting things (assuming it is given forward iterators), so it need not reallocate a vector's underlying memory more than once. As you can imagine, the savings can be considerable.

The analysis I've just performed is for vectors, but the same reasoning applies to strings, too. For deques, the reasoning is similar, but deques manage their memory differently from vectors and strings, so the argument about repeated memory allocations doesn't apply. The argument about moving elements an unnecessarily large number of times, however, generally does apply (though the details are different), as does the observation about the number of function calls.

Among the standard sequence containers, that leaves only list, but here, too, there is a performance advantage to using a range form of insert instead of a single-element form. The argument about repeated function calls continues to be valid, of course, but, because of the way linked lists work, the copying and memory allocation issues fail to arise. Instead, there is a new problem: repeated superfluous assignments to the next and prev pointers of some nodes in the list.

Each time an element is added to a linked list, the list node holding that element must have its next and prev pointers set, and of course the node preceding the new node (let's call it B, for "before") must set its next pointer and the node following the new node (we'll call it A, for "after") must set its prev pointer:

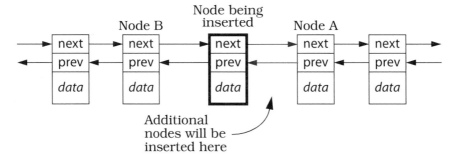

When a series of new nodes is added one by one by calling list's single-element insert, all but the last new node will set its next pointer *twice*, once to point to A, a second time to point to the element inserted after it. A will set its prev pointer to point to a new node each time one is inserted in front of it. If numValues nodes are inserted in front of A, numValues-1 superfluous assignments will be made to the inserted nodes' next pointers, and numValues-1 superfluous assignments will be made to A's prev pointer. All told, that's 2*(numValues-1) unnecessary pointer assignments. Pointer assignments are cheap, of course, but why pay for them if you don't have to?

By now it should be clear that you don't have to, and the key to evading the cost is to use list's range form of insert. Because that function knows how many nodes will ultimately be inserted, it can avoid the superfluous pointer assignments, using only a single assignment to each pointer to set it to its proper post-insertion value.

For the standard sequence containers, then, a lot more than programming style is on the line when choosing between single-element insertions and range insertions. For the associative containers, the efficiency case is harder to make, though the issue of extra function call overhead for repeated calls to single-element insert continues to apply. Furthermore, certain special kinds of range insertions may lead to optimization possibilities in associative containers, too, but as far as I can tell, such optimizations currently exist only in theory. By the time you read this, of course, theory may have become practice, so range insertions into associative containers may indeed be more efficient than repeated single-element insertions. Certainly they are never *less* efficient, so you have nothing to lose by preferring them.

Even without the efficiency argument, the fact remains that using range member functions requires less typing as you write the code, and it also yields code that is easier to understand, thus enhancing your software's long-term maintainability. Those two characteristics alone should convince you to prefer range member functions. The efficiency edge is really just a bonus.

Having droned on this long about the wonder of range member functions, it seems only appropriate that I summarize them for you. Knowing which member functions support ranges makes it a lot easier to recognize opportunities to use them. In the signatures below, the parameter type iterator literally means the iterator type for the container, i.e, *container*::iterator. The parameter type InputIterator, on the other hand, means that any input iterator is acceptable.

- **Range construction**. All standard containers offer a constructor of this form:

```
container::container( InputIterator begin,    // beginning of range
                      InputIterator end);     // end of range
```

When the iterators passed to this constructor are istream_iterators or istreambuf_iterators (see Item 29), you may encounter C++'s most astonishing parse, one that causes your compilers to interpret this construct as a function declaration instead of as the definition of a new container object. Item 6 tells you everything you need to know about that parse, including how to defeat it.

- **Range insertion**. All standard sequence containers offer this form of insert:

      void *container*::insert(iterator position,   // where to insert the range
                          InputIterator begin,   // start of range to insert
                          InputIterator end);   // end of range to insert

  Associative containers use their comparison function to determine where elements go, so they offer a signature that omits the position parameter:

      void *container*::insert(InputIterator begin, InputIterator end);

  When looking for ways to replace single-element inserts with range versions, don't forget that some single-element variants camouflage themselves by adopting different function names. For example, push_front and push_back both insert single elements into containers, even though they're not called insert. If you see a loop calling push_front or push_back, or if you see an algorithm such as copy being passed front_inserter or back_inserter as a parameter, you've discovered a place where a range form of insert is likely to be a superior strategy.

- **Range erasure**. Every standard container offers a range form of erase, but the return types differ for sequence and associative containers. Sequence containers provide this,

      iterator *container*::erase(iterator begin, iterator end);

  while associative containers offer this:

      void *container*::erase(iterator begin, iterator end);

  Why the difference? The claim is that having the associative container version of erase return an iterator (to the element following the one that was erased) would incur an unacceptable performance penalty. I'm one of many who find this claim specious, but the Standard says what the Standard says, and what the Standard says is that sequence and associative container versions of erase have different return types.

  Most of this Item's efficiency analysis for insert has analogues for erase. The number of function calls is still greater for repeated calls to single-element erase than for a single call to range erase. Element values must still be shifted one position at a time towards their final destination when using single-element erase, while range erase can move them into their final positions in a single move.

  One argument about vector's and string's insert that fails to apply to erase has to do with repeated allocations. (For erase, of course, it would concern repeated *de*allocations.) That's because the memory for vectors and strings automatically grows to accommodate new elements, but it doesn't automatically shrink when the number of elements is reduced. (Item 17 describes how you may reduce the unnecessary memory held by a vector or string.)

One particularly important manifestation of range erase is the erase-remove idiom. You can read all about it in Item 32.

- **Range assignment**. As I noted at the beginning of this Item, all standard sequence containers offer a range form of assign:

```
void container::assign(InputIterator begin, InputIterator end);
```

So there you have it, three solid arguments for preferring range member functions to their single-element counterparts. Range member functions are easier to write, they express your intent more clearly, and they exhibit higher performance. That's a troika that's hard to beat.

Item 6:   Be alert for C++'s most vexing parse.

Suppose you have a file of ints and you'd like to copy those ints into a list. This seems like a reasonable way to do it:

```
ifstream dataFile("ints.dat");

list<int> data(istream_iterator<int>(dataFile),    // warning! this doesn't do
                istream_iterator<int>());            // what you think it does
```

The idea here is to pass a pair of istream_iterators to list's range constructor (see Item 5), thus copying the ints in the file into the list.

This code will compile, but at runtime, it won't do anything. It won't read any data out of a file. It won't even create a list. That's because the second statement doesn't declare a list and it doesn't call a constructor. What it does is ... well, what it does is so strange, I dare not tell you straight out, because you won't believe me. Instead, I have to develop the explanation, bit by bit. Are you sitting down? If not, you might want to look around for a chair...

We'll start with the basics. This line declares a function f taking a double and returning an int:

```
int f(double d);
```

This next line does the same thing. The parentheses around the parameter name d are superfluous and are ignored:

```
int f(double (d));          // same as above; parens around d are ignored
```

The line below declares the same function. It simply omits the parameter name:

```
int f(double);            // same as above; parameter name is omitted
```

Those three declaration forms should be familiar to you, though the ability to put parentheses around a parameter name may have been new. (It wasn't long ago that it was new to me.)

Let's now look at three more function declarations. The first one declares a function g taking a parameter that's a pointer to a function taking nothing and returning a double:

```
int g(double (*pf)());    // g takes a pointer to a function as a parameter
```

Here's another way to say the same thing. The only difference is that pf is declared using non-pointer syntax (a syntax that's valid in both C and C++):

```
int g(double pf());       // same as above; pf is implicitly a pointer
```

As usual, parameter names may be omitted, so here's a third declaration for g, one where the name pf has been eliminated:

```
int g(double ());         // same as above; parameter name is omitted
```

Notice the difference between parentheses *around a parameter name* (such as d in the second declaration for f) and *standing by themselves* (as in this example). Parentheses around a parameter name are ignored, but parentheses standing by themselves indicate the existence of a parameter list; they announce the presence of a parameter that is itself a pointer to a function.

Having warmed ourselves up with these declarations for f and g, we are ready to examine the code that began this Item. Here it is again:

```
list<int> data(istream_iterator<int>(dataFile),
               istream_iterator<int>());
```

Brace yourself. This declares a *function*, data, whose return type is list<int>. The function data takes two parameters:

- The first parameter is named dataFile. It's type is istream_iterator<int>. The parentheses around dataFile are superfluous and are ignored.

- The second parameter has no name. Its type is pointer to function taking nothing and returning an istream_iterator<int>.

Amazing, huh? But it's consistent with a universal rule in C++, which says that pretty much anything that can be parsed as a function declaration will be. If you've been programming in C++ for a while, you've

almost certainly encountered another manifestation of this rule. How
many times have you seen this mistake?

```
class Widget { ... };              // assume Widget has a default constructor
Widget w();                        // uh oh...
```

This doesn't declare a Widget named w, it declares a function named w
that takes nothing and returns a Widget. Learning to recognize this
faux pas is a veritable rite of passage for C++ programmers.

All of which is interesting (in its own twisted way), but it doesn't help
us say what we want to say, which is that a list<int> object should be
initialized with the contents of a file. Now that we know what parse we
have to defeat, that's easy to express. It's not legal to surround a formal parameter declaration with parentheses, but it is legal to surround an argument to a function call with parentheses, so by adding
a pair of parentheses, we force compilers to see things our way:

```
list<int> data( istream_iterator<int>(dataFile) ,   // note new parens
                istream_iterator<int>());            // around first argument
                                                     // to list's constructor
```

This is the proper way to declare data, and given the utility of
istream_iterators and range constructors (again, see Item 5), it's worth
knowing how to do it.

Unfortunately, not all compilers currently know it themselves. Of the
several I tested, almost half refused to accept data's declaration unless
it was *incorrectly* declared without the additional parentheses! To pla-
cate such compilers, you could roll your eyes and use the declaration
for data that I've painstakingly explained is incorrect, but that would
be both unportable and short-sighted. After all, compilers that currently get the parse wrong will surely correct it in the future, right?
(Surely!)

A better solution is to step back from the trendy use of anonymous
istream_iterator objects in data's declaration and simply give those iterators names. The following code should work everywhere:

```
ifstream dataFile("ints.dat");

istream_iterator<int> dataBegin(dataFile);
istream_iterator<int> dataEnd;

list<int> data(dataBegin, dataEnd );
```

This use of named iterator objects runs contrary to common STL programming style, but you may decide that's a price worth paying for
code that's unambiguous to both compilers and the humans who
have to work with them.

Item 7: When using containers of newed pointers, remember to delete the pointers before the container is destroyed.

Containers in the STL are remarkably smart. They serve up iterators for both forward and reverse traversals (via begin, end, rbegin, etc.); they tell you what type of objects they contain (via their value_type typedef); during insertions and erasures, they take care of any necessary memory management; they report both how many objects they hold and the most they may contain (via size and max_size, respectively); and of course they automatically destroy each object they hold when they (the containers) are themselves destroyed.

Given such brainy containers, many programmers stop worrying about cleaning up after themselves. Heck, they figure, their containers will do the worrying for them. In many cases, they're right, but when the containers hold *pointers* to objects allocated with new, they're not right enough. Sure, a container of pointers will destroy each element it contains when it (the container) is destroyed, but the "destructor" for a pointer is a no-op! It certainly doesn't call delete.

As a result, the following code leads straight to a resource leak:

```
void doSomething()
{
  vector<Widget*> vwp;

  for (int i = 0; i < SOME_MAGIC_NUMBER; ++i)
    vwp.push_back(new Widget);

  ...                              // use vwp

}                                  // Widgets are leaked here!
```

Each of vwp's elements is destroyed when vwp goes out of scope, but that doesn't change the fact that delete was never used for the objects conjured up with new. Such deletion is your responsibility, not that of your vector. This is a feature. Only you know whether the pointers *should* be deleted.

Usually, you want them to be. When that's the case, making it happen seems easy enough:

```
void doSomething()
{
  vector<Widget*> vwp;

  ...                              // as before
```

```
  for( vector<Widget*>::iterator i = vwp.begin();
      i != vwp.end();
      ++i)
    delete *i;
}
```

This works, but only if you're not terribly picky about what you mean by "works". One problem is that the new for loop does pretty much what for_each does, but it's not as clear as using for_each (see Item 43). Another is that the code isn't exception safe. If an exception is thrown between the time vwp is filled with pointers and the time you get around to deleteing them, you've leaked resources again. Fortunately, both problems can be overcome.

To turn your for_each-like loop into an actual use of for_each, you need to turn delete into a function object. That's child's play, assuming you have a child who likes to play with the STL:

```
template<typename T>
struct DeleteObject:                          // Item 40 describes why
  public unary_function<const T*, void> {     // this inheritance is here

    void operator()(const T* ptr) const
    {
      delete ptr;
    }

};
```

Now you can do this:

```
void doSomething()
{
    ...                                   // as before
  for_each(vwp.begin(), vwp.end(), DeleteObject<Widget>());
}
```

Unfortunately, this makes you specify the type of objects that Delete-Object will be deleting (in this case, Widget). That's annoying. vwp is a vector<Widget*>, so *of course* DeleteObject will be deleting Widget* pointers! Duh! This kind of redundancy is more than just annoying, because it can lead to bugs that are difficult to track down. Suppose, for example, somebody ill-advisedly decides to inherit from string:

```
class SpecialString: public string { ... };
```

This is risky from the get-go, because string, like all the standard STL containers, lacks a virtual destructor, and publicly inheriting from classes without virtual destructors is a major C++ no-no. (For details, consult any good book on C++. In *Effective C++*, the place to look is

Item 14.) Still, some people do this kind of thing, so let's consider how the following code would behave:

```
void doSomething()
{
  deque<SpecialString*> dssp;

  ...

  for_each( dssp.begin(), dssp.end(),        // undefined behavior! Deletion
       DeleteObject<string>());              // of a derived object via a base
  }                                          // class pointer where there is
                                             // no virtual destructor
```

Note how dssp is declared to hold SpecialString* pointers, but the author of the for_each loop has told DeleteObject that it will be deleting string* pointers. It's easy to understand how such an error could arise. SpecialString undoubtedly acts a lot like a string, so one can forgive its clients if they occasionally forget that they are using SpecialStrings instead of strings.

We can eliminate the error (as well as reduce the number of key-strokes required of DeleteObject's clients) by having compilers deduce the type of pointer being passed to DeleteObject::operator(). All we need to do is move the templatization from DeleteObject to its operator():

```
struct DeleteObject {                        // templatization and base
                                             // class removed here

  template<typename T>                       // templatization added here
  void operator()(const T* ptr) const
  {
    delete ptr;
  }
};
```

Compilers know the type of pointer being passed to DeleteObject::operator(), so we have them automatically instantiate an operator() taking that type of pointer. The downside to this type deduction is that we give up the ability to make DeleteObject adaptable (see Item 40). Considering how DeleteObject is designed to be used, it's difficult to imagine how that could be a problem.

With this new version of DeleteObject, the code for SpecialString clients looks like this:

```
void doSomething()
{
  deque<SpecialString*> dssp;

  ...
```

```
        for_each( dssp.begin(), dssp.end(),
                     DeleteObject());                   // ah! well-defined behavior!
    }
```

Straightforward and type-safe, just the way we like it.

But still not exception-safe. If an exception is thrown after the Special-Strings are newed but before invocation of the call to for_each, it's Leakapalooza. That problem can be addressed in a variety of ways, but the simplest is probably to replace the container of pointers with a container of *smart pointers*, typically reference-counted pointers. (If you're unfamiliar with the notion of smart pointers, you should be able to find a description in any intermediate or advanced C++ book. In *More Effective C++*, the material is in Item 28.)

The STL itself contains no reference-counting smart pointer, and writing a good one — one that works correctly all the time — is tricky enough that you don't want to do it unless you have to. I published the code for a reference-counting smart pointer in *More Effective C++* in 1996, and despite basing it on established smart pointer implementations and submitting it to extensive pre-publication reviewing by experienced developers, a small parade of valid bug reports has trickled in for years. The number of subtle ways in which reference-counting smart pointers can fail is remarkable. (For details, consult the *More Effective C++* errata list [28].)

Fortunately, there's rarely a need to write your own, because proven implementations are not difficult to find. One such smart pointer is shared_ptr in the Boost library (see Item 50). With Boost's shared_ptr, this Item's original example can be rewritten as follows:

```
    void doSomething()
    {
      typedef boost::shared_ptr<Widget> SPW;    // SPW = "shared_ptr
                                                 //         to Widget"
      vector<SPW> vwp;

      for (int i = 0; i < SOME_MAGIC_NUMBER; ++i)
        vwp.push_back(SPW(new Widget));         // create a SPW from a
                                                 // Widget*, then do a
                                                 // push_back on it

      ...                                        // use vwp

    }                                            // no Widgets are leaked here, not
                                                 // even if an exception is thrown
                                                 // in the code above
```

One thing you must *never* be fooled into thinking is that you can arrange for pointers to be deleted automatically by creating containers of auto_ptrs. That's a horrible thought, one so perilous, I've devoted Item 8 to why you should avoid it.

All you really need to remember is that STL containers are smart, but they're not smart enough to know whether to delete the pointers they contain. To avoid resource leaks when you have containers of pointers that should be deleted, you must either replace the pointers with smart reference-counting pointer objects (such as Boost's shared_ptr) or you must manually delete each pointer in the container before the container is destroyed.

Finally, it may have crossed your mind that if a struct like DeleteObject can make it easier to avoid resource leaks for containers holding pointers to objects, it should be possible to create a similar DeleteArray struct to make it easier to avoid resource leaks for containers holding pointers to arrays. Certainly it is *possible*, but whether it is advisable is a different matter. Item 13 explains why dynamically allocated arrays are almost always inferior to vector and string objects, so before you sit down to write DeleteArray, please review Item 13 first. With luck, you'll decide that DeleteArray is a struct whose time will never come.

Item 8:   **Never create containers of** auto_ptrs.

Frankly, this Item shouldn't need to be in *Effective STL*. Containers of auto_ptr (COAPs) are prohibited. Code attempting to use them shouldn't compile. The C++ Standardization Committee expended untold effort to arrange for that to be the case.[†] I shouldn't have to say anything about COAPs, because your compilers should have plenty to say about such containers, and all of it should be uncomplimentary.

Alas, many programmers use STL platforms that fail to reject COAPs. Alas even more, many programmers see in COAPs the chimera of a simple, straightforward, efficient solution to the resource leaks that often accompany containers of pointers (see Items 7 and 33). As a result, many programmers are tempted to use COAPs, even though it's not supposed to be possible to create them.

I'll explain in a moment why the spectre of COAPs was so alarming that the Standardization Committee took specific steps to make them illegal. Right now, I want to focus on a disadvantage that requires no knowledge of auto_ptr, or even of containers: COAPs aren't portable. How could they be? The Standard for C++ forbids them, and better

---

[†] If you're interested in the tortured history of auto_ptr standardization, point your web browser to the *auto_ptr Update page* [29] at the *More Effective C++* web site.

STL platforms already enforce this. It's reasonable to assume that as time goes by, STL platforms that currently fail to enforce this aspect of the Standard will become more compliant, and when that happens, code that uses COAPs will be even less portable than it is now. If you value portability (and you should), you'll reject COAPs simply because they fail the portability test.

But maybe you're not of a portability mind-set. If that's the case, kindly allow me to remind you of the unique — some would say bizarre — definition of what it means to copy an auto_ptr.

When you copy an auto_ptr, ownership of the object pointed to by the auto_ptr is transferred to the copying auto_ptr, and the copied auto_ptr is set to NULL. You read that right: *to copy an auto_ptr is to change its value*:

```
auto_ptr<Widget> pw1(new Widget);     // pw1 points to a Widget

auto_ptr<Widget> pw2(pw1);            // pw2 points to pw1's Widget;
                                      // pw1 is set to NULL. (Ownership
                                      // of the Widget is transferred
                                      // from pw1 to pw2.)

pw1 = pw2;                            // pw1 now points to the Widget
                                      // again; pw2 is set to NULL
```

This is certainly unusual, and perhaps it's interesting, but the reason you (as a user of the STL) care is that it leads to some *very* surprising behavior. For example, consider this innocent-looking code, which creates a vector of auto_ptr<Widget> and then sorts it using a function that compares the values of the pointed-to Widgets:

```
bool widgetAPCompare(const auto_ptr<Widget>& lhs,
                     const auto_ptr<Widget>& rhs)
{
   return *lhs < *rhs;                // for this example, assume that
}                                     // operator< exists for Widgets

vector<auto_ptr<Widget> > widgets;    // create a vector and then fill it
...                                   // with auto_ptrs to Widgets;
                                      // remember that this should
                                      // not compile!

sort( widgets.begin(), widgets.end(), // sort the vector
      widgetAPCompare);
```

Everything here looks reasonable, and conceptually, everything *is* reasonable, but the results need not be reasonable at all. For example, one or more of the auto_ptrs in widgets may have been set to NULL during the sort. The act of sorting the vector may have changed its contents! It is worthwhile understanding how this can be.

It can be because one approach to implementing sort — a common approach, as it turns out — is to use some variation on the quicksort algorithm. The fine points of quicksort need not concern us, but the basic idea is that to sort a container, some element of the container is chosen as the "pivot element," then a recursive sort is done on the values greater than and less than or equal to the pivot element. Within sort, such an approach could look something like this:

```
template<class RandomAccessIterator,      // this declaration for
         class Compare>                    // sort is copied straight
void sort(RandomAccessIterator first,      // out of the Standard
          RandomAccessIterator last,
          Compare comp)
{
  // this typedef is described below
  typedef typename iterator_traits<RandomAccessIterator>::value_type
    ElementType;

  RandomAccessIterator i;

  ...                                      // make i point to the pivot element

  ElementType pivotValue(*i);              // copy the pivot element into a
                                           // local temporary variable; see
                                           // discussion below

  ...                                      // do the rest of the sorting work
}
```

Unless you're an experienced reader of STL source code, this may look intimidating, but it's really not that bad. The only tricky part is the reference to iterator_traits<RandomAccessIterator>::value_type, and that's just the fancy STL way of referring to the type of object pointed to by the iterators passed to sort. (When we refer to iterator_traits<RandomAccessIterator>::value_type, we must precede it by typename, because it's the name of a type that's dependent on a template parameter, in this case, RandomAccessIterator. For more information about this use of typename, turn to page 7.)

The troublesome statement in the code above is this one,

```
ElementType pivotValue(*i);
```

because it copies an element from the range being sorted into a local temporary object. In our case, the element is an auto_ptr<Widget>, so this act of copying silently sets the copied auto_ptr — the one in the vector — to NULL. Furthermore, when pivotValue goes out of scope, it will automatically delete the Widget it points to. By the time the call to sort returns, the contents of the vector will have changed, and at least one Widget will have been deleted. It's possible that several vector elements will have been set to NULL and several Widgets will have been deleted, because quicksort is a recursive algorithm, so it could well have copied a pivot element at each level of recursion.

This is a nasty trap to fall into, and that's why the Standardization Committee worked so hard to make sure you're not supposed to be able to fall into it. Honor its work on your behalf, then, by never creating containers of auto_ptrs, even if your STL platforms allow it.

If your goal is a container of smart pointers, this doesn't mean you're out of luck. Containers of smart pointers are fine, and Item 50 describes where you can find smart pointers that mesh well with STL containers. It's just that auto_ptr is not such a smart pointer. Not at all.

Item 9: Choose carefully among erasing options.

Suppose you have a standard STL container, c, that holds ints,

```
Container<int> c;
```

and you'd like to get rid of all the objects in c with the value 1963. Surprisingly, the way to accomplish this task varies from container type to container type; no single approach works for all of them.

If you have a contiguous-memory container (vector, deque, or string — see Item 1), the best approach is the erase-remove idiom (see Item 32):

```
c.erase(remove(c.begin(), c.end(), 1963),     // the erase-remove idiom is
        c.end());                              // the best way to get rid of
                                               // elements with a specific
                                               // value when c is a vector,
                                               // string, or deque
```

This approach works for lists, too, but, as Item 44 explains, the list member function remove is more efficient:

```
c.remove(1963);                    // the remove member function is the
                                   // best way to get rid of elements with
                                   // a specific value when c is a list
```

When c is a standard associative container (i.e., a set, multiset, map, or multimap), the use of anything named remove is completely wrong. Such containers have no member function named remove, and using the remove algorithm might overwrite container values (see Item 32), potentially corrupting the container. (For details on such corruption, consult Item 22, which also explains why trying to use remove on maps and multimaps won't compile, and trying to use it on sets and multisets may not compile.)

No, for associative containers, the proper way to approach the problem is to call erase:

```
c. erase(1963);            // the erase member function is the
                           // best way to get rid of elements with
                           // a specific value when c is a
                           // standard associative container
```

Not only does this do the right thing, it does it efficiently, taking only logarithmic time. (The remove-based techniques for sequence containers require linear time.) Furthermore, the associative container erase member function has the advantage of being based on equivalence instead of equality, a distinction whose importance is explained in Item 19.

Let's now revise the problem slightly. Instead of getting rid of every object in c that has a particular value, let's eliminate every object for which the following predicate (see Item 39) returns true:

```
bool badValue(int x);           // returns whether x is "bad"
```

For the sequence containers (vector, string, deque, and list), all we need to do is replace each use of remove with remove_if, and we're done:

```
c.erase( remove_if(c.begin(), c.end(), badValue),    // this is the best way to
         c.end());                                    // get rid of objects
                                                      // where badValue
                                                      // returns true when c is
                                                      // a vector, string, or
                                                      // deque

c. remove_if(badValue);          // this is the best way to get rid of
                                 // objects where badValue returns
                                 // true when c is a list
```

For the standard associative containers, it's not quite so straightforward. There are two ways to approach the problem, one easier to code, one more efficient. The easier-but-less-efficient solution uses remove_copy_if to copy the values we want into a new container, then swaps the contents of the original container with those of the new one:

```
AssocContainer<int> c;           // c is now one of the
...                              // standard associative
                                 // containers

AssocContainer<int> goodValues;  // temporary container
                                 // to hold unremoved
                                 // values

remove_copy_if(c.begin(), c.end(),    // copy unremoved
               inserter( goodValues,   // values from c to
                         goodValues.end()),  // goodValues
               badValue);

c. swap(goodValues);             // swap the contents of
                                 // c and goodValues
```

The drawback to this approach is that it involves copying all the elements that aren't being removed, and such copying might cost us more than we're interested in paying.

We can dodge that bill by removing the elements from the original container directly. However, because associative containers offer no member function akin to remove_if, we must write a loop to iterate over the elements in c, erasing elements as we go.

Conceptually, the task is simple, and in fact, the code is simple, too. Unfortunately, the code that does the job correctly is rarely the code that springs to mind. For example, this is what many programmers come up with first:

```
AssocContainer<int> c;
...

for (AssocContainer<int>::iterator i = c.begin();    // clear, straightforward,
    i != c.end();                                     // and buggy code to
      ++i) {                                          // erase every element
  if (badValue(*i)) c.erase(i);                       // in c where badValue
}                                                     // returns true; don't
                                                      // do this!
```

Alas, this has undefined behavior. When an element of a container is erased, all iterators that point to that element are invalidated. Once c.erase(i) returns, i has been invalidated. That's bad news for this loop, because after erase returns, i is incremented via the ++i part of the for loop.

To avoid this problem, we have to make sure we have an iterator to the next element of c before we call erase. The easiest way to do that is to use postfix increment on i when we make the call:

```
AssocContainer<int> c;
...

for (AssocContainer<int>::iterator i = c.begin();    // the 3rd part of the for
    i != c.end();                                     // loop is empty; i is now
      /* nothing */ {                                 // incremented below
  if (badValue(*i)) c.erase(i ++);                    // for bad values, pass the
  else   ++i                                          // current i to erase and
}                                                     // increment i as a side
                                                      // effect; for good values,
                                                      // just increment i
```

This approach to calling erase works, because the value of the expression i++ is i's old value, but as a side effect, i is incremented. Hence, we pass i's old (unincremented) value to erase, but we also increment i itself before erase begins executing. That's exactly what we want. As I said, the code is simple, it's just not what most programmers come up with the first time they try.

Let's now revise the problem further. Instead of merely erasing each element for which badValue returns true, we also want to write a message to a log file each time an element is erased.

For the associative containers, this is as easy as easy can be, because it requires only a trivial modification to the loop we just developed:

```
ofstream logFile;                             // log file to write to
AssocContainer<int> c;
...

for (AssocContainer<int>::iterator i = c.begin();  // loop conditions are the
    i != c.end(); ) {                              // same as before
  if (badValue(*i)) {
    logFile << "Erasing " << *i << '\n';           // write log file
    c.erase(i++);                                  // erase element
  }
  else ++i;
}
```

It's vector, string, and deque that now give us trouble. We can't use the erase-remove idiom any longer, because there's no way to get erase or remove to write the log file. Furthermore, we can't use the loop we just developed for associative containers, because it yields undefined behavior for vectors, strings, and deques! Recall that for such containers, invoking erase not only invalidates all iterators pointing to the erased element, it also invalidates all iterators *beyond* the erased element. In our case, that includes all iterators beyond i. It doesn't matter if we write i++, ++i, or anything else you can think of, because none of the resulting iterators is valid.

We must take a different tack with vector, string, and deque. In particular, we must take advantage of erase's return value. That return value is exactly what we need: it's a valid iterator pointing to the element following the erased element once the erase has been accomplished. In other words, we write this:

```
for (SeqContainer<int>::iterator i = c.begin();
    i != c.end(); ) {
  if (badValue(*i)) {
    logFile << "Erasing " << *i << '\n';
    i = c.erase(i);                                // keep i valid by assigning
  }                                                // erase's return value to it
  else ++i;
}
```

This works wonderfully, but only for the standard sequence containers. Due to reasoning one might question (Item 5 does), erase's return type for the standard associative containers is void. For those containers, you have to use the postincrement-the-iterator-you-pass-to-erase technique. (Incidentally, this kind of difference between coding for sequence containers and coding for associative containers is an example of why it's generally ill-advised to try to write container-independent code — see Item 2.)

Lest you be left wondering what the appropriate approach for list is, it turns out that for purposes of iterating and erasing, you can treat list like a vector/string/deque or you can treat it like an associative container; both approaches work for list. The convention is to work with list in the same way as vector, string, and deque, because these are all sequence containers. Experienced STL hands would find it odd to come across list code that iterates and erases using the associative container technique.

If we take stock of everything we've covered in this Item, we come to the following conclusions:

- **To eliminate all objects in a container that have a particular value:**

    If the container is a vector, string, or deque, use the erase-remove idiom.

    If the container is a list, use list::remove.

    If the container is a standard associative container, use its erase member function.

- **To eliminate all objects in a container that satisfy a particular predicate:**

    If the container is a vector, string, or deque, use the erase-remove_if idiom.

    If the container is a list, use list::remove_if.

    If the container is a standard associative container, use remove_copy_if and swap, or write a loop to walk the container elements, being sure to postincrement your iterator when you pass it to erase.

- **To do something inside the loop (in addition to erasing objects):**

    If the container is a standard sequence container, write a loop to walk the container elements, being sure to update your iterator with erase's return value each time you call it.

If the container is a standard associative container, write a loop to walk the container elements, being sure to postincrement your iterator when you pass it to erase.

As you can see, there's more to erasing container elements effectively than just calling erase. The best way to approach the matter depends on how you identify which objects to erase, the type of container they're stored in, and what (if anything) you want to do while you're erasing them. As long as you're careful and heed the advice in this Item, you'll have no trouble. If you're not careful, you run the risk of producing code that's needlessly inefficient or that yields undefined behavior.

Item 10: Be aware of allocator conventions and restrictions.

Allocators are weird. They were originally developed as an abstraction for memory models that would allow library developers to ignore the distinction between near and far pointers in certain 16-bit operating systems (i.e., DOS and its pernicious spawn), but that effort failed. Allocators were also designed to facilitate the development of memory managers that are full-fledged objects, but it turned out that that approach led to efficiency degradations in some parts of the STL. To avoid the efficiency hits, the C++ Standardization Committee added wording to the Standard that emasculated allocators as objects, yet simultaneously expressed the hope that they would suffer no loss of potency from the operation.

There's more. Like operator new and operator new[], STL allocators are responsible for allocating (and deallocating) raw memory, but an allocator's client interface bears little resemblance to that of operator new, operator new[], or even malloc. Finally (and perhaps most remarkable), most of the standard containers *never ask* their associated allocator for memory. Never. The end result is that allocators are, well, allocators are weird.

That's not their fault, of course, and at any rate, it doesn't mean they're useless. However, before I explain what allocators are good for (that's the topic of Item 11), I need to explain what they're not good for. There are a number of things that allocators *seem* to be able to do, but can't, and it's important that you know the boundaries of the field before you try to start playing. If you don't, you'll get injured for sure. Besides, the truth about allocators is so peculiar, the mere act of summarizing it is both enlightening and entertaining. At least I hope it is.

The list of restrictions on allocators begins with their vestigial typedefs for pointers and references. As I mentioned, allocators were originally conceived of as abstractions for memory models, and as such it made sense for allocators to provide typedefs for pointers and references in the memory model they defined. In the C++ standard, the default allocator for objects of type T (cunningly known as allocator<T>) offers the typedefs allocator<T>::pointer and allocator<T>::reference, and it is expected that user-defined allocators will provide these typedefs, too.

Old C++ hands immediately recognize that this is suspect, because there's no way to fake a reference in C++. Doing so would require the ability to overload operator. ("operator dot"), and that's not permitted. In addition, creating objects that act like references is an example of the use of *proxy objects*, and proxy objects lead to a number of problems. (One such problem motivates Item 18. For a comprehensive discussion of proxy objects, turn to Item 30 of *More Effective C++*, where you can read about when they work as well as when they do not.)

In the case of allocators in the STL, it's not any technical shortcomings of proxy objects that render the pointer and reference typedefs impotent, it's the fact that the Standard explicitly allows library implementers to assume that every allocator's pointer typedef is a synonym for T* and every allocator's reference typedef is the same as T&. That's right, library implementers may ignore the typedefs and use raw pointers and references directly! So even if you could somehow find a way to write an allocator that successfully provided new pointer and reference types, it wouldn't do any good, because the STL implementations you were using would be free to ignore your typedefs. Neat, huh?

While you're admiring that quirk of standardization, I'll introduce another. Allocators are objects, and that means they may have member functions, nested types and typedefs (such as pointer and reference), etc., but the Standard says that an implementation of the STL is permitted to assume that all allocator objects of the same type are equivalent and always compare equal. Offhand, that doesn't sound so awful, and there's certainly good motivation for it. Consider this code:

```
template<typename T>                     // a user-defined allocator
class SpecialAllocator { ... };          // template

typedef SpecialAllocator<Widget> SAW;    // SAW = "SpecialAllocator
                                         //          for Widgets"

list<Widget, SAW> L1;
list<Widget, SAW> L2;

...

L1.splice(L1.begin(), L2);               // move L2's nodes to the
                                         // front of L1
```

Recall that when list elements are spliced from one list to another, nothing is copied. Instead, a few pointers are adjusted, and the list nodes that used to be in one list find themselves in another. This makes splicing operations both fast and exception-safe. In the example above, the nodes that were in L2 prior to the splice are in L1 after the splice.

When L1 is destroyed, of course, it must destroy all its nodes (and deallocate their memory), and because it now contains nodes that were originally part of L2, L1's allocator must deallocate the nodes that were originally allocated by L2's allocator. Now it should be clear why the Standard permits implementers of the STL to assume that allocators of the same type are equivalent. It's so memory allocated by one allocator object (such as L2's) may be safely deallocated by another allocator object (such as L1's). Without being able to make such an assumption, splicing operations would be more difficult to implement. Certainly they wouldn't be as efficient as they can be now. (The existence of splicing operations affects other parts of the STL, too. For another example, see Item 4.)

That's all well and good, but the more you think about it, the more you'll realize just how draconian a restriction it is that STL implementations may assume that allocators of the same type are equivalent. It means that portable allocator objects — allocators that will function correctly under different STL implementations — may not have state. Let's be explicit about this: it means that *portable allocators may not have any nonstatic data members*, at least not any that affect their behavior. None. Nada. That means, for example, you can't have one SpecialAllocator<int> that allocates from one heap and a different SpecialAllocator<int> that allocates from a different heap. Such allocators wouldn't be equivalent, and STL implementations exist where attempts to use both allocators could lead to corrupt runtime data structures.

Notice that this is a *runtime* issue. Allocators with state will compile just fine. They just may not run the way you expect them to. The responsibility for ensuring that all allocators of a given type are equivalent is yours. Don't expect compilers to issue a warning if you violate this constraint.

In fairness to the Standardization Committee, I should point out that it included the following statement immediately after the text that permits STL implementers to assume that allocators of the same type are equivalent:

> Implementors are encouraged to supply libraries that ... support non-equal instances. In such implementations, ... the

semantics of containers and algorithms when allocator instances compare non-equal are implementation-defined.

This is a lovely sentiment, but as a user of the STL who is considering the development of a custom allocator with state, it offers you next to nothing. You can take advantage of this statement only if (1) you know that the STL implementations you are using support inequivalent allocators, (2) you are willing to delve into their documentation to determine whether the implementation-defined behavior of "non-equal" allocators is acceptable to you, and (3) you're not concerned about porting your code to STL implementations that may take advantage of the latitude expressly extended to them by the Standard. In short, this paragraph — paragraph 5 of section 20.1.5, for those who insist on knowing — is the Standard's "I have a dream" speech for allocators. Until that dream becomes common reality, programmers concerned about portability will limit themselves to custom allocators with no state.

I remarked earlier that allocators are like operator new in that they allocate raw memory, but their interface is different. This becomes apparent if you look at the declaration of the most common forms of operator new and allocator<T>::allocate:

```
void* operator new(size_t bytes);

pointer allocator<T>::allocate(size_type numObjects);
                              // recall that "pointer" is a typedef
                              // that's virtually always T*
```

Both take a parameter specifying how much memory to allocate, but in the case of operator new, this parameter specifies a certain number of bytes, while in the case of allocator<T>::allocate, it specifies how many T objects are to fit in the memory. On a platform where sizeof(int) == 4, for example, you'd pass 4 to operator new if you wanted enough memory to hold an int, but you'd pass 1 to allocator<int>::allocate. (The type of this parameter is size_t in the case of operator new, while it's allocator<T>::size_type in the case of allocate. In both cases, it's an unsigned integral value, and typically allocator<T>::size_type is a typedef for size_t, anyway.) There's nothing "wrong" about this discrepancy, but the inconsistent conventions between operator new and allocator<T>::allocate complicate the process of applying experience with custom versions of operator new to the development of custom allocators.

operator new and allocator<T>::allocate differ in return types, too. operator new returns a void*, which is the traditional C++ way of representing a pointer to uninitialized memory. allocator<T>::allocate returns a T* (via the pointer typedef), which is not only untraditional, it's premeditated fraud. The pointer returned from allocator<T>::allocate doesn't point to a T object, because no T has yet been constructed! Implicit in the STL is the expectation that allocator<T>::allocate's caller will eventually construct one or more T objects in the memory it returns (possibly via allocator<T>::construct, via uninitialized_fill, or via some application of raw_storage_iterators), though in the case of vector::reserve or string::reserve, that may never happen (see Item 14). The difference in return type between operator new and allocator<T>::allocate indicates a change in the conceptual model for uninitialized memory, and it again makes it harder to apply knowledge about implementing operator new to the development of custom allocators.

That brings us to the final curiosity of STL allocators, that most of the standard containers never make a single call to the allocators with which they are instantiated. Here are two examples:

```
list<int> L;                          // same as list<int, allocator<int> >;
                                      // allocator<int> is never asked to
                                      // allocate memory!

set<Widget, SAW> s;                   // recall that SAW is a typedef for
                                      // SpecialAllocator<Widget>; no
                                      // SAW will ever allocate memory!
```

This oddity is true for list and all the standard associative containers (set, multiset, map, and multimap). That's because these are *node-based* containers, i.e., containers based on data structures in which a new node is dynamically allocated each time a value is to be stored. In the case of list, the nodes are list nodes. In the case of the standard associative containers, the nodes are usually tree nodes, because the standard associative containers are typically implemented as balanced binary search trees.

Think for a moment about how a list<T> is likely to be implemented. The list itself will be made up of nodes, each of which holds a T object as well as pointers to the next and previous nodes in the list:

```
template<typename T,                       // possible list
         typename Allocator = allocator<T> >   // implementation
class list {
private:
   Allocator alloc;                        // allocator for objects of type T

   struct ListNode {                       // nodes in the linked list
      T data;
      ListNode *prev;
      ListNode *next;
   };

   ...

};
```

When a new node is added to the list, we need to get memory for it from an allocator, but we don't need memory for a T, we need memory for a ListNode that contains a T. That makes our Allocator object all but useless, because it doesn't allocate memory for ListNodes, it allocates memory for Ts. Now you understand why list never asks its Allocator to do any allocation: the allocator can't provide what list needs.

What list needs is a way to get from the allocator type it has to the corresponding allocator for ListNodes. This would be tough were it not that, by convention, allocators provide a typedef that does the job. The typedef is called other, but it's not quite that simple, because other is a typedef nested inside a struct called rebind, which itself is a template nested inside the allocator — which itself is a template!

Please don't try to think about that last sentence. Instead, look at the code below, then proceed directly to the explanation that follows.

```
template<typename T>           // the standard allocator is declared
class allocator {              // like this, but this could be a user-
public:                        // written allocator template, too

    template<typename U>
    struct rebind {
        typedef allocator<U> other;
    };

    ...
};
```

In the code implementing list<T>, there is a need to determine the type of the allocator for ListNodes that corresponds to the allocator we have for Ts. The type of the allocator we have for Ts is the template parameter Allocator. That being the case, the type of the corresponding allocator for ListNodes is this:

Allocator::rebind<ListNode>::other

Stay with me here. Every allocator template A (e.g., std::allocator, SpecialAllocator, etc.) is expected to have a nested struct template called rebind. rebind takes a single type parameter, U, and defines nothing but a typedef, other. other is simply a name for A<U>. As a result, list<T> can get from its allocator for T objects (called Allocator) to the corresponding allocator for ListNode objects by referring to Allocator::rebind<ListNode>::other.

Maybe this makes sense to you, maybe it doesn't. (If you stare at it long enough, it will, but you may have to stare a while. I know I had to.) As a user of the STL who may want to write a custom allocator, you don't really need to know how it works. What you do need to know is that if you choose to write allocators and use them with the standard containers, your allocators must provide the rebind template, because standard containers assume it will be there. (For debugging purposes, it's also helpful to know why node-based containers of T objects never ask for memory from the allocators for T objects.)

Hallelujah! We are finally done examining the idiosyncrasies of allocators. Let us therefore summarize the things you need to remember if you ever want to write a custom allocator.

- Make your allocator a template, with the template parameter T representing the type of objects for which you are allocating memory.

- Provide the typedefs pointer and reference, but always have pointer be T* and reference be T&.

- Never give your allocators per-object state. In general, allocators should have no nonstatic data members.

- Remember that an allocator's allocate member functions are passed the number of *objects* for which memory is required, not the number of bytes needed. Also remember that these functions return T* pointers (via the pointer typedef), even though no T objects have yet been constructed.

- Be sure to provide the nested rebind template on which standard containers depend.

Most of what you have to do to write your own allocator is reproduce a fair amount of boilerplate code, then tinker with a few member functions, notably allocate and deallocate. Rather than writing the boilerplate from scratch, I suggest you begin with the code at Josuttis' sample allocator web page [23] or in Austern's article, "What Are Allocators Good For?" [24].

Once you've digested the information in this Item, you'll know a lot about what allocators *cannot* do, but that's probably not what you want to know. Instead, you'd probably like to know what allocators *can* do. That's a rich topic in its own right, a topic I call "Item 11."

Item 11: Understand the legitimate uses of custom allocators.

So you've benchmarked, profiled, and experimented your way to the conclusion that the default STL memory manager (i.e., allocator<T>) is too slow, wastes memory, or suffers excessive fragmentation for your STL needs, and you're certain you can do a better job yourself. Or you discover that allocator<T> takes precautions to be thread-safe, but you're interested only in single-threaded execution and you don't want to pay for the synchronization overhead you don't need. Or you know that objects in certain containers are typically used together, so you'd like to place them near one another in a special heap to maximize locality of reference. Or you'd like to set up a unique heap that corresponds to shared memory, then put one or more containers in that memory so they can be shared by other processes. Congratulations! Each of these scenarios corresponds to a situation where custom allocators are well suited to the problem.

For example, suppose you have special routines modeled after malloc and free for managing a heap of shared memory,

```
void* mallocShared(size_t bytesNeeded);

void freeShared(void *ptr);
```

and you'd like to make it possible to put the contents of STL containers in that shared memory. No problem:

```
template<typename T>
class SharedMemoryAllocator {
public:
    ...
    pointer allocate(size_type numObjects, const void *localityHint = 0)
    {
        return static_cast<pointer>(mallocShared(numObjects * sizeof(T)));
    }
    void deallocate(pointer ptrToMemory, size_type numObjects)
    {
        freeShared(ptrToMemory);
    }

    ...
};
```

For information on the pointer type as well as the cast and the multiplication inside allocate, see Item 10.

You could use SharedMemoryAllocator like this:

```
// convenience typedef
typedef
    vector<double, SharedMemoryAllocator<double> > SharedDoubleVec;
...
{                                              // begin some block
    ...
    SharedDoubleVec v;                         // create a vector whose elements
                                               // are in shared memory

    ...
}                                              // end the block
```

The wording in the comment next to v's definition is important. v is using a SharedMemoryAllocator, so the memory v allocates to hold its elements will come from shared memory. v itself, however — including all its data members — will almost certainly *not* be placed in shared memory. v is just a normal stack-based object, so it will be located in whatever memory the runtime system uses for all normal stack-based objects. That's almost never shared memory. To put both v's contents and v itself into shared memory, you'd have to do something like this:

```
void *pVectorMemory =                       // allocate enough shared
    mallocShared(sizeof(SharedDoubleVec));  // memory to hold a
                                            // SharedDoubleVec object

SharedDoubleVec *pv =                        // use "placement new" to
    new (pVectorMemory) SharedDoubleVec;    // create a SharedDoubleVec
                                            // object in the memory;
                                            // see below

...                                         // use the object (via pv)

pv->~SharedDoubleVec();                      // destroy the object in the
                                            // shared memory

freeShared(pVectorMemory);                   // deallocate the initial
                                            // chunk of shared memory
```

I hope the comments make clear how this works. Fundamentally, you acquire some shared memory, then construct a vector in it that uses shared memory for its own internal allocations. When you're done with the vector, you invoke its destructor, then release the memory the vector occupied. The code isn't terribly complicated, but it's a lot more demanding than just declaring a local variable as we did above. Unless you really need a container (as opposed to its elements) to be in shared memory, I encourage you to avoid this manual four-step allocate/construct/destroy/deallocate process.

In this example, you've doubtless noticed that the code ignores the possibility that mallocShared might return a null pointer. Obviously, production code would have to take such a possibility into account. Also, construction of the vector in the shared memory is accomplished by "placement new." If you're unfamiliar with placement new, your favorite C++ text should be able to introduce you. If that text happens to be *More Effective C++*, you'll find that the pleasantries are exchanged in Item 8.

As a second example of the utility of allocators, suppose you have two heaps, identified by the classes Heap1 and Heap2. Each heap class has static member functions for performing allocation and deallocation:

```
class Heap1 {
public:
   ...
   static void* alloc(size_t numBytes, const void *memoryBlockToBeNear);
   static void dealloc(void *ptr);
   ...
};

class Heap2 { ... };                    // has the same alloc/dealloc interface
```

Further suppose you'd like to co-locate the contents of some STL containers in different heaps. Again, no problem. First you write an allocator designed to use classes like Heap1 and Heap2 for the actual memory management:

```
template<typename T, typename Heap>
SpecificHeapAllocator {
public:
   ...
   pointer allocate(size_type numObjects, const void *localityHint = 0)
   {
      return static_cast<pointer> (Heap::alloc (numObjects * sizeof(T),
                                                localityHint));
   }

   void deallocate(pointer ptrToMemory, size_type numObjects)
   {
      Heap::dealloc (ptrToMemory);
   }

   ...
};
```

Then you use SpecialHeapAllocator to cluster containers' elements together:

```
vector<int, SpecificHeapAllocator<int, Heap1> > v;     // put both v's and
set<int, SpecificHeapAllocator<int, Heap1> > s;        // s's elements in
                                                       // Heap1

list<Widget,
     SpecificHeapAllocator<Widget, Heap2> > L;         // put both L's and
map< int, string, less<int>,                           // m's elements in
     SpecificHeapAllocator<pair<const int, string>,    // Heap2
                           Heap2> > m;
```

In this example, it's quite important that Heap1 and Heap2 be *types* and not objects. The STL offers a syntax for initializing different STL containers with different allocator objects of the same type, but I'm not going to show you what it is. That's because if Heap1 and Heap2 were *objects* instead of types, they'd be inequivalent allocators, and that would violate the equivalence constraint on allocators that is detailed in Item 10.

As these examples demonstrate, allocators are useful in a number of contexts. As long as you obey the constraint that all allocators of the same type must be equivalent, you'll have no trouble employing custom allocators to control general memory management strategies, clustering relationships, and use of shared memory and other special heaps.

Item 12: Have realistic expectations about the thread safety of STL containers.

The world of standard C++ is rather sheltered and old-fashioned. In this rarefied world, all executables are statically linked. Neither memory-mapped files nor shared memory exist. There are no window systems, no networks, no databases, no other processes. That being the case, you should not be surprised to learn that the Standard says not a word about threading. The first expectation you should have about the thread safety of the STL, then, is that it will vary from implementation to implementation.

Of course, multithreaded programs are common, so most STL vendors strive to make their implementations work well in a threaded environment. Even when they do a good job, however, much of the burden remains on your shoulders, and it's important to understand why. There's only so much STL vendors can do to ease your multithreading pain, and you need to know what it is.

The gold standard in support for multithreading in STL containers (and the aspiration of most vendors) has been defined by SGI and is published at their STL Web Site [21]. In essence, it says that the most you can hope for from an implementation is the following.

- **Multiple readers are safe**. Multiple threads may simultaneously read the contents of a single container, and this will work correctly. Naturally, there must not be any writers acting on the container during the reads.

- **Multiple writers to different containers are safe**. Multiple threads may simultaneously write to different containers.

That's all, and let me make clear that this is what you can *hope for*, not what you can *expect*. Some implementations offer these guarantees, but some do not.

Writing multithreaded code is hard, and many programmers wish that STL implementations were completely thread safe out of the box. Were that the case, programmers might hope to be relieved of the need to attend to concurrency control themselves. There's no doubt this would be convenient state of affairs, but it would also be very difficult to achieve. Consider the following ways a library might try to implement such comprehensive container thread safety:

- Lock a container for the duration of each call to its member functions.

- Lock a container for the lifetime of each iterator it returns (via, e.g., calls to begin or end).

- Lock a container for the duration of each algorithm invoked on that container. (This actually makes no sense, because, as Item 32 explains, algorithms have no way to identify the container on which they are operating. Nevertheless, we'll examine this option here, because it's instructive to see why it wouldn't work even if it were possible.)

Now consider the following code. It searches a vector<int> for the first occurrence of the value 5, and, if it finds one, changes that value to 0.

```
vector<int> v;

...

vector<int>::iterator first5(find(v.begin(), v.end(), 5));    // Line 1
if (first5 != v.end()) {                                      // Line 2
   *first5 = 0;                                               // Line 3
}
```

In a multithreaded environment, it's possible that a different thread will modify the data in v immediately after completion of Line 1. If that were to happen, the test of first5 against v.end on Line 2 would be meaningless, because v's values would be different from what they were at the end of Line 1. In fact, such a test could yield undefined results, because another thread could have intervened between Lines 1 and 2 and invalidated first5, perhaps by performing an insertion that caused the vector to reallocate its underlying memory. (That would invalidate all the vector's iterators. For details on this reallocation behavior, turn to Item 14.) Similarly, the assignment to *first5 on Line 3 is unsafe, because another thread might execute between Lines 2 and 3 in such a way as to invalidate first5, perhaps by erasing the element it points to (or at least *used* to point to).

None of the approaches to locking listed above would prevent these problems. The calls to begin and end in Line 1 both return too quickly to offer any help, the iterators they generate last only until the end of that line, and find also returns at the end of that line.

For the code above to be thread safe, v must remain locked from Line 1 through Line 3, and it's difficult to imagine how an STL implementation could deduce that automatically. Bearing in mind the typically high cost of synchronization primitives (e.g., semaphores, mutexes, etc.), it's even more difficult to imagine how an implementation could do it without imposing a significant performance penalty on programs that knew *a priori* — that were *designed* in such a way — that no more than one thread had access to v during the course of Lines 1-3.

Such considerations explain why you can't expect any STL implementation to make your threading woes disappear. Instead, you'll have to manually take charge of synchronization control in these kinds of scenarios. In this example, you might do it like this:

```
vector<int> v;

...

getMutexFor(v);
vector<int>::iterator first5(find(v.begin(), v.end(), 5));
if (first5 != v.end()) {                      // this is now safe
   *first5 = 0;                               // so is this
}
releaseMutexFor(v);
```

A more object-oriented solution is to create a Lock class that acquires a mutex in its constructor and releases it in its destructor, thus minimizing the chances that a call to getMutexFor will go unmatched by a call to releaseMutexFor. The essence of such a class (really a class template) is this:

```
template<typename Container>      // skeletal template for classes
class Lock {                      // that acquire and release mutexes
public:                           // for containers; many details
                                  // have been omitted

   Lock(const Container& container)
   : c(container)
   {
      getMutexFor(c);            // acquire mutex in the constructor
   }

   ~Lock()
   {
      releaseMutexFor(c);        // release it in the destructor
   }
private:
   const Container& c;
};
```

The idea of using a class (like Lock) to manage the lifetime of resources (such as mutexes) is generally known as *resource acquisition is initialization*, and you should be able to read about it in any comprehensive C++ textbook. A good place to start is Stroustrup's *The C++ Programming Language* [7], because Stroustrup popularized the idiom, but you can also turn to Item 9 of *More Effective C++*. No matter what source you consult, bear in mind that the above Lock is stripped to the bare essentials. An industrial-strength version would require a number of enhancements, but such a fleshing-out would have nothing to do with the STL. Furthermore, this minimalist Lock is enough to see how we could apply it to the example we've been considering:

```
vector<int> v;

...

{                                           // create new block
    Lock<vector<int> > lock(v);             // acquire mutex
    vector<int>::iterator first5(find(v.begin(), v.end(), 5));
    if (first5 != v.end()) {
        *first5 = 0;
    }
}                                           // close block, automatically
                                            // releasing the mutex
```

Because a Lock object releases the container's mutex in the Lock's destructor, it's important that the Lock be destroyed as soon as the mutex should be released. To make that happen, we create a new block in which to define the Lock, and we close that block as soon as we no longer need the mutex. This sounds like we're just trading the need to call releaseMutexFor with the need to close a new block, but that's not an accurate assessment. If we forget to create a new block for the Lock, the mutex will still be released, but it may happen later than it should — when control reaches the end of the enclosing block. If we forget to call releaseMutexFor, we never release the mutex.

Furthermore, the Lock-based approach is robust in the presence of exceptions. C++ guarantees that local objects are destroyed if an exception is thrown, so Lock will release its mutex even if an exception is thrown while we're using the Lock object. If we relied on manual calls to getMutexFor and releaseMutexFor, we'd never relinquish the mutex if an exception was thrown after calling getMutexFor but before calling releaseMutexFor.

Exceptions and resource management are important, but they're not the subject of this Item. This Item is about thread safety in the STL. When it comes to thread safety and STL containers, you can hope for a library implementation that allows multiple readers on one container and multiple writers on separate containers. You *can't* hope for the library to eliminate the need for manual concurrency control, and you can't *rely* on any thread support at all.

vector **and** string

All the STL containers are useful, but if you're like most C++ program-mers, you'll find yourself reaching for vector and string more often than their compatriots. That's to be expected. vector and string are designed to replace most applications of arrays, and arrays are so useful, they've been included in every commercially successful programming language from COBOL to Java.

The Items in this chapter cover vectors and strings from a number of perspectives. We begin with a discussion of why the switch from arrays is worthwhile, then look at ways to improve vector and string performance, identify important variations in string implementations, examine how to pass vector and string data to APIs that understand only C, and learn how to eliminate excess memory allocation. We con-clude with an examination of an instructive anomaly, vector<bool>, the little vector that couldn't.

Each of the Items in this chapter will help you take the two most use-ful containers in the STL and refine their application. By the time we're done, you'll know how to make them serve you even better.

Item 13: **Prefer** vector **and** string **to dynamically allocated arrays.**

The minute you decide to use new for a dynamic allocation, you adopt the following responsibilities:

1. You must make sure that somebody will later delete the alloca-tion. Without a subsequent delete, your new will yield a resource leak.

2. You must ensure that the correct form of delete is used. For an allocation of a single object, "delete" must be used. For an array allocation, "delete []" is required. If the wrong form of delete is

used, results will be undefined. On some platforms, the program will crash at runtime. On others, it will silently blunder forward, sometimes leaking resources and corrupting memory as it goes.

3. You must make sure that delete is used exactly once. If an allocation is deleted more than once, results are again undefined.

That's quite a set of responsibilities, and I can't understand why you'd want to adopt them if it wasn't necessary. Thanks to vector and string, it isn't necessary anywhere near as often as it used to be.

Any time you find yourself getting ready to dynamically allocate an array (i.e., plotting to write "new T[...]"), you should consider using a vector or a string instead. (In general, use string when T is a character type and use vector when it's not, though later in this Item, we'll encounter a scenario where a vector<char> may be a reasonable design choice.) vector and string eliminate the burdens above, because they manage their own memory. Their memory grows as elements are added to these containers, and when a vector or string is destroyed, its destructor automatically destroys the elements in the container and deallocates the memory holding those elements.

In addition, vector and string are full-fledged STL sequence containers, so they put at your disposal the complete arsenal of STL algorithms that work on such containers. True, arrays can be used with STL algorithms, too, but arrays don't offer member functions like begin, end, and size, nor do they have nested typedefs like iterator, reverse_iterator, or value_type. And of course char* pointers can hardly compete with the scores of specialized member functions proffered by string. The more you work with the STL, the more jaundiced the eye with which you'll come to view built-in arrays.

If you're concerned about the legacy code you must continue to support, all of which is based on arrays, relax and use vectors and strings anyway. Item 16 shows how easy it is to pass the data in vectors and strings to APIs that expect arrays, so integration with legacy code is generally not a problem.

Frankly, I can think of only one legitimate cause for concern in replacing dynamically allocated arrays with vectors or strings, and it applies only to strings. Many string implementations employ reference counting behind the scenes (see Item 15), a strategy that eliminates some unnecessary memory allocations and copying of characters and that can improve performance for many applications. In fact, the ability to optimize strings via reference counting was considered so important, the C++ Standardization Committee took specific steps to make sure it was a valid implementation.

Alas, one programmer's optimization is another's pessimization, and if you use reference-counted strings in a multithreaded environment, you may find that the time saved by avoiding allocations and copying is dwarfed by the time spent on behind-the-scenes concurrency control. (For details, consult Sutter's article, "Optimizations That Aren't (In a Multithreaded World)" [20].) If you're using reference-counted strings in a multithreaded environment, then, it makes sense to keep an eye out for performance problems arising from their support for thread safety.

To determine whether you're using a reference-counting implementation for string, it's often easiest to consult the documentation for your library. Because reference counting is considered an optimization, vendors generally tout it as a feature. An alternative is to look at the source code for your libraries' implementations of string. I don't generally recommend trying to figure things out from library source code, but sometimes it's the only way to find out what you need to know. If you choose this approach, remember that string is a typedef for basic_string<char> (and wstring is a typedef for basic_string<wchar_t>), so what you really want to look at is the template basic_string. The easiest thing to check is probably the class's copy constructor. Look to see if it increments a reference count somewhere. If it does, string is reference counted. If it doesn't, either string isn't reference counted or you misread the code. Ahem.

If the string implementations available to you are reference counted and you are running in a multithreaded environment where you've determined that string's reference counting support is a performance problem, you have at least three reasonable choices, none of which involves abandoning the STL. First, check to see if your library implementation is one that makes it possible to disable reference counting, often by changing the value of a preprocessor variable. This won't be portable, of course, but given the amount of work involved, it's worth investigating. Second, find or develop an alternative string implementation (or partial implementation) that doesn't use reference counting. Third, consider using a vector<char> instead of a string. vector implementations are not allowed to be reference counted, so hidden multithreading performance issues fail to arise. Of course, you forgo string's fancy member functions if you switch to vector<char>, but most of that functionality is available through STL algorithms anyway, so you're not so much giving up functionality as you are trading one syntax for another.

The upshot of all this is simple. If you're dynamically allocating arrays, you're probably taking on more work than you need to. To lighten your load, use vectors or strings instead.

Item 14: Use reserve **to avoid unnecessary reallocations.**

One of the most marvelous things about STL containers is that they automatically grow to accommodate as much data as you put into them, provided only that you don't exceed their maximum size. (To discover this maximum, just call the aptly named max_size member function.) For vector and string, growth is handled by doing the moral equivalent of a realloc whenever more space is needed. This realloc-like operation has four parts:

1. Allocate a new block of memory that is some multiple of the container's current capacity. In most implementations, vector and string capacities grow by a factor of two each time, i.e, their capacity is doubled each time the container must be expanded.

2. Copy all the elements from the container's old memory into its new memory.

3. Destroy the objects in the old memory.

4. Deallocate the old memory.

Given all that allocation, deallocation, copying, and destruction, It should not stun you to learn that these steps can be expensive. Naturally, you don't want to perform them any more frequently than you have to. If that doesn't strike you as natural, perhaps it will when you consider that each time these steps occur, all iterators, pointers, and references into the vector or string are invalidated. That means that the simple act of inserting an element into a vector or string may also require updating other data structures that use iterators, pointers, or references into the vector or string being expanded.

The reserve member function allows you to minimize the number of reallocations that must be performed, thus avoiding the costs of reallocation and iterator/pointer/reference invalidation. Before I explain how reserve can do that, however, let me briefly recap four interrelated member functions that are sometimes confused. Among the standard containers, only vector and string offer all of these functions.

- size() tells you how many elements are in the container. It does *not* tell you how much memory the container has allocated for the elements it holds.

- capacity() tells you how many elements the container can hold in the memory it has already allocated. This is how many *total elements* the container can hold in that memory, not how many *more* elements it can hold. If you'd like to find out how much unoccupied memory a vector or string has, you must subtract size() from capacity(). If size and capacity return the same value, there is no empty space in the container, and the next insertion (via insert or push_back, etc.) will trigger the reallocation steps above.

- resize(size_t n) forces the container to change to n the number of elements it holds. After the call to resize, size will return n. If n is smaller than the current size, elements at the end of the container will be destroyed. If n is larger than the current size, new default-constructed elements will be added to the end of the container. If n is larger than the current capacity, a reallocation will take place before the elements are added.

- reserve(size_t n) forces the container to change its capacity to at least n, provided n is no less than the current size. This typically forces a reallocation, because the capacity needs to be increased. (If n is less than the current capacity, vector ignores the call and does nothing. string *may* reduce its capacity to the maximum of size() and n, but the string's size definitely remains unchanged. In my experience, using reserve to trim the excess capacity from a string is generally less successful than using "the swap trick," which is the topic of Item 17.)

This recap should make it clear that reallocations (including their constituent raw memory allocations and deallocations, object copying and destruction, and invalidation of iterators, pointers, and references) occur whenever an element needs to be inserted and the container's capacity is insufficient. The key to avoiding reallocations, then, is to use reserve to set a container's capacity to a sufficiently large value as soon as possible, ideally right after the container is constructed.

For example, suppose you'd like to create a vector<int> holding the values 1–1000. Without using reserve, you might do it like this:

```
vector<int> v;
for (int i = 1; i <= 1000; ++i) v.push_back(i);
```

In most STL implementations, this code will result in between two and 10 reallocations during the course of the loop. (There's no magic to the number 10. Recall that vectors typically double in capacity each time a reallocation occurs, and 1000 is roughly 2^{10}.)

Modifying the code to use reserve gives us this:

```
vector<int> v;
v.reserve(1000);

for (int i = 1; i <= 1000; ++i) v.push_back(i);
```

This should result in zero reallocations during the loop.

The relationship between size and capacity makes it possible to predict when an insertion will cause a vector or string to perform a reallocation, and that, in turn, makes it possible to predict when an insertion will invalidate iterators, pointers, and references into a container. For example, given this code,

```
string s;

...

if (s.size() < s.capacity()) {
   s.push_back('x');
}
```

the call to push_back can't invalidate iterators, pointers, or references into the string, because the string's capacity is guaranteed to be greater than its size. If, instead of performing a push_back, the code did an insert into an arbitrary location in the string, we'd still be guaranteed that no reallocation would take place during the insertion, but, in accord with the usual rule for iterator invalidation accompanying a string insertion, all iterators/pointers/references from the insertion point to the end of the string would be invalidated.

Getting back to the main point of this Item, there are two common ways to use reserve to avoid unneeded reallocations. The first is applicable when you know exactly or approximately how many elements will ultimately end up in your container. In that case, as in the vector code above, you simply reserve the appropriate amount of space in advance. The second way is to reserve the maximum space you could ever need, then, once you've added all your data, trim off any excess capacity. The trimming part isn't difficult, but I'm not going to show it here, because there's a trick to it. To learn the trick, turn to Item 17.

Item 15: Be aware of variations in string implementations.

Bjarne Stroustrup once wrote an article with the curious title, "Sixteen Ways to Stack a Cat" [27]. It turns out that there are almost as many ways to implement strings. As experienced and sophisticated software engineers, of course, we're supposed to pooh-pooh "implementation details," but if Einstein is right and God is in the details, reality requires that we sometimes get religion. Even when the details don't matter, having some idea about them puts us in a position to be *sure* they don't matter.

For example, what is the size of a string object? In other words, what value does sizeof(string) return? This could be an important question if you're keeping a close eye on memory consumption, and you're thinking of replacing a raw char* pointer with a string object.

The news about sizeof(string) is "interesting," which is almost certainly what you do not want to hear if you're concerned about space. While it's not uncommon to find string implementations in which strings are the same size as char* pointers, it's also easy to find string implementations where each string is seven times that size. Why the difference? To understand that, we have to know what data a string is likely to store as well as where it might decide to store it.

Virtually every string implementation holds the following information:

- The **size** of the string, i.e., the number of characters it contains.

- The **capacity** of the memory holding the string's characters. (For a review of the difference between a string's size and its capacity, see Item 14.)

- The **value** of the string, i.e., the characters making up the string.

In addition, a string may hold

- A copy of its **allocator**. For an explanation of why this field is optional, turn to Item 10 and read about the curious rules governing allocators.

string implementations that depend on reference counting also contain

- The **reference count** for the value.

Different string implementations put these pieces of information together in different ways. To demonstrate what I mean, I'll show you the data structures used by four different string implementations. There's nothing special about these selections. They all come from STL implementations that are commonly used. They just happen to be the string implementations in the first four libraries I checked.

In implementation A, each string object contains a copy of its allocator, the string's size, its capacity, and a pointer to a dynamically allocated buffer containing both the reference count (the "RefCnt") and the string's value. In this implementation, a string object using the default allocator is four times the size of a pointer. With a custom allocator, the string object would be bigger by about the size of the allocator object:

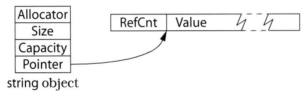

string object

Implementation A

Implementation B's string objects are the same size as a pointer, because they contain nothing but a pointer to a struct. Again, this assumes that the default allocator is used. As in Implementation A, if a custom allocator is used, the string object's size will increase by about the size of the allocator object. In this implementation, use of the default allocator requires no space, thanks to an optimization present here but not present in Implementation A.

The object pointed to by B's string contains the string's size, capacity, and reference count, as well as a pointer to a dynamically allocated buffer holding the string's value. The object also contains some additional data related to concurrency control in multithreaded systems. Such data is outside our purview here, so I've just labeled that part of the data structure "Other:"

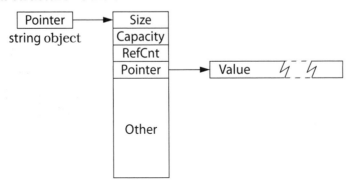

Implementation B

The box for "Other" is larger than the other boxes, because I've drawn the boxes to scale. If one box is twice the size of another, the larger box uses twice as many bytes as the smaller one. In Implementation B, the data for concurrency control is six times the size of a pointer.

string objects under Implementation C are always the size of a pointer, but this pointer points to a dynamically allocated buffer containing everything related to the string: its size, capacity, reference count, and value. There is no per-object allocator support. The buffer also holds some data concerning the shareability of the value, a topic we'll not consider here, so I've labeled it "X". (If you're interested in why a reference counted value might not be shareable in the first place, consult Item 29 of *More Effective C++*.)

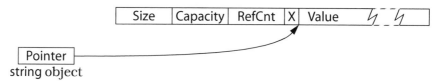

string object

Implementation C

Implementation D's string objects are seven times the size of a pointer (still assuming use of the default allocator). This implementation employs no reference counting, but each string contains an internal buffer large enough to represent string values of up to 15 characters. Small strings can thus be stored entirely within the string object, a feature sometimes known as the "small string optimization." When a string's capacity exceeds 15, the first part of the buffer is used as a pointer to dynamically allocated memory, and the string's value resides in that memory:

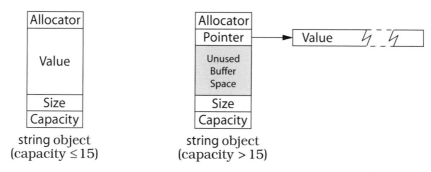

string object   string object
(capacity ≤ 15)   (capacity > 15)

Implementation D

These diagrams do more than just prove I can read source code and draw pretty pictures. They also allow you to deduce that creation of a string in a statement such as this,

    string s("Perse");   // Our dog is named "Persephone", but we
                                     // usually just call her "Perse". Visit her web site
                                     // at http://www.aristeia.com/Persephone/

will cost you zero dynamic allocations under Implementation D, one under Implementations A and C, and two under Implementation B (one for the object pointed to by the string object, one for the character buffer pointed to by that object). If you're concerned about the number of times you dynamically allocate and deallocate memory, or if you're concerned about the memory overhead that often accompanies such allocations, you might want to shy away from Implementation B. On the other hand, the fact that Implementation B's data structure includes specific support for concurrency control in multithreaded systems might mean that it meets your needs better than implementations A or C, the number of dynamic allocations notwithstanding. (Implementation D requires no special support for multithreading, because it doesn't use reference counting. For more on the interaction of threading and reference counted strings, see Item 13. For information on what you may reasonably hope for in the way of threading support in STL containers, consult Item 12.)

In a design based on reference counting, everything outside the string object can be shared by multiple strings (if they have the same value), so something else we can observe from the diagrams is that Implementation A offers less sharing than B or C. In particular, Implementations B and C can share a string's size and capacity, thus potentially reducing the amortized per-object cost of storing that data. Interestingly, the fact that Implementation C fails to support per-object allocators means that it is the only implementation that can share allocators: all strings must use the same one! (Again, for details on the rules governing allocators, turn to Item 10.) Implementation D shares no data across string objects.

An interesting aspect of string behavior you can't fully deduce from the diagrams is the policy regarding memory allocation for small strings. Some implementations refuse to allocate memory for fewer than a certain number of characters, and Implementations A, C, and D are among them. Look again at this statement:

```
string s("Perse");                        // s is a string of size 5
```

Implementation A has a minimum allocation size of 32 characters, so though s's size is 5 under all implementations, its capacity under Implementation A is 31. (The 32nd character is presumably reserved for a trailing null, thus making it easy to implement the c_str member function.) Implementation C also has a minimum, but it's 16, and no space is reserved for a trailing null, so under Implementation C, s's capacity is 16. Implementation D's minimum buffer size is also 16, including room for a trailing null. Of course, what distinguishes Implementation D in this area is that the memory for strings with capacity less than 16 is contained within the string object itself. Implementation B has no minimum allocation, and under Implementation

B, s's capacity is 7. (Why it's not 6 or 5, I don't know. I didn't read the source code that closely, sorry.)

I hope it's obvious that the various implementations' policies on minimum allocations might be important to you if you expect to have lots of short strings and either (1) your release environment has very little memory or (2) you are concerned about locality of reference and want to cluster strings on as few pages as possible.

Clearly, string implementations have more degrees of freedom than are apparent at first glance, and equally clearly, different implementers have taken advantage of this design flexibility in different ways. Let's summarize the things that vary:

- string values may or may not be reference counted. By default, many implementations do use reference counting, but they usually offer a way to turn it off, often via a preprocessor macro. Item 13 gives an example of specific conditions under which you might want to turn it off, but you might want to do so for other reasons, too. For example, reference counting helps only when strings are frequently copied, and some applications just don't copy strings often enough to justify the overhead.

- string objects may range in size from one to at least seven times the size of char* pointers.

- Creation of a new string value may require zero, one, or two dynamic allocations.

- string objects may or may not share information on the string's size and capacity.

- strings may or may not support per-object allocators.

- Different implementations have different policies regarding minimum allocations for character buffers.

Now, don't get me wrong. I think string is one of the most important components of the standard library, and I encourage you to use it as often as you can. Item 13, for example, is devoted to why you should use string in place of dynamically allocated character arrays. At the same time, if you're to make effective use of the STL, you need to be aware of the variability in string implementations, especially if you're writing code that must run on different STL platforms and you face stringent performance requirements.

Besides, string seems so conceptually simple. Who'd have thought the implementations could be so interesting?

Item 16: Know how to pass vector and string data to legacy APIs.

Since C++ was standardized in 1998, the C++ elite haven't been terribly subtle in their attempt to nudge programmers away from arrays and towards vectors. They've been similarly overt in trying to get developers to shift from char* pointers to string objects. There are good reasons for making these changes, including the elimination of common programming errors (see Item 13) and the ability to take full advantage of the power of the STL algorithms (see, e.g., Item 31).

Still, obstacles remain, and one of the most common is the existence of legacy C APIs that traffic in arrays and char* pointers instead of vector and string objects. Such APIs will exist for a long time, so we must make peace with them if we are to use the STL effectively.

Fortunately, it's easy. If you have a vector v and you need to get a pointer to the data in v that can be viewed as an array, just use &v[0]. For a string s, the corresponding incantation is simply s.c_str(). But read on. As the fine print in advertising often points out, certain restrictions apply.

Given

```
vector<int> v;
```

the expression v[0] yields a reference to the first element in the vector, so &v[0] is a pointer to that first element. The elements in a vector are constrained by the C++ Standard to be stored in contiguous memory, just like an array, so if we wish to pass v to a C API that looks something like this,

```
void doSomething(const int* pInts, size_t numInts);
```

we can do it like this:

```
doSomething(&v[0], v.size());
```

Maybe. Probably. The only sticking point is if v is empty. If it is, v.size() is zero, and &v[0] attempts to produce a pointer to something that does not exist. Not good. Undefined results. A safer way to code the call is this:

```
if (!v.empty()) {
    doSomething(&v[0], v.size());
}
```

If you travel in the wrong circles, you may run across shady characters who will tell you that you can use v.begin() in place of &v[0], because (these loathsome creatures will tell you) begin returns an iterator into the vector, and for vectors, iterators are really pointers. That's often true, but as Item 50 reveals, it's not always true, and you should never rely on it. The return type of begin is an iterator, not a pointer, and you should never use begin when you need to get a pointer to the data in a vector. If you're determined to type v.begin() for some reason, type &*v.begin(), because that will yield the same pointer as &v[0], though it's more work for you as a typist and more obscure for people trying to make sense of your code. Frankly, if you're hanging out with people who tell you to use v.begin() instead of &v[0], you need to rethink your social circle.

The approach to getting a pointer to container data that works for vectors isn't reliable for strings, because (1) the data for strings are not guaranteed to be stored in contiguous memory, and (2) the internal representation of a string is not guaranteed to end with a null character. This explains the existence of the string member function c_str, which returns a pointer to the value of the string in a form designed for C. We can thus pass a string s to this function,

```
void doSomething(const char *pString);
```

like this:

```
doSomething(s.c_str());
```

This works even if the string is of length zero. In that case, c_str will return a pointer to a null character. It also works if the string has embedded nulls. If it does, however, doSomething is likely to interpret the first embedded null as the end of the string. string objects don't care if they contain null characters, but char*-based C APIs do.

Look again at the doSomething declarations:

```
void doSomething(const int* pInts, size_t numInts);
void doSomething(const char *pString);
```

In both cases, the pointers being passed are pointers to const. The vector or string data are being passed to an API that will *read* it, not modify it. This is by far the safest thing to do. For strings, it's the only thing to do, because there is no guarantee that c_str yields a pointer to the internal representation of the string data; it could return a pointer to an unmodifiable *copy* of the string's data, one that's correctly formatted for a C API. (If this makes the efficiency hairs on the back of your neck rise up in alarm, rest assured that the alarm is probably false. I don't know of any contemporary library implementation that takes advantage of this latitude.)

For a vector, you have a little more flexibility. If you pass v to a C API that modifies v's elements, that's typically okay, but the called routine must not attempt to change the number of elements in the vector. For example, it must not try to "create" new elements in a vector's unused capacity. If it does, v will become internally inconsistent, because it won't know its correct size any longer. v.size() will yield incorrect results. And if the called routine attempts to add data to a vector whose size and capacity (see Item 14) are the same, truly horrible things could happen. I don't even want to contemplate them. They're just too awful.

Did you notice my use of the word "typically" in the phrase "that's typically okay" in the preceding paragraph? Of course you did. Some vectors have extra constraints on their data, and if you pass a vector to an API that modifies the vector's data, you must ensure that the additional constraints continue to be satisfied. For example, Item 23 explains how sorted vectors can often be a viable alternative to associative containers, but it's important for such vectors to remain sorted. If you pass a sorted vector to an API that may modify the vector's data, you'll need to take into account that the vector may no longer be sorted after the call has returned.

If you have a vector that you'd like to initialize with elements from a C API, you can take advantage of the underlying layout compatibility of vectors and arrays by passing to the API the storage for the vector's elements:

```
// C API: this function takes a pointer to an array of at most arraySize
// doubles and writes data to it. It returns the number of doubles written,
// which is never more than maxNumDoubles.
size_t fillArray(double *pArray, size_t arraySize);

vector<double> vd(maxNumDoubles);          // create a vector whose
                                           // size is maxNumDoubles

vd.resize(fillArray(&vd[0], vd.size()));   // have fillArray write data
                                           // into vd, then resize vd
                                           // to the number of
                                           // elements fillArray wrote
```

This technique works only for vectors, because only vectors are guaranteed to have the same underlying memory layout as arrays. If you want to initialize a string with data from a C API, however, you can do it easily enough. Just have the API put the data into a vector<char>, then copy the data from the vector to the string:

```
// C API: this function takes a pointer to an array of at most arraySize
// chars and writes data to it. It returns the number of chars written,
// which is never more than maxNumChars.
size_t fillString(char *pArray, size_t arraySize);
```

```
vector<char> vc(maxNumChars);                          // create a vector whose
                                                       // size is maxNumChars

size_t charsWritten = fillString(&vc[0], vc.size());   // have fillString write
                                                       // into vc

string s(vc.begin(), vc.begin()+charsWritten);         // copy data from vc to s
                                                       // via range constructor
                                                       // ( see Item 5)
```

In fact, the idea of having a C API put data into a vector and then copying the data into the STL container you really want it in always works:

```
size_t fillArray(double *pArray, size_t arraySize);    // as above

vector<double> vd(maxNumDoubles);                      // also as above
vd.resize(fillArray(&vd[0], vd.size()));

deque<double> d(vd.begin(), vd.end());                 // copy data into
                                                       // deque

list<double> l(vd.begin(), vd.end());                  // copy data into list

set<double> s(vd.begin(), vd.end());                   // copy data into set
```

Furthermore, this hints at how STL containers other than vector or
string can pass their data to C APIs. Just copy each container's data
into a vector, then pass it to the API:

```
void doSomething(const int* pInts, size_t numInts);  // C API (from above)
set<int> intSet;                                       // set that will hold
...                                                    // data to pass to API
vector<int> v(intSet.begin(), intSet.end());           // copy set data into
                                                       // a vector
if (!v.empty()) doSomething(&v[0], v.size());          // pass the data to
                                                       // the API
```

You could copy the data into an array, too, then pass the array to the
C API, but why would you want to? Unless you know the size of the
container during compilation, you'd have to allocate the array dynamically, and Item 13 explains why you should prefer vectors to dynamically allocated arrays anyway.

Item 17: Use "the swap trick" to trim excess capacity.

So you're writing software to support the TV game show *Give Me Lots
Of Money — Now!*, and you're keeping track of the potential contestants, whom you have stored in a vector:

```
class Contestant { ... };

vector<Contestant> contestants;
```

When the show puts out a call for new contestants, it's inundated with applicants, and your vector quickly acquires a lot of elements. As the show's producers vet the prospective players, however, a relatively small number of viable candidates get moved to the front of the vector (perhaps via partial_sort or partition — see Item 31), and the candidates no longer in the running are removed from the vector (typically by calling a range form of erase — see Item 5). This does a fine job of reducing the size of the vector, but it does nothing to reduce its capacity. If your vector held a hundred thousand potential candidates at some point, its capacity would continue to be at least 100,000, even if later it held only, say, 10.

To avoid having your vector hold onto memory it no longer needs, you'd like to have a way to reduce its capacity from the maximum it used to the amount it currently needs. Such a reduction in capacity is commonly known as "shrink to fit." Shrink-to-fit is easy to program, but the code is — how shall I put this? — something less than intuitive. Let me show it to you, then I'll explain how it works.

This is how you trim the excess capacity from your contestants vector:

```
vector<Contestant>(contestants).swap(contestants);
```

The expression vector<Contestant>(contestants) creates a temporary vector that is a copy of contestants; vector's copy constructor does the work. However, vector's copy constructor allocates *only as much memory as is needed for the elements being copied*, so this temporary vector has no excess capacity. We then swap the data in the temporary vector with that in contestants, and by the time we're done, contestants has the trimmed capacity of the temporary, and the temporary holds the bloated capacity that used to be in contestants. At that point (the end of the statement), the temporary vector is destroyed, thus freeing the memory formerly used by contestants. *Voilà!* Shrink-to-fit.

The same trick is applicable to strings:

```
string s;
...                         // make s large, then erase most
                            // of its characters
string(s).swap(s);          // do a "shrink-to-fit" on s
```

Now, the language police require that I inform you that there's no guarantee that this technique will truly eliminate excess capacity. Implementers are free to give vectors and strings excess capacity if they want to, and sometimes they want to. For example, they may have a minimum capacity below which they never go, or they may constrain a vector's or string's capacity to be a power of two. (In my experience, such anomalies are more common in string implementations than in vector implementations. For examples, see Item 15.) This approach to "shrink-to-fit," then, doesn't really mean "make the capacity as small as possible," it means "make the capacity as small as this implementation is willing to make it given the current size of the container." Short of switching to a different implementation of the STL, however, this is the best you can do, so when you think "shrink-to-fit" for vectors and strings, think "the swap trick."

As an aside, a variant of the swap trick can be used both to clear a container and to reduce its capacity to the minimum your implementation offers. You simply do the swap with a temporary vector or string that is default-constructed:

```
vector<Contestant> v;
string s;

...                              // use v and s

vector<Contestant>().swap(v);    // clear v and minimize its capacity
string().swap(s);                // clear s and minimize its capacity
```

One final observation about the swap trick, or, rather, about swap in general. Swapping the contents of two containers also swaps their iterators, pointers, and references. Iterators, pointers, and references that used to point to elements in one container remain valid and point to the same elements — *but in the other container* — after the swap.

Item 18: Avoid using vector<bool>.

As an STL container, there are really only two things wrong with vector<bool>. First, it's not an STL container. Second, it doesn't hold bools. Other than that, there's not much to object to.

An object doesn't become an STL container just because somebody says it's one. An object becomes an STL container only if it fulfills all the container requirements laid down in section 23.1 of the Standard for C++. Among the requirements is that if c is a container of objects of type T and c supports operator[], the following must compile:

```
T *p = &c[0];                    // initialize a T* with the address
                                 // of whatever operator[] returns
```

In other words, if you use operator[] to get at one of the T objects in a Container<T>, you can get a pointer to that object by taking its address. (This assumes that T hasn't perversely overloaded operator&.) If vector<bool> is to be a container, then, this code must compile:

```
vector<bool> v;

bool *pb = &v[0];                // initialize a bool* with the address of
                                 // what vector<bool>::operator[] returns
```

But it won't compile. It won't, because vector<bool> is a pseudo-container that contains not actual bools, but a packed representation of bools that is designed to save space. In a typical implementation, each "bool" stored in the "vector" occupies a single bit, and an eight-bit byte holds eight "bools." Internally, vector<bool> uses the moral equivalent of bitfields to represent the bools it pretends to be holding.

Like bools, bitfields represent only two possible values, but there is an important difference between true bools and bitfields masquerading as bools. You may create a pointer to a real bool, but pointers to individual bits are forbidden.

References to individual bits are forbidden, too, and this posed a problem for the design of vector<bool>'s interface, because the return type of vector<T>::operator[] is supposed to be T&. That wouldn't be a problem if vector<bool> really held bools, but because it doesn't, vector<bool>::operator[] would need somehow to return a reference to a bit, and there's no such thing.

To deal with this difficulty, vector<bool>::operator[] returns an object that *acts like* a reference to a bit, a so-called *proxy object*. (You don't need to understand proxy objects to use the STL, but they're a C++ technique worth knowing about. For information about them, consult Item 30 of *More Effective C++* as well as the "Proxy" chapter in Gamma *et al.*'s *Design Patterns* [6].) Stripped down to the bare essentials, vector<bool> looks like this:

```
template <typename Allocator>
vector<bool, Allocator> {
public:

    class reference { ... };            // class to generate proxies for
                                        // references to individual bits

    reference operator[](size_type n);  // operator[] returns a proxy

    ...

};
```

Now it's clear why this code won't compile:

```
vector<bool> v;

bool *pb = &v[0];                       // error! the expression on the right is
                                        // of type vector<bool>::reference*,
                                        // not bool*
```

Because it won't compile, vector<bool> fails to satisfy the requirements for STL containers. Yes, vector<bool> is in the Standard, and yes, it *almost* satisfies the requirements for STL containers, but almost just isn't good enough. The more you write your own templates designed to work with the STL, the more you'll appreciate that. The day will come, I assure you, when you'll write a template that will work only if taking the address of a container element yields a pointer to the contained type, and when that day comes, you'll suddenly understand the difference between being a container and *almost* being a container.

You may wonder why vector<bool> is in the Standard, given that it's not a container and all. The answer has to do with a noble experiment that failed, but let me defer that discussion for a moment while I address a more pressing question. To wit, if vector<bool> should be avoided because it's not a container, what should you use when you *need* a vector<bool>?

The standard library provides two alternatives that suffice almost all the time. The first is deque<bool>. A deque offers almost everything a vector does (the only notable omissions are reserve and capacity), and a deque<bool> is an STL container that really contains bools. Of course, the underlying memory for a deque isn't contiguous, so you can't pass the data behind a deque<bool> to a C API[†] that expects an array of bool (see Item 16), but you couldn't do that with a vector<bool> anyway because there's no portable way to get at the data for a vector<bool>. (The techniques that work for vectors in Item 16 fail to compile for vector<bool>, because they depend on being able to get a pointer to the type of element contained in the vector. Have I mentioned that a vector<bool> doesn't contain bools?)

The second alternative to vector<bool> is bitset. bitset isn't an STL container, but it is part of the standard C++ library. Unlike STL containers, its size (number of elements) is fixed during compilation, so there is no support for inserting or erasing elements. Furthermore, because it's not an STL container, it offers no support for iterators. Like vector<bool>, however, it uses a compact representation that devotes only a single bit to each value it contains. It offers vector<bool>'s special flip member function, as well as a number of other special member functions that make sense for collections of bits. If you can live without iterators and dynamic changes in size, you'll probably find that a bitset will serve you well.

And now let me discuss the noble experiment that failed, the one that left behind as its residue the STL non-container vector<bool>. I mentioned earlier that proxy objects are often useful in C++ software development. The members of the C++ Standardization Committee

---

† This would presumably be a C99 API, because bool was added to C only as of that version of the language.

were well aware of this, so they decided to develop vector<bool> as a demonstration of how the STL could support containers whose elements are accessed via proxies. With this example in the Standard, they reasoned, practitioners would have a ready reference for implementing their own proxy-based containers.

Alas, what they discovered was that it was *not* possible to create proxy-based containers that satisfy all the requirements of STL containers. For one reason or another, however, their failed attempt at developing one remained in the Standard. One can speculate on why vector<bool> was retained, but practically speaking, it doesn't matter. What does matter is this: vector<bool> doesn't satisfy the requirements of an STL container; you're best off not using it; and deque<bool> and bitset are alternative data structures that will almost certainly satisfy your need for the capabilities promised by vector<bool>.

Associative Containers

Somewhat like the polychromatic horse in *The Wizard of Oz* movie, the associative containers are creatures of a different color. True, they share many characteristics with the sequence containers, but they differ in a number of fundamental ways. For example, they automatically keep themselves sorted; they view their contents through the lens of equivalence instead of equality; sets and maps reject duplicate entries; and maps and multimaps generally ignore half of each object they contain. Yes, the associative containers are containers, but if you'll excuse my likening vectors and strings to Kansas, we are definitely not in Kansas any more.

In the Items that follow, I explain the critical notion of equivalence, describe an important restriction on comparison functions, motivate custom comparison functions for associative containers of pointers, discuss the official and practical sides of key constness, and offer advice on improving the efficiency of associative containers.

At the end of the chapter, I examine the STL's lack of containers based on hash tables, and I survey two common (nonstandard) implementations. Though the STL proper doesn't offer hash tables, you need not write your own or do without. High-quality implementations are readily available.

Item 19: Understand the difference between equality and equivalence.

The STL is awash in comparisons of objects to see if they have the same value. For example, when you ask find to locate the first object in a range with a particular value, find has to be able to compare two objects to see if the value of one is the same as the value of the other. Similarly, when you attempt to insert a new element into a set, set::insert has to be able to determine whether that element's value is already in the set.

The find algorithm and set's insert member function are representative of many functions that must determine whether two values are the same. Yet they do it in different ways. find's definition of "the same" is *equality*, which is based on operator==. set::insert's definition of "the same" is *equivalence*, which is usually based on operator<. Because these are different definitions, it's possible for one definition to dictate that two objects have the same value while the other definition decrees that they do not. As a result, you must understand the difference between equality and equivalence if you are to make effective use of the STL.

Operationally, the notion of equality is based on operator==. If the expression "x == y" returns true, x and y have equal values, otherwise they don't. That's pretty straightforward, though it's useful to bear in mind that just because x and y have equal values does not necessarily imply that all of their data members have equal values. For example, we might have a Widget class that internally keeps track of its last time of access,

```
class Widget {
public:
    ...
private:
    TimeStamp lastAccessed;
    ...
};
```

and we might have an operator== for Widgets that ignores this field:

```
bool operator==(const Widget& lhs, const Widget& rhs)
{
    // code that ignores the lastAccessed field
}
```

In that case, two Widgets would have equal values even if their lastAccessed fields were different.

Equivalence is based on the relative ordering of object values in a sorted range. Equivalence makes the most sense if you think about it in terms of the sort order that is part of every standard associative container (i.e., set, multiset, map, and multimap). Two objects x and y have equivalent values with respect to the sort order used by an associative container c if neither precedes the other in c's sort order. That sounds complicated, but in practice, it's not. Consider, as an example, a set<Widget> s. Two Widgets w1 and w2 have equivalent values with respect to s if neither precedes the other in s's sort order. The default comparison function for a set<Widget> is less<Widget>, and by default less<Widget> simply calls operator< for Widgets, so w1 and w2 have equivalent values with respect to operator< if the following expression is true:

```
!(w1 < w2)                              // it's not true that w1 < w2
&&                                      // and
!(w2 < w1)                              // it's not true that w2 < w1
```

This makes sense: two values are equivalent (with respect to some ordering criterion) if neither precedes the other (according to that criterion).

In the general case, the comparison function for an associative container isn't operator< or even less, it's a user-defined predicate. (See Item 39 for more information on predicates.) Every standard associative container makes its sorting predicate available through its key_comp member function, so two objects x and y have equivalent values with respect to an associative container c's sorting criterion if the following evaluates to true:

```
!c.key_comp()(x, y) && !c.key_comp()(y, x)   // it's not true that x precedes
                                             // y in c's sort order and it's
                                             // also not true that y precedes
                                             // x in c's sort order
```

The expression !c.key_comp()(x, y) looks nasty, but once you understand that c.key_comp() is returning a function (or a function object), the nastiness dissipates. !c.key_comp()(x, y) is just calling the function (or function object) returned by key_comp, and it's passing x and y as arguments. Then it negates the result. c.key_comp()(x, y) returns true only when x precedes y in c's sort order, so !c.key_comp()(x, y) is true only when x *doesn't* precede y in c's sort order.

To fully grasp the implications of equality versus equivalence, consider a case-insensitive set<string>, i.e., a set<string> where the set's comparison function ignores the case of the characters in the strings. Such a comparison function would consider "STL" and "stL" to be equivalent. Item 35 shows how to implement a function, ciStringCompare, that performs a case-insensitive comparison, but set wants a comparison function *type*, not an actual function. To bridge this gap, we write a functor class whose operator() calls ciStringCompare:

```
struct CIStringCompare:                 // class for case-insensitive
  public                                // string comparisons;
  binary_function<string, string, bool> {  // see Item 40 for info on
                                        // this base class
  bool operator()(const string& lhs,
              const string& rhs) const
  {
    return ciStringCompare(lhs, rhs);   // see Item 35 for how
  }                                     // ciStringCompare is
                                        // implemented
};
```

Given CIStringCompare, it's easy to create a case-insensitive set<string>:

```
set<string, CIStringCompare> ciss;      // ciss = "case-insensitive
                                        //        string set"
```

If we insert "Persephone" and "persephone" into the set, only the first string is added, because the second one is equivalent to the first:

```
ciss.insert("Persephone");          // a new element is added to the set

ciss.insert("persephone");          // no new element is added to the set
```

If we now search for the string "persephone" using set's find member function, the search will succeed,

```
if (ciss.find("persephone") != ciss.end()) ...      // this test will succeed
```

but if we use the non-member find algorithm, the search will fail:

```
if (find( ciss.begin(), ciss.end(),
          "persephone") != ciss.end()) ...          // this test will fail
```

That's because "persephone" is *equivalent* to "Persephone" (with respect to the comparison functor CIStringCompare), but it's not *equal* to it (because string("persephone") != string("Persephone")). This example demonstrates one reason why you should follow the advice in Item 44 and prefer member functions (like set::find) to their non-member counterparts (like find).

You might wonder why the standard associative containers are based on equivalence instead of equality. After all, most programmers have an intuition about equality that they lack for equivalence. (Were that not the case, there'd be no need for this Item.) The answer is simple at first glance, but the more closely you look, the more subtle it becomes.

The standard associative containers are kept in sorted order, so each container must have a comparison function (less, by default) that defines how to keep things sorted. Equivalence is defined in terms of this comparison function, so clients of a standard associative container need to specify only one comparison function (the one determining the sort order) for any container they use. If the associative containers used equality to determine when two objects have the same value, each associative container would need, in addition to its comparison function for sorting, a second comparison function for determining when two values are equal. (By default, this comparison function would presumably be equal_to, but it's interesting to note that equal_to is never used as a default comparison function in the STL. When equality is needed in the STL, the convention is to simply call operator== directly. For example, this is what the non-member find algorithm does.)

Let's suppose we had a set-like STL container called set2CF, "set with two comparison functions." The first comparison function would be used to determine the sort order of the set, the second would be used to determine whether two objects had the same value. Now consider this set2CF:

```
set2CF<string, CIStringCompare, equal_to<string> > s;
```

Here, s sorts its strings internally without regard to case, and the equality criterion is the intuitive one: two strings have the same value if they are equal to one another. Let's insert our two spellings of Hades' reluctant bride (Persephone) into s:

```
s.insert("Persephone");
s.insert("persephone");
```

What should this do? If we observe that "Persephone" != "persephone" and insert them both into s, what order should they go in? Remember that the sorting function can't tell them apart. Do we insert them in some arbitrary order, thus giving up the ability to traverse the contents of the set in deterministic order? (This inability to traverse associative container elements in a deterministic order already afflicts multisets and multimaps, because the Standard places no constraints on the relative ordering of equivalent values (for multisets) or keys (for multimaps).) Or do we insist on a deterministic ordering of s's contents and ignore the second attempted insertion (the one for "persephone")? If we do that, what happens here?

```
if (s.find("persephone") != s.end()) ...        // does this test succeed or fail?
```

Presumably find employs the equality check, but if we ignored the second call to insert in order to maintain a deterministic ordering of the elements in s, this find will fail, even though the insertion of "persephone" was ignored on the basis of its being a duplicate value!

The long and short of it is that by using only a single comparison function and by employing equivalence as the arbiter of what it means for two values to be "the same," the standard associative containers sidestep a whole host of difficulties that would arise if two comparison functions were allowed. Their behavior may seem a little odd at first (especially when one realizes that member and non-member find may return different results), but in the long run, it avoids the kind of confusion that would arise from mixing uses of equality and equivalence within standard associative containers.

Interestingly, once you leave the realm of *sorted* associative containers, the situation changes, and the issue of equality versus equivalence can be — and has been — revisited. There are two common designs for nonstandard (but widely available) associative containers based on hash tables. One design is based on equality, while the other is based on equivalence. I encourage you to turn to Item 25 to learn more about these containers and the design decisions they've adopted.

Item 20: Specify comparison types for associative containers of pointers.

Suppose you have a set of string* pointers and you insert the names of some animals into the set:

```
set<string*> ssp;                          // ssp = "set of string ptrs"

ssp.insert(new string("Anteater"));
ssp.insert(new string("Wombat"));
ssp.insert(new string("Lemur"));
ssp.insert(new string("Penguin"));
```

You then write the following code to print the contents of the set, expecting the strings to come out in alphabetical order. After all, sets keep their contents sorted.

```
for (set<string*>::const_iterator i = ssp.begin();   // you expect to see
     i != ssp.end();                                  // this: "Anteater",
     ++i)                                              // "Lemur", "Penguin",
    cout << *i << endl;                                // "Wombat"
```

The comment describes what you expect to see, but you don't see that at all. Instead, you see four hexadecimal numbers. They are pointer values. Because the set holds pointers, *i isn't a string, it's a *pointer* to a string. Let this be a lesson that reminds you to adhere to the guidance of Item 43 and avoid writing your own loops. If you'd used a call to the copy algorithm instead,

```
copy(ssp.begin(), ssp.end(),                      // copy the strings in
     ostream_iterator<string>(cout, "\n"));       // ssp to cout (but this
                                                  // won't compile)
```

you'd not only have typed fewer characters, you'd have found out about your error sooner, because this call to copy won't compile. ostream_iterator insists on knowing the type of object being printed, so when you tell it it's a string (by passing that as the template parameter), your compilers detect the mismatch between that and the type of objects stored in ssp (which is string*), and they refuse to compile the code. Score another one for type safety.

If you exasperatedly change the *i in your explicit loop to **i, you *might* get the output you want, but you probably won't. Yes, the animal names will be printed, but the chances of their coming out in alphabetical order are only 1 in 24. ssp keeps its contents in sorted order, but it holds pointers, so it sorts by *pointer value*, not by string value. There are 24 possible permutations for four pointer values, so there are 24 possible orders for the pointers to be stored in. Hence the odds of 1 in 24 of your seeing the strings in alphabetical order.[†]

To surmount this problem, it helps to recall that

```
set<string*> ssp;
```

is shorthand for this:

```
set<string*, less<string*> > ssp;
```

Well, to be completely accurate, it's shorthand for

```
set<string*, less<string*>, allocator<string*> > ssp;
```

but allocators don't concern us in this Item, so we'll ignore them.

If you want the string* pointers to be stored in the set in an order determined by the string values, you can't use the default comparison functor class less<string*>. You must instead write your own comparison functor class, one whose objects take string* pointers and order them by the values of the strings they point to. Like this:

```
struct StringPtrLess:
    public binary_function<const string*,       // see Item 40 for the
                           const string*,        // reason for this base
                           bool> {               // class
    bool operator()(const string *ps1, const string *ps2) const
    {
        return *ps1 < *ps2;
    }
};
```

Then you can use StringPtrLess as ssp's comparison type:

```
typedef set<string*, StringPtrLess> StringPtrSet;

StringPtrSet ssp;                    // create a set of strings and order
                                     // them as defined by StringPtrLess

...                                  // insert the same four strings as
                                     // before
```

Now your loop will finally do what you want it to do (provided you've fixed the earlier problem whereby you used *i instead of **i):

[†] Practically speaking, the 24 permutations are not equally likely, so the "1 in 24" statement is a bit misleading. Still, there *are* 24 different orders, and you *could* get any one of them.

```
for (StringPtrSet::const_iterator i = ssp.begin();   // prints "Anteater",
     i != ssp.end();                                 // "Lemur",
     ++i)                                            // "Penguin",
   cout << **i << endl;                              // "Wombat"
```

If you want to use an algorithm instead, you could write a function that knows how to dereference string* pointers before printing them, then use that function in conjunction with for_each:

```
void print(const string *ps)                         // print to cout the
{                                                    // object pointed to
   cout << *ps << endl;                              // by ps
}

for_each(ssp.begin(), ssp.end(), print);            // invoke print on each
                                                    // element in ssp
```

Or you could get fancy and write a generic dereferencing functor class, then use that with transform and an ostream_iterator:

```
// when functors of this type are passed a T*, they return a const T&
struct Dereference {

   template <typename T>
   const T& operator()(const T *ptr) const
   {
      return *ptr;
   }

};

transform( ssp.begin(), ssp.end(),                  // "transform" each
           ostream_iterator<string>(cout, "\n"),   // element in ssp by
           Dereference());                          // dereferencing it,
                                                    // writing the results
                                                    // to cout
```

Replacement of loops with algorithms, however, is not the point, at least not for this Item. (It *is* the point for Item 43.) The point is that anytime you create a standard associative container of pointers, you must bear in mind that the container will be sorted by the values of the pointers. Only rarely will this be what you want, so you'll almost always want to create your own functor class to serve as a comparison type.

Notice that I wrote "comparison *type.*" You may wonder why you have to go to the trouble of creating a functor class instead of simply writing a comparison function for the set. For example, you might think to try

```
bool stringPtrLess(const string* ps1,          // would-be comparison
               const string* ps2)              // function for string*
{                                               // pointers to be sorted by
   return *ps1 < *ps2;                          // string value
}

set<string, stringPtrLess> ssp;                 // attempt to use stringPtrLess
                                                // as ssp's comparison function;
                                                // this won't compile
```

The problem here is that each of the set template's three parameters is a *type*. Unfortunately, stringPtrLess isn't a type, it's a function. That's why the attempt to use stringPtrLess as set's comparison function won't compile. set doesn't want a function, it wants a type that it can internally instantiate to *create* a function.

Anytime you create associative containers of pointers, figure you're probably going to have to specify the container's comparison type, too. Most of the time, your comparison type will just dereference the pointers and compare the pointed-to objects (as is done in StringPtrLess above). That being the case, you might as well keep a template for such comparison functors close at hand. Like this:

```
struct DereferenceLess {

   template <typename PtrType>
   bool operator()(PtrType pT1,             // parameters are passed by
                PtrType pT2) const          // value, because we expect them
   {                                        // to be (or to act like) pointers
      return *pT1 < *pT2;
   }

};
```

Such a template eliminates the need to write classes like StringPtrLess, because we can use DereferenceLess instead:

```
set<string*, DereferenceLess> ssp;           // behaves the same as
                                             // set<string*, StringPtrLess>
```

Oh, one more thing. This Item is about associative containers of pointers, but it applies equally well to containers of objects that *act* like pointers, e.g., smart pointers and iterators. If you have an associative container of smart pointers or of iterators, plan on specifying the comparison type for it, too. Fortunately, the solution for pointers tends to work for pointeresque objects, too. Just as DereferenceLess is likely to be suitable as the comparison type for an associative container of T*, it's likely to work as the comparison type for containers of iterators and smart pointers to T objects, too.

Item 21: Always have comparison functions return false for equal values.

Let me show you something kind of cool. Create a set where less_equal is the comparison type, then insert 10 into the set:

```
set<int, less_equal<int> > s;        // s is sorted by "<="
s.insert(10);                        // insert the value 10
```

Now try inserting 10 again:

```
s.insert(10);
```

For this call to insert, the set has to figure out whether 10 is already present. We know that it is, but the set is dumb as toast, so it has to check. To make it easier to understand what happens when the set does this, we'll call the 10 that was initially inserted 10_A and the 10 that we're trying to insert 10_B.

The set runs through its internal data structures looking for the place to insert 10_B. It ultimately has to check 10_B to see if it's the same as 10_A. The definition of "the same" for associative containers is equivalence (see Item 19), so the set tests to see whether 10_B is equivalent to 10_A. When performing this test, it naturally uses the set's comparison function. In this example, that's operator<=, because we specified less_equal as the set's comparison function, and less_equal means operator<=. The set thus checks to see whether this expression is true:

```
!(10A <= 10B) && !(10B <= 10A)       // test 10A and 10B for equivalence
```

Well, 10_A and 10_B are both 10, so it's clearly true that $10_A <= 10_B$. Equally clearly, $10_B <= 10_A$. The above expression thus simplifies to

```
!(true) && !(true)
```

and that simplifies to

```
false && false
```

which is simply false. That is, the set concludes that 10_A and 10_B are *not* equivalent, hence *not* the same, and it thus goes about inserting 10_B into the container alongside 10_A. Technically, this action yields undefined behavior, but the nearly universal outcome is that the set ends up with *two* copies of the value 10, and that means it's not a set any longer. By using less_equal as our comparison type, we've corrupted the container! Furthermore, *any* comparison function where equal values return true will do the same thing. Equal values are, by definition, *not* equivalent! Isn't that cool?

Okay, maybe your definition of cool isn't the same as mine. Even so, you'll still want to make sure that the comparison functions you use for associative containers always return false for equal values. You'll need to be vigilant, however. It's surprisingly easy to run afoul of this constraint.

For example, Item 20 describes how to write a comparison function for containers of string* pointers such that the container sorts its contents by the values of the strings instead of the values of the pointers. That comparison function sorts them in ascending order, but let's suppose you're in need of a comparison function for a container of string* pointers that sorts in descending order. The natural thing to do is to grab the existing code and modify it. If you're not careful, you might come up with this, where I've highlighted the changes to the code in Item 20:

```
struct StringPtrGreater:                      // highlights show how
    public binary_function<const string*,     // this code was changed
                           const string*,      // from page 89. Beware,
                           bool> {             // this code is flawed!

    bool operator()(const string *ps1, const string *ps2) const
    {
        return !(*ps1 < *ps2);                // just negate the old test;
    }                                          // this is incorrect!
};
```

The idea here is to reverse the sort order by negating the test inside the comparison function. Unfortunately, negating "<" doesn't give you ">" (which is what you want), it gives you ">=". And you now understand that ">=", because it will return true for equal values, is an invalid comparison function for associative containers.

The comparison type you really want is this one:

```
struct StringPtrGreater:                      // this is a valid
    public binary_function<const string*,     // comparison type for
                           const string*,      // associative containers
                           bool> {

    bool operator()(const string *ps1, const string *ps2) const
    {
        return *ps2 < *ps1;                   // return whether *ps2
    }                                          // precedes *ps1 (i.e., swap
                                               // the order of the
};                                             // operands)
```

To avoid falling into this trap, all you need to remember is that the return value of a comparison function indicates whether one value precedes another in the sort order defined by that function. Equal values never precede one another, so comparison functions should always return false for equal values.

Sigh.

I know what you're thinking. You're thinking, "Sure, that makes sense for set and map, because those containers can't hold duplicates. But what about multiset and multimap? Those containers may contain duplicates, so what do I care if the container thinks that two objects of equal value aren't equivalent? It will store them both, which is what the multi containers are supposed to do. No problem, right?"

Wrong. To see why, let's go back to the original example, but this time we'll use a multiset:

```
multiset<int, less_equal<int> > s;          // s is still sorted by "<="
s.insert(10);                               // insert 10_A
s.insert(10);                               // insert 10_B
```

s now has two copies of 10 in it, so we'd expect that if we do an equal_range on it, we'll get back a pair of iterators that define a range containing both copies. But that's not possible. equal_range, its name notwithstanding, doesn't identify a range of equal values, it identifies a range of *equivalent* values. In this example, s's comparison function says that 10_A and 10_B are not equivalent, so there's no way that both can be in the range identified by equal_range.

You see? Unless your comparison functions always return false for equal values, you break all standard associative containers, regardless of whether they are allowed to store duplicates.

Technically speaking, comparison functions used to sort associative containers must define a "strict weak ordering" over the objects they compare. (Comparison functions passed to algorithms like sort (see Item 31) are similarly constrained.) If you're interested in the details of what it means to be a strict weak ordering, you can find them in many comprehensive STL references, including Josuttis' *The C++ Standard Library* [3], Austern's *Generic Programming and the STL* [4], and the SGI STL Web Site [21]. I've never found the details terribly illuminating, but one of the requirements of a strict weak ordering bears directly on this Item. That requirement is that any function defining a strict weak ordering must return false if it's passed two copies of the same value.

Hey! That *is* this Item!

Item 22: Avoid in-place key modification in set and multiset.

The motivation for this Item is easy to understand. Like all the standard associative containers, set and multiset keep their elements in sorted order, and the proper behavior of these containers is dependent on their remaining sorted. If you change the value of an element in an associative container (e.g., change a 10 to a 1000), the new value might not be in the correct location, and that would break the sortedness of the container. Simple, right?

It's especially simple for map and multimap, because programs that attempt to change the value of a key in these containers won't compile:

```
map<int, string> m;
...
m.begin()->first = 10;              // error! map keys can't be changed
multimap<int, string> mm;
...
mm.begin()->first = 20;             // error! multimap keys can't
                                    // be changed, either
```

That's because the elements in an object of type map<K, V> or multimap<K, V> are of type pair<const K, V>. Because the type of the key is const K, it can't be changed. (Well, you can probably change it if you employ a const_cast, as we'll see below. Believe it or not, sometimes that's what you *want* to do.)

But notice that the title of this Item doesn't mention map or multimap. There's a reason for that. As the example above demonstrates, in-place key modification is impossible for map and multimap (unless you use a cast), but it may be possible for set and multiset. For objects of type set<T> or multiset<T>, the type of the elements stored in the container is simply T, not const T. Hence, the elements in a set or multiset may be changed anytime you want to. No cast is required. (Actually, things aren't quite that straightforward, but we'll come to that presently. There's no reason to get ahead of ourselves. First we crawl. Later we crawl on broken glass.)

Let us begin with an understanding of why the elements in a set or multiset aren't const. Suppose we have a class for employees:

```
class Employee {
public:
    ...
    const string& name() const;            // get employee name
    void setName(const string& name);      // set employee name

    const string& title() const;           // get employee title
    void setTitle(const string& title);    // set employee title

    int idNumber() const;                  // get employee ID number
    ...
};
```

96   Item 22   Associative Containers

As you can see, there are various bits of information we can get about employees. Let us make the reasonable assumption, however, that each employee has a unique ID number, a number that is returned by the idNumber function. To create a set of employees, then, it could easily make sense to order the set by ID number only, like this:

```
struct IDNumberLess:
  public binary_function<Employee, Employee, bool> {       // see Item 40
  bool operator()( const Employee& lhs,
                   const Employee& rhs) const
  {
    return lhs.idNumber() < rhs.idNumber();
  }
};

typedef set<Employee, IDNumberLess> EmpIDSet;

EmpIDSet se;                         // se is a set of employees
                                     // sorted by ID number
```

Practically speaking, the employee ID number is the *key* for the elements in this set. The rest of the employee data is just along for the ride. That being the case, there's no reason why we shouldn't be able to change the title of a particular employee to something interesting. Like so:

```
Employee selectedID;                 // variable to hold employee
                                     // with selected ID number
...
EmpIDSet::iterator i = se.find(selectedID);
if (i != se.end()) {
  i->setTitle("Corporate Deity");    // give employee new title
}
```

Because all we're doing here is changing an aspect of an employee that is unrelated to the way the set is sorted (a *non-key* part of the employee), this code can't corrupt the set. That's why it's legal. But making it legal precludes having the elements of a set/multiset be const. And that's why they aren't.

Why, you might wonder, doesn't the same logic apply to the keys in maps and multimaps? Wouldn't it make sense to create a map from employees to, say, the country in which they live, a map where the comparison function was IDNumberLess, just as in the previous example? And given such a map, wouldn't it be reasonable to change an employee's title without affecting the employee's ID number, just as in the previous example?

To be brutally frank, I think it would. Being equally frank, however, it doesn't matter what I think. What matters is what the Standardization Committee thought, and what it thought is that map/multimap keys should be const and set/multiset values shouldn't be.

Because the values in a set or multiset are not const, attempts to change them may compile. The purpose of this Item is to alert you that if you do change an element in a set or multiset, you must be sure not to change a *key part* — a part of the element that affects the sortedness of the container. If you do, you may corrupt the container, using the container will yield undefined results, and it will be your fault. On the other hand, this constraint applies only to the key parts of the contained objects. For all other parts of the contained elements, it's open season; change away!

Except for the broken glass. Remember the broken glass I referred to earlier? We're there now. Grab some bandages and follow me.

Even if set and multiset elements aren't const, there are ways for implementations to keep them from being modified. For example, an implementation could have operator* for a set<T>::iterator return a const T&. That is, it could have the result of dereferencing a set iterator be a reference-to-*const* element of the set. Under such an implementation, there'd be no way to modify set or multiset elements, because all the ways of accessing the elements would add a const before letting you at them.

Are such implementations legal? Arguably yes. And arguably no. The Standard is inconsistent in this area, and in accord with Murphy's Law, different implementers have interpreted it in different ways. The result is that it's not uncommon to find STL implementations where this code, which I earlier claimed should compile, won't compile:

```
EmpIDSet se;                        // as before, se is a set of employees
                                    // sorted by ID number

Employee selectedID;                // as before, selectedID is a dummy
                                    // employee with the selected ID
                                    // number
...
EmpIDSet::iterator i = se.find(selectedID);
if (i != se.end()) {
  i->setTitle("Corporate Deity");   // some STL implementations will
}                                   // reject this line
```

Because of the equivocal state of the Standard and the differing interpretations it has engendered, code that attempts to modify elements in a set or multiset isn't portable.

So where do we stand? Encouragingly, things aren't complicated:

- If portability is not a concern, you want to change the value of an element in a set or multiset, and your STL implementation will let you get away with it, go ahead and do it. Just be sure not to change a key part of the element, i.e., a part of the element that could affect the sortedness of the container.

- If you value portability, assume that the elements in sets and multisets cannot be modified, at least not without a cast.

Ah, casts. We've seen that it can be entirely reasonable to change a non-key portion of an element in a set or a multiset, so I feel compelled to show you how to do it. How to do it correctly and portably, that is. It's not hard, but it requires a subtlety too many programmers overlook: you must cast to a *reference*. As an example, look again at the setTitle call we just saw that failed to compile under some implementations:

```
EmpIDSet::iterator i = se.find(selectedID);
if (i != se.end()) {
   i->setTitle("Corporate Deity");        // some STL implementations will
}                                          // reject this line because *i is const
```

To get this to compile and behave correctly, we must cast away the constness of *i. Here's the correct way to do it:

```
if (i != se.end()) {                                    // cast away
   const_cast<Employee&>(*i).setTitle("Corporate Deity");   // constness
}                                                       // of *i
```

This takes the object pointed to by i, tells your compilers to treat the result of the cast as a reference to a (non-const) Employee, then invoke setTitle on the reference. Rather than explain why this works, I'll explain why an alternative approach fails to behave the way people often expect it to.

Many people come up with this code,

```
if (i != se.end()) {                                   // cast *i
   static_cast<Employee>(*i).setTitle("Corporate Deity");   // to an
}                                                      // Employee
```

which is equivalent to the following:

```
if (i != se.end()) {                                   // same as above,
   ((Employee)(*i)).setTitle("Corporate Deity");       // but using C
}                                                      // cast syntax
```

Both of these compile, and because these are equivalent, they're wrong for the same reason. At runtime, they don't modify *i! In both cases, the result of the cast is a temporary anonymous object that is a *copy* of *i, and setTitle is invoked on the anonymous object, not on *i! *i isn't modified, because setTitle is never invoked on that object, it's invoked on a *copy* of that object. Both syntactic forms are equivalent to this:

```
if (i != se.end()) {
    Employee tempCopy(*i);                      // copy *i into tempCopy
    tempCopy.setTitle("Corporate Deity");       // modify tempCopy
}
```

Now the importance of a cast to a reference should be clear. By casting to a reference, we avoid creating a new object. Instead, the result of the cast is a reference to an *existing* object, the object pointed to by i. When we invoke setTitle on the object indicated by the reference, we're invoking setTitle on *i, and that's exactly what we want.

What I've just written is fine for sets and multisets, but when we turn to maps and multimaps, the plot thickens. Recall that a map<K, V> or a multimap<K, V> contains elements of type pair<*const* K, V>. That const means that the first component of the pair is *defined* to be const, and *that* means that attempts to cast away its constness are undefined. In theory, an STL implementation could write such values to a read-only memory location (such as a virtual memory page that, once written, is made write-protected by a system call), and attempts to cast away its constness would, at best, have no effect. I've never heard of an implementation that does that, but if you're a stickler for following the rules laid down by the Standard, you'll *never* try to cast away the constness of a map or multimap key.

You've surely heard that casts are dangerous, and I hope this book makes clear that I believe you should avoid them whenever you can. To perform a cast is to shuck temporarily the safety of the type system, and the pitfalls we've discussed exemplify what can happen when you leave your safety net behind.

Most casts can be avoided, and that includes the ones we've just considered. If you want to change an element in a set, multiset, map, or multimap in a way that always works and is always safe, do it in five simple steps:

1. Locate the container element you want to change. If you're not sure of the best way to do that, Item 45 offers guidance on how to perform an appropriate search.

2. Make a copy of the element to be modified. In the case of a map or multimap, be sure not to declare the first component of the copy const. After all, you want to change it!

3. Remove the element from the container, typically via a call to erase (see Item 9).

4. Modify the copy so it has the value you want to be in the container.

5. Insert the new value into the container. If the location of the new element in the container's sort order is likely to be the same or adjacent to that of the removed element, use the "hint" form of insert to improve the efficiency of the insertion from logarithmic-time to constant-time. Use the iterator you got from Step 1 as the hint.

Here's the same tired employee example, this time written in a safe, portable manner:

```
EmpIDSet se;                      // as before, se is a set of employees
                                  // sorted by ID number

Employee selectedID;              // as before, selectedID is a dummy
                                  // employee with the desired ID number

...

EmpIDSet::iterator i =
    se.find(selectedID);          // Step 1: find element to change

if (i != se.end()) {
    Employee e(*i);               // Step 2: copy the element

    se.erase(i++);                // Step 3: remove the element;
                                  // increment the iterator to maintain
                                  // its validity (see Item 9)

    e.setTitle("Corporate Deity");  // Step 4: modify the copy

    se.insert(i, e);              // Step 5: insert new value; hint that its
                                  // location is the same as that of the
}                                 // original element
```

You'll excuse my putting it this way, but the *key* thing to remember is that with set and multiset, if you perform any in-place modifications of container elements, you are responsible for making sure that the container remains sorted.

Item 23: Consider replacing associative containers with sorted vectors.

Many STL programmers, when faced with the need for a data structure offering fast lookups, immediately think of the standard associative containers, set, multiset, map, and multimap. That's fine, as far as it goes, but it doesn't go far enough. If lookup speed is really important, it's almost certainly worthwhile to consider the nonstandard hashed containers as well (see Item 25). With suitable hashing functions, hashed containers can be expected to offer constant-time lookups. (With poorly chosen hashing functions or with table sizes that are too small, the performance of hash table lookups may degrade significantly, but this is relatively uncommon in practice.) For many applications, the expected constant-time lookups of hashed containers are preferable to the guaranteed logarithmic-time lookups that are the hallmark of set, map and their multi companions.

Even if guaranteed logarithmic-time lookup is what you want, the standard associative containers still may not be your best bet. Counterintuitively, it's not uncommon for the standard associative containers to offer performance that is inferior to that of the lowly vector. If you want to make effective use of the STL, you need to understand when and how a vector can offer faster lookups than a standard associative container.

The standard associative containers are typically implemented as balanced binary search trees. A balanced binary search tree is a data structure that is optimized for a mixed combination of insertions, erasures, and lookups. That is, it's designed for applications that do some insertions, then some lookups, then maybe some more insertions, then perhaps some erasures, then a few more lookups, then more insertions or erasures, then more lookups, etc. The key characteristic of this sequence of events is that the insertions, erasures, and lookups are all mixed up. In general, there's no way to predict what the next operation on the tree will be.

Many applications use their data structures in a less chaotic manner. Their use of data structures fall into three distinct phases, which can be summarized like this:

1. **Setup**. Create a new data structure by inserting lots of elements into it. During this phase, almost all operations are insertions and erasures. Lookups are rare or nonexistent.

2. **Lookup**. Consult the data structure to find specific pieces of information. During this phase, almost all operations are lookups. Insertions and erasures are rare or nonexistent.

3. **Reorganize**. Modify the contents of the data structure, perhaps by erasing all the current data and inserting new data in its place. Behaviorally, this phase is equivalent to phase 1. Once this phase is completed, the application returns to phase 2.

For applications that use their data structures in this way, a vector is likely to offer better performance (in both time and space) than an associative container. But not just any vector will do. It has to be a *sorted* vector, because only sorted containers work correctly with the lookup algorithms binary_search, lower_bound, equal_range, etc. (see Item 34). But why should a binary search through a (sorted) vector offer better performance than a binary search through a binary search tree? Because some things are trite but true, and one of them is that size matters. Others are less trite but no less true, and one of those is that locality of reference matters, too.

Consider first the size issue. Suppose we need a container to hold Widget objects, and, because lookup speed is important to us, we are considering both an associative container of Widgets and a sorted vector<Widget>. If we choose an associative container, we'll almost certainly be using a balanced binary tree. Such a tree would be made up of tree nodes, each holding not only a Widget, but also a pointer to the node's left child, a pointer to its right child, and (typically) a pointer to its parent. That means that the space overhead for storing a Widget in an associative container would be at least three pointers.

In contrast, there is no overhead when we store a Widget in a vector; we simply store a Widget. The vector itself has overhead, of course, and there may be empty (reserved) space at the end of the vector (see Item 14), but the per-vector overhead is typically insignificant (usually three machine words, e.g., three pointers or two pointers and an int), and the empty space at the end can be lopped off via "the swap trick" if necessary (see Item 17). Even if the extra space is not eliminated, it's unimportant for the analysis below, because that memory won't be referenced when doing a lookup.

Assuming our data structures are big enough, they'll be split across multiple memory pages, but the vector will require fewer pages than the associative container. That's because the vector requires no per-Widget overhead, while the associative container exacts three pointers per Widget. To see why this is important, suppose you're working on a system where a Widget is 12 bytes in size, pointers are 4 bytes, and a memory page holds 4096 (4K) bytes. Ignoring the per-container overhead, you can fit 341 Widgets on a page when they are stored in a vector, but you can fit at most 170 when they are stored in an associative container. You'll thus use about twice as much memory for the associative container as you would for the vector. If you're working in an environment where virtual memory is available, it's easy to see how that can translate into a lot more page faults, therefore a system that is significantly slower for large sets of data.

I'm actually being optimistic about the associative containers here, because I'm assuming that the nodes in the binary trees are clustered together on a relatively small set of memory pages. Most STL implementations use custom memory managers (implemented on top of the containers' allocators — see Items 10 and 11) to achieve such clustering, but if your STL implementation fails to take steps to improve locality of reference among tree nodes, the nodes could end up scattered all over your address space. That would lead to even more page faults. Even with the customary clustering memory managers, associative containers tend to have more problems with page faults, because, unlike contiguous-memory containers such as vector, node-based containers find it more difficult to guarantee that container elements that are close to one another in a container's traversal order are also close to one another in physical memory. Yet this is precisely the kind of memory organization that minimizes page faults when performing a binary search.

Bottom line: storing data in a sorted vector is likely to consume less memory than storing the same data in a standard associative container, and searching a sorted vector via binary search is likely to be faster than searching a standard associative container when page faults are taken into account.

Of course, the big drawback of a sorted vector is that it must remain sorted! When a new element is inserted, everything beyond the new element must be moved up by one. That's as expensive as it sounds, and it gets even more expensive if the vector has to reallocate its underlying memory (see Item 14), because then *all* the elements in the vector typically have to be copied. Similarly, if an element is removed from the vector, all the elements beyond it must be moved down. Insertions and erasures are expensive for vectors, but they're cheap for associative containers. That's why it makes sense to consider using a sorted vector instead of an associative container only when you know that your data structure is used in such a way that lookups are almost never mixed with insertions and erasures.

This Item has featured a lot of text, but it's been woefully short on examples, so let's take a look at a code skeleton for using a sorted vector instead of a set:

```
vector<Widget> vw;                    // alternative to set<Widget>

...                                   // Setup phase: lots of
                                      // insertions, few lookups

sort(vw.begin(), vw.end());           // end of Setup phase. (When
                                      // simulating a multiset, you
                                      // might prefer stable_sort
                                      // instead; see Item 31.)
```

```
Widget w;                                    // object for value to look up
...                                          // start Lookup phase
if (binary_search(vw.begin(), vw.end(), w)) ... // lookup via binary_search
vector<Widget>::iterator i =
    lower_bound(vw.begin(), vw.end(), w);    // lookup via lower_bound;
if (i != vw.end() && !(*i < w)) ...          // see Item 45 for an explana-
                                             // tion of the "!(*i < w)" test

pair<vector<Widget>::iterator,
    vector<Widget>::iterator> range =
    equal_range(vw.begin(), vw.end(), w);    // lookup via equal_range
if (range.first != range.second) ...

...                                          // end Lookup phase, start
                                             // Reorganize phase
sort(vw.begin(), vw.end());                  // begin new Lookup phase...
```

As you can see, it's all pretty straightforward. The hardest thing about it is deciding among the search algorithms (e.g., binary_search, lower_bound, etc.), and Item 45 helps you do that.

Things get a bit more interesting when you decide to replace a map or multimap with a vector, because the vector must hold pair objects. After all, that's what map and multimap hold. Recall, however, that if you declare an object of type map<K, V> (or its multimap equivalent), the type of elements stored in the map is pair<*const* K, V>. To emulate a map or multimap using a vector, you must omit the const, because when you sort the vector, the values of its elements will get moved around via assignment, and that means that both components of the pair must be assignable. When using a vector to emulate a map<K, V>, then, the type of the data stored in the vector will be pair<K, V>, not pair<const K, V>.

maps and multimaps keep their elements in sorted order, but they look only at the key part of the element (the first component of the pair) for sorting purposes, and you must do the same when sorting a vector. You'll need to write a custom comparison function for your pairs, because pair's operator< looks at *both* components of the pair.

Interestingly, you'll need a second comparison function for performing lookups. The comparison function you'll use for sorting will take two pair objects, but lookups are performed given only a key value. The comparison function for lookups, then, must take an object of the key type (the value being searched for) and a pair (one of the pairs stored in the vector) — two different types. As an additional twist, you can't know whether the key value or the pair will be passed as the first argument, so you really need two comparison functions for lookups: one where the key value is passed first and one where the pair is passed first.

Here's an example of how to put all the pieces together:

```
typedef pair<string, int> Data;          // type held in the "map"
                                          // in this example

class DataCompare {                       // class for comparison
public:                                   // functions
    bool operator()(const Data& lhs,              // comparison func
                    const Data& rhs) const        // for sorting
    {
        return keyLess(lhs.first, rhs.first);     // keyLess is below
    }
    bool operator()(const Data& lhs,              // comparison func
                    const Data::first_type& k) const    // for lookups
    {                                                   // (form 1)
        return keyLess(lhs.first, k);
    }
    bool operator()(const Data::first_type& k,    // comparison func
                    const Data& rhs) const        // for lookups
    {                                             // (form 2)
        return keyLess(k, rhs.first);
    }
private:
    bool keyLess(const Data::first_type& k1,      // the "real"
                 const Data::first_type& k2) const    // comparison
    {                                                 // function
        return k1 < k2;
    }
};
```

In this example, we assume that our sorted vector will be emulating a map<string, int>. The code is pretty much a literal translation of the discussion above, except for the presence of the member function key-Less. That function exists to ensure consistency between the various operator() functions. Each such function simply compares two key values, so rather than duplicate the logic, we put the test inside keyLess and have the operator() functions return whatever keyLess does. This admirable act of software engineering enhances the maintainability of DataCompare, but there is a minor drawback. Its provision for operator() functions with different parameter types renders the resulting function objects unadaptable (see Item 40). Oh well.

Using a sorted vector as a map is essentially the same as using it as a set. The only major difference is the need to use DataCompare objects as comparison functions:

```
vector<Data> vd;                              // alternative to
                                              // map<string, int>

...                                           // Setup phase: lots of
                                              // insertions, few lookups

sort(vd.begin(), vd.end(), DataCompare());    // end of Setup phase. (When
                                              // simulating a multimap, you
                                              // might prefer stable_sort
                                              // instead; see Item 31.)

string s;                                     // object for value to look up

...                                           // start Lookup phase

if (binary_search(vd.begin(), vd.end(), s,
          DataCompare())) ...                 // lookup via binary_search

vector<Data>::iterator i =
    lower_bound(vd.begin(), vd.end(), s,
          DataCompare());                     // lookup via lower_bound;
if (i != vd.end() && !(i->first < s)) ...     // again, see Item 45 for info
                                              // on the "!(i->first < s)" test

pair<vector<Data>::iterator,
    vector<Data>::iterator> range =
    equal_range(vd.begin(), vd.end(), s,
          DataCompare());                     // lookup via equal_range
if (range.first != range.second) ...

...                                           // end Lookup phase, start
                                              // Reorganize phase

sort(vd.begin(), vd.end(), DataCompare());    // begin new Lookup phase...
```

As you can see, once you've written DataCompare, things pretty much fall into place. And once in place, they'll often run faster and use less memory than the corresponding design using a real map *as long as your program uses the data structure in the phased manner described on page 101.* If your program doesn't operate on the data structure in a phased manner, use of a sorted vector instead of a standard associative container will almost certainly end up wasting time.

Item 24: Choose carefully between map::operator[] and map::insert when efficiency is important.

Let's suppose we have a Widget class that supports default construction as well as construction and assignment from a double:

```
class Widget {
public:
  Widget();
  Widget(double weight);

  Widget& operator=(double weight);
  ...
};
```

Let's now suppose we'd like to create a map from ints to Widgets, and we'd like to initialize the map with particular values. 'Tis simplicity itself:

```
map<int, Widget> m;
m[1] = 1.50;
m[2] = 3.67;
m[3] = 10.5;
m[4] = 45.8;
m[5] = 0.0003;
```

In fact, the only thing simpler is forgetting what's really going on. That's too bad, because what's going on could incur a considerable performance hit.

The operator[] function for maps is a novel creature, unrelated to the operator[] functions for vectors, deques, and strings and equally unrelated to the built-in operator[] that works with arrays. Instead, map::operator[] is designed to facilitate "add or update" functionality. That is, given

```
map<K, V> m;
```

the expression

```
m[k] = v;
```

checks to see if the key k is already in the map. If not, it's added, along with v as its corresponding value. If k is already in the map, its associated value is updated to v.

The way this works is that operator[] returns a reference to the value object associated with k. v is then assigned to the object to which the reference (the one returned from operator[]) refers. This is straightforward when an existing key's associated value is being updated, because there's already a value object to which operator[] can return a reference. But if k isn't yet in the map, there's no value object for operator[] to refer to. In that case, it creates one from scratch by using the value type's default constructor. operator[] then returns a reference to this newly-created object.

Let's look again at the first part of our original example:

```
map<int, Widget> m;
m[1] = 1.50;
```

The expression m[1] is shorthand for m.operator[](1), so this is a call to map::operator[]. That function must return a reference to a Widget, because m's mapped type is Widget. In this case, m doesn't yet have anything in it, so there is no entry in the map for the key 1. operator[]

therefore default-constructs a Widget to act as the value associated with 1, then returns a reference to that Widget. Finally, the Widget becomes the target of an assignment; the assigned value is 1.50.

In other words, the statement

```
m[1] = 1.50;
```

is functionally equivalent to this:

```
typedef map<int, Widget> IntWidgetMap;          // convenience
                                                // typedef

pair<IntWidgetMap::iterator, bool> result =     // create new map
    m.insert(IntWidgetMap::value_type(1, Widget()));  // entry with key 1
                                                // and a default-
                                                // constructed value
                                                // object; see below
                                                // for a comment on
                                                // value_type

result.first->second = 1.50;                    // assign to the
                                                // newly-constructed
                                                // value object
```

Now it should be clear why this approach may degrade performance. We first default-construct a Widget, then we immediately assign it a new value. If it's measurably more efficient to construct a Widget with the value we want instead of default-constructing the Widget and then doing the assignment, we'd be better off replacing our use of operator[] (including its attendant construction plus assignment) with a straightforward call to insert:

```
m.insert(IntWidgetMap::value_type(1, 1.50));
```

This has precisely the same ultimate effect as the code above, except it typically saves you three function calls: one to create a temporary default-constructed Widget object, one to destruct that temporary object, and one to Widget's assignment operator. The more expensive those function calls, the more you save by using map::insert instead of map::operator[].

The code above takes advantage of the value_type typedef that's provided by every standard container. There's nothing particularly significant about this typedef, but it's important to remember that for map and multimap (as well as the nonstandard containers hash_map and hash_multimap — see Item 25), the type of the contained elements will always be some kind of pair.

I remarked earlier that operator[] is designed to facilitate "add or update" functionality, and we now understand that when an "add" is performed, insert is more efficient than operator[]. The situation is reversed when we do an update, i.e., when an equivalent key (see Item 19) is already in the map. To see why that is the case, look at our update options:

```
m[k] = v;                                                  // use operator[]
                                                           // to update k's
                                                           // value to be v

m.insert(IntWidgetMap::value_type(k, v)).first->second = v;  // use insert to
                                                           // update k's
                                                           // value to be v
```

The syntax alone is probably enough to convince you to favor operator[], but we're focusing on efficiency here, so we'll overlook that.

The call to insert requires an argument of type IntWidgetMap::value_type (i.e., pair<int, Widget>), so when we call insert, we must construct and destruct an object of that type. That costs us a pair constructor and destructor. That, in turn, entails a Widget construction and destruction, because a pair<int, Widget> itself contains a Widget object. operator[] uses no pair object, so it constructs and destructs no pair and no Widget.

Efficiency considerations thus lead us to conclude that insert is preferable to operator[] when adding an element to a map, and both efficiency and aesthetics dictate that operator[] is preferable when updating the value of an element that's already in the map.

It would be nice if the STL provided a function that offered the best of both worlds, i.e., efficient add-or-update functionality in a syntactically attractive package. For example, it's not hard to envision a calling interface such as this:

```
iterator affectedPair =           // if key k isn't in map m, efficiently
    efficientAddOrUpdate(m, k, v); // add pair (k,v) to m; otherwise
                                   // efficiently update to v the value
                                   // associated with k. Return an
                                   // iterator to the added or
                                   // modified pair
```

There's no function like this in the STL, but, as the code below demonstrates, it's not terribly hard to write yourself. The comments summarize what's going on, and the paragraphs that follow provide some additional explanation.

```
template< typename MapType,                    // type of map
          typename KeyArgType,                 // see below for why
          typename ValueArgType>               // KeyArgType and
                                               // ValueArgType are type
typename MapType::iterator                      // parameters
efficientAddOrUpdate(MapType& m,
                     const KeyArgType& k,
                     const ValueArgType& v)
{
    typename MapType::iterator lb =            // find where k is or should
        m.lower_bound(k);                      // be; see page 7 for why
                                               // "typename" is needed
                                               // here

    if ( lb != m.end() &&                      // if lb points to a pair
         !(m.key_comp()(k, lb->first))) {      // whose key is equiv to k...

        lb->second = v;                        // update the pair's value
        return lb;                             // and return an iterator
    }                                          // to that pair

    else {
        typedef typename MapType::value_type MVT;
        return m.insert(lb, MVT(k, v));        // add pair(k, v) to m and
    }                                          // return an iterator to the
}                                              // new map element
```

To perform an efficient add or update, we need to be able to find out if k's value is in the map; if so, where it is; and if not, where it should be inserted. That job is tailor-made for lower_bound (see Item 45), so that's the function we call. To determine whether lower_bound found an element with the key we were looking for, we perform the second half of an equivalence test (see Item 19), being sure to use the correct comparison function for the map; that comparison function is available via map::key_comp. The result of the equivalence test tells us whether we're performing an add or an update.

If it's an update, the code is straightforward. The insert branch is more interesting, because it uses the "hint" form of insert. The construct m.insert(lb, MVT(k, v)) "hints" that lb identifies the correct insertion location for a new element with key equivalent to k, and the Standard guarantees that if the hint is correct, the insertion will occur in constant, rather than logarithmic, time. In efficientAddOrUpdate, we know that lb identifies the proper insertion location, so the call to insert is guaranteed to be a constant-time operation.

An interesting aspect of this implementation is that KeyArgType and ValueArgType need not be the types stored in the map. They need only be *convertible* to the types stored in the map. The alternative would be to eliminate the type parameters KeyArgType and ValueArgType, using instead MapType::key_type and MapType::mapped_type. However, if we did that, we might force unnecessary type conversions to occur at the point of call. For instance, look again at the definition of the map we've been using in this Item's examples:

```
map<int, Widget> m;                              // as before
```

And recall that Widget accepts assignment from a double:

```
class Widget {                                   // also as before
public:
    ...
    Widget& operator=(double weight);
    ...
};
```

Now consider this call to efficientAddOrUpdate:

```
efficientAddOrUpdate(m, 10, 1.5);
```

Suppose that it's an update operation, i.e., m already contains an element whose key is 10. In that case, the template above deduces that ValueArgType is double, and the body of the function directly assigns 1.5 as a double to the Widget associated with the key 10. That's accomplished by an invocation of Widget::operator=(double). If we had used MapType::mapped_type as the type of efficientAddOrUpdate's third parameter, we'd have converted 1.5 to a Widget at the point of call, and we'd thus have paid for a Widget construction (and subsequent destruction) we didn't need.

Subtleties in the implementation of efficientAddOrUpdate may be interesting, but they're not as important as the main point of this Item, which is that you should choose carefully between map::operator[] and map::insert when efficiency is important. If you're updating an existing map element, operator[] is preferable, but if you're adding a new element, insert has the edge.

Item 25: Familiarize yourself with the nonstandard hashed containers.

It generally doesn't take much time for STL programmers to begin to wonder, "Vectors, lists, maps, sure, but where are the hash tables?" Alas, there aren't any hash tables in the standard C++ library. Everyone agrees that this is unfortunate, but the Standardization Committee felt that the work needed to add them would have unduly delayed completion of the Standard. It's a foregone conclusion that the next version of the Standard will include hash tables, but for the time being, the STL doesn't do hashing.

If you like hash tables, however, take heart. You need not do without or roll your own. STL-compatible hashed associative containers are available from multiple sources, and they even have *de facto* standard names: hash_set, hash_multiset, hash_map, and hash_multimap.

Behind these common names, different implementations, er, differ. They differ in their interfaces, their capabilities, their underlying data structures, and the relative efficiency of the operations they support. It's still possible to write reasonably portable code using hash tables, but it's not as easy as it would be had the hashed containers been standardized. (Now you know why standards are important.)

Of the several available implementations for hashed containers, the two most common are from SGI (see Item 50) and Dinkumware (see Appendix B), so in what follows, I restrict myself to the designs of the hashed containers from these vendors. STLport (again, see Item 50) also offers hashed containers, but the STLport hashed containers are based on those from SGI. For purposes of this Item, assume that whatever I write about the SGI hashed containers applies to the STLport hashed containers, too.

Hashed containers are associative containers, so it should not surprise you that, like all associative containers, they need to know the type of objects stored in the container, the comparison function for such objects, and the allocator for these objects. In addition, hashed containers require specification of a hashing function. That suggests the following declaration for hashed containers:

```
template<typename T,
        typename HashFunction,
        typename CompareFunction,
        typename Allocator = allocator<T> >
class hash_container;
```

This is quite close to the SGI declaration for hashed containers, the primary difference being that SGI provides default types for HashFunction and CompareFunction. The SGI declaration for hash_set looks essentially like this (I've tweaked it a bit for presentation purposes):

```
template<typename T,
        typename HashFunction = hash<T>,
        typename CompareFunction = equal_to<T>,
        typename Allocator = allocator<T> >
class hash_set;
```

A noteworthy aspect of the SGI design is the use of equal_to as the default comparison function. This is a departure from the conventions of the standard associative containers, where the default comparison function is less. This design decision signifies more than a simple change in default comparison functions. SGI's hashed containers determine whether two objects in a hashed container have the same value by testing for *equality*, not equivalence (see Item 19). For hashed containers, this is not an unreasonable decision, because hashed associative containers, unlike their standard (typically tree-based) counterparts, are not kept in sorted order.

The Dinkumware design for hashed containers adopts some different strategies. It still allows you to specify object types, hash function types, comparison function types, and allocator types, but it moves the default hash and comparison functions into a separate traits-like class called hash_compare, and it makes hash_compare the default argument for the HashingInfo parameter of the container templates. (If you're unfamiliar with the notion of a "traits" class, open a good STL reference like Josuttis' *The C++ Standard Library* [3] and study the motivation and implementation of the char_traits and iterator_traits templates.)

For example, here's the Dinkumware hash_set declaration (again, tweaked for presentation):

```
template<typename T, typename CompareFunction>
class hash_compare;

template<typename T,
         typename HashingInfo = hash_compare<T, less<T> >,
         typename Allocator = allocator<T> >
class hash_set;
```

The interesting part of this interface design is the use of HashingInfo. The container's hashing and comparison functions are stored there, but the HashingInfo type also holds enums controlling the minimum number of buckets in the table as well as the maximum allowable ratio of container elements to buckets. When this ratio is exceeded, the number of buckets in the table is increased, and some elements in the table are rehashed. (SGI provides member functions that afford similar control over the number of table buckets and, hence, the ratio of table elements to buckets.)

After some tweaks for presentation, hash_compare (the default value for HashingInfo) looks more or less like this:

```
template<typename T, typename CompareFunction = less<T> >
class hash_compare {
public:

  enum {
    bucket_size = 4,          // max ratio of elements to buckets
    min_buckets = 8           // minimum number of buckets
  };
```

```
    size_t operator()(const T&) const;      // hash function
    bool operator()(const T&,               // comparison function
              const T&) const;

    ...                                     // a few things omitted, including
};                                          // the use of CompareFunction
```

The overloading of operator() (in this case, to implement both the hashing and comparison functions) is a strategy that crops up more frequently than you might imagine. For another application of the same idea, take a look at Item 23.

The Dinkumware design allows you to write your own hash_compare-like class (possibly by deriving from hash_compare itself), and as long as your class provides definitions for bucket_size, min_buckets, two operator() functions (one taking one argument, one taking two), plus a few things I've left out, you can use it to control the configuration and behavior of a Dinkumware hash_set or hash_multiset. Configuration control for hash_map and hash_multimap is similar.

Notice that with both the SGI and the Dinkumware designs, you can leave all the decision-making to the implementations and simply write something like this:

```
    hash_set<int> intTable;               // create a hashed set of ints
```

For this to compile, the hash table must hold an integral type (such as int), because the default hashing functions are generally limited to integral types. (SGI's default hashing function is slightly more flexible. Item 50 will tell you where to find all the details.)

Under the hood, the SGI and Dinkumware implementations go their very separate ways. SGI employs a conventional open hashing scheme composed of an array (the buckets) of pointers to singly linked lists of elements. Dinkumware also employs open hashing, but it's design is based on a novel data structure consisting of an array of iterators (essentially the buckets) into a doubly linked list of elements, where adjacent pairs of iterators identify the extent of the elements in each bucket. (For details, consult Plauger's aptly titled column, "Hash Tables" [16].)

As a user of these implementations, it's likely you'll be interested in the fact that the SGI implementation stores the table elements in singly linked lists, while the Dinkumware implementation uses a doubly linked list. The difference is noteworthy, because it affects the iterator categories for the two implementations. SGI's hashed containers offer forward iterators, so you forgo the ability to perform reverse iterations; there are no rbegin or rend member functions in SGI's hashed containers. The iterators for Dinkumware's hashed containers are bidirectional, so they offer both forward and reverse traversals. In terms of memory usage, the SGI design is a bit more parsimonious than that from Dinkumware.

Which design is best for you and your applications? I can't possibly know. Only you can determine that, and this Item hasn't tried to give you enough information to come to a reasonable conclusion. Instead, the goal of this Item is to make sure you know that though the STL itself lacks hashed containers, STL-compatible hashed containers (with varying interfaces, capabilities, and behavioral trade-offs) are not difficult to come by. In the case of the SGI and STLport implementations, you can even come by them for free, because they're available for free download.

Iterators

At first glance, iterators appear straightforward. Look more closely, however, and you'll notice that the standard STL containers offer four different iterator types: iterator, const_iterator, reverse_iterator, and const_reverse_iterator. From there it's only a matter of time until you note that of these four types, only one is accepted by containers in certain forms of insert and erase. That's when the questions begin. Why four iterator types? What is the relationship among them? Are they interconvertible? Can the different types be mixed in calls to algorithms and STL utility functions? How do these types relate to containers and their member functions?

This chapter answers these questions, and it introduces an iterator type that deserves more notice than it usually gets: istreambuf_iterator. If you like the STL, but you're unhappy with the performance of istream_iterators when reading character streams, istreambuf_iterator could be just the tool you're looking for.

Item 26: Prefer iterator to const_iterator, reverse_iterator, and const_reverse_iterator.

As you know, every standard container offers four types of iterator. For a container<T>, the type iterator acts like a T*, while const_iterator acts like a const T* (which you may also see written as a T const *; they mean the same thing). Incrementing an iterator or a const_iterator moves you to the next element in the container in a traversal starting at the front of the container and proceeding to the back. reverse_iterator and const_reverse_iterator also act like T* and const T*, respectively, except that incrementing these iterator types moves you to the next element in the container in a traversal from back to front.

Let me show you two things. First, take a look at some signatures for insert and erase in vector<T>:

```
iterator insert(iterator position, const T& x);
iterator erase(iterator position);
iterator erase(iterator rangeBegin, iterator rangeEnd);
```

Every standard container offers functions analogous to these, though the return types vary, depending on the container type. The thing to notice is that these functions demand parameters of type iterator. Not const_iterator, not reverse_iterator, not const_reverse_iterator. Always iterator. Though containers support four iterator types, one of those types has privileges the others do not have. That type is iterator. iterator is special.

The second thing I want to show you is this diagram, which displays the conversions that exist among iterator types.

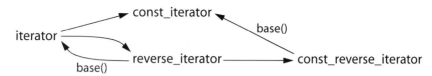

The diagram shows that there are implicit conversions from iterator to const_iterator, from iterator to reverse_iterator, and from reverse_iterator to const_reverse_iterator. It also shows that a reverse_iterator may be converted into an iterator by using the reverse_iterator's base member function, and a const_reverse_iterator may similarly be converted into a const_iterator via base. The diagram does not show that the iterators obtained from base may not be the ones you want. For the story on that, turn to Item 28.

You'll observe that there is no way to get from a const_iterator to an iterator or from a const_reverse_iterator to a reverse_iterator. This is important, because it means that if you have a const_iterator or a const_reverse_iterator, you'll find it difficult to use those iterators with some container member functions. Such functions demand iterators, and since there's no conversion path from the const iterator types back to iterator, the const iterator types are largely useless if you want to use them to specify insertion positions or elements to be erased.

Don't be fooled into thinking that this means const iterators are useless in general. They're not. They're perfectly useful with algorithms, because algorithms don't usually care what kind of iterators they work with, as long as they are of the appropriate category. const iterators are also acceptable for many container member functions. It's only some forms of insert and erase that are picky.

I wrote that const iterators are "largely" useless if you want to specify insertion positions or elements to be erased. The implication is that they are not completely useless. That's true. They can be useful if you can find a way to get an iterator from a const_iterator or from a const_reverse_iterator. That's often possible. It isn't *always* possible, however, and even when it is, the way to do it isn't terribly obvious. It may not be terribly efficient, either. The topic is meaty enough to justify its own Item, so turn to Item 27 if you're interested in the details. For now, we have enough information to understand why it often makes sense to prefer iterators to const and reverse iterators:

- Some versions of insert and erase require iterators. If you want to call those functions, you're going to have to produce iterators. const and reverse iterators won't do.

- It's not possible to implicitly convert a const iterator to an iterator, and the technique described in Item 27 for generating an iterator from a const_iterator is neither universally applicable nor guaranteed to be efficient.

- Conversion from a reverse_iterator to an iterator may require iterator adjustment after the conversion. Item 28 explains when and why.

All these things conspire to make working with containers easiest, most efficient, and least likely to harbor subtle bugs if you prefer iterators to their const and reverse colleagues.

Practically speaking, you are more likely to have a choice when it comes to iterators and const_iterators. The decision between iterator and reverse_iterator is often made for you. You either need a front-to-back traversal or a back-to-front traversal, and that's pretty much that. You choose the one you need, and if that means choosing reverse_iterator, you choose reverse_iterator and use base to convert it to an iterator (possibly preceded by an offset adjustment — see Item 28) when you want to make calls to container member functions that require iterators.

When choosing between iterators and const_iterators, there are reasons to choose iterators even when you could use a const_iterator and when you have no need to use the iterator as a parameter to a container member function. One of the most irksome involves comparisons between iterators and const_iterators. I hope we can all agree that this is reasonable code:

```
typedef deque<int> IntDeque;              // STL container and
typedef IntDeque::iterator Iter;          // iterator types are easier
typedef IntDeque::const_iterator ConstIter;  // to work with if you
                                          // use some typedefs

Iter i;
ConstIter ci;
```

```
...                                          // make i and ci point into
                                             // the same container
if (i == ci) ...                             // compare an iterator
                                             // and a const_iterator
```

All we're doing here is comparing two iterators into a container, the kind of comparison that's the bread and butter of the STL. The only twist is that one object is of type iterator and one is of type const_iterator. This should be no problem. The iterator should be implicitly converted into a const_iterator, and the comparison should be performed between two const_iterators.

With well-designed STL implementations, this is precisely what happens, but with other implementations, the code will not compile. The reason is that such implementations declare operator== for const_iterators as a member function instead of as a non-member function, but the cause of the problem is likely to be of less interest to you than the workaround, which is to swap the order of the iterators, like this:

```
if (ci == i) ...                             // workaround for when the
                                             // comparison above won't compile
```

This kind of problem can arise whenever you mix iterators and const_iterators (or reverse_iterators and const_reverse_iterators) in the same expression, not just when you are comparing them. For example, if you try to subtract one random access iterator from another,

```
if (i - ci >= 3) ...                         // if i is at least 3 beyond ci ...
```

your (valid) code may be (incorrectly) rejected if the iterators aren't of the same type. The workaround is what you'd expect (swap the order of i and ci), but in this case you have to take into account that you can't just replace i - ci with ci - i:

```
if (ci + 3 <= i) ...                         // workaround for when the above
                                             // won't compile
```

The easiest way to guard against these kinds of problems is to minimize your mixing of iterator types, and that, in turn, leads back to preferring iterators to const_iterators. From the perspective of const correctness (a worthy perspective, to be sure), staying away from const_iterators simply to avoid potential implementation shortcomings (all of which have workarounds) seems unjustified, but in conjunction with the anointed status of iterators in some container member functions, it's hard to avoid the practical conclusion that const_iterators are not only less useful than iterators, sometimes they're just not worth the trouble.

Item 27: Use distance and advance to convert a container's const_iterators to iterators.

Item 26 points out that some container member functions that take iterators as parameters insist on *iterators*; const_iterators won't do. So what do you do if you have a const_iterator in hand and you want to, say, insert a new value into a container at the position indicated by the iterator? Somehow you've got to turn your const_iterator into an iterator, and you have to take an active role in doing it, because, as Item 26 explains, there is no implicit conversion from const_iterator to iterator.

I know what you're thinking. You're thinking, "When all else fails, get a bigger hammer." In the world of C++, that can mean only one thing: casting. Shame on you for such thoughts. Where do you get these ideas?

Let us confront this cast obsession of yours head on. Look what happens when you try to cast a const_iterator to an iterator:

```
typedef deque<int> IntDeque;              // convenience typedefs
typedef IntDeque::iterator Iter;
typedef IntDeque::const_iterator ConstIter;

ConstIter ci;                             // ci is a const_iterator

...

Iter i(ci);                               // error! no implicit conversion from
                                          // const_iterator to iterator

Iter i(const_cast<Iter>(ci));             // still an error! can't cast a
                                          // const_iterator to an iterator
```

This example happens to use deque, but the outcome would be the same for list, set, multiset, map, multimap, and the hashed containers described in Item 25. The line using the cast *might* compile in the case of vector or string, but those are special cases we'll consider in a moment.

The reason the cast won't compile is that for these container types, iterator and const_iterator are different classes, barely more closely related to one another than string and complex<double>. Trying to cast one type to the other is nonsensical, and that's why the const_cast is rejected. static_cast, reinterpret_cast, and a C-style cast would lead to the same end.

Alas, the cast that won't compile might compile if the iterators' container were a vector or a string. That's because it is common for implementations of these containers to use pointers as iterators. For such implementations, vector<T>::iterator is a typedef for T*, vector<T>::const_iterator is a typedef for const T*, string::iterator is a typedef for char*, and string::const_iterator is a typedef for const char*. With such implementations, the const_cast from a const_iterator to an iterator will compile and do the right thing, because the cast is converting a const T* into a T*. Even under such implementations, however, reverse_iterators and const_reverse_iterators are true classes, so you can't const_cast a const_reverse_iterator to a reverse_iterator. Also, as Item 50 explains, even implementations where vector and string iterators are pointers might use that representation only when compiling in release mode. All these factors lead to the conclusion that casting const iterators to iterators is ill-advised even for vector and string, because its portability is doubtful.

If you have access to the container a const_iterator came from, there is a safe, portable way to get its corresponding iterator, and it involves no circumvention of the type system. Here's the essence of the solution, though it must be modified slightly before it will compile:

```
typedef deque<int> IntDeque;              // as before
typedef IntDeque::iterator Iter;
typedef IntDeque::const_iterator ConstIter;

IntDeque d;

ConstIter ci;
...                                       // make ci point into d

Iter i(d.begin());                        // initialize i to d.begin()

advance(i, distance(i, ci));              // move i up to where ci is
                                          // (but see below for why this must
                                          // be tweaked before it will compile)
```

This approach is so simple and direct, it's startling. To get an iterator pointing to the same container element as a const_iterator, create a new iterator at the beginning of the container, then move it forward it until it's as far from the beginning of the container as the const_iterator is! This task is facilitated by the function templates advance and distance, both of which are declared in <iterator>. distance reports how far apart two iterators into the same container are, and advance moves an iterator a specified distance. When i and ci point into the same container, the expression advance(i, distance(i, ci)) makes i and ci point to the same place in the container.

Well, it would if it would compile, but it won't. To see why, look at the declaration for distance:

```
template <typename InputIterator>
typename iterator_traits<InputIterator>::difference_type
distance(InputIterator first, InputIterator last);
```

Don't get hung up on the fact that the return type of the function is 56 characters long and mentions dependent types like difference_type. Instead, focus your attention on the uses of the type parameter Input-Iterator:

```
template <typename InputIterator>
typename iterator_traits<InputIterator>::difference_type
distance(InputIterator first, InputIterator last);
```

When faced with a call to distance, your compilers must deduce the type represented by InputIterator by examining the arguments used in the call. Look again at the call to distance in the code I said wasn't quite right:

```
advance(i, distance(i, ci));                    // move i up to where ci is
```

Two parameters are passed to distance, i and ci. i is of type Iter, which is a typedef for deque<int>::iterator. To compilers, that implies that InputIterator in the call to distance is deque<int>::iterator. ci, however, is of type ConstIter, which is a typedef for deque<int>::const_iterator. *That* implies that InputIterator is of type deque<int>::const_iterator. It's not possible for InputIterator to be two different types at the same time, so the call to distance fails, typically yielding some long-winded error message that may or may not indicate that the compiler couldn't figure out what type InputIterator is supposed to be.

To get the call to compile, you must eliminate the ambiguity. The easiest way to do that is to explicitly specify the type parameter to be used by distance, thus obviating the need for your compilers to figure it out for themselves:

```
advance(i, distance<ConstIter>(i, ci));    // figure the distance between
                                           // i and ci (as const_iterators),
                                           // then move i that distance
```

We now know how to use advance and distance to get an iterator corresponding to a const_iterator, but we have so far sidestepped a question of considerable practical interest: How efficient is this technique? The answer is simple. It's as efficient as the iterators allow it to be. For random access iterators (such as those sported by vector, string, and deque), it's a constant-time operation. For bidirectional iterators (i.e., those for all other standard containers and for some implementations of the hashed containers (see Item 25)), it's a linear-time operation.

Because it may take linear time to produce an iterator equivalent to a const_iterator, and because it can't be done at all unless the container for the const_iterator is available when the const_iterator is, you may wish to rethink designs that require producing iterators from const_iterators. Such considerations, in fact, help motivate Item 26, which advises you to prefer iterators over const and reverse iterators when dealing with containers.

Item 28: Understand how to use a reverse_iterator's base iterator.

Invoking the base member function on a reverse_iterator yields the "corresponding" iterator, but it's not really clear what that means. As an example, take a look at this code, which puts the numbers 1-5 in a vector, sets a reverse_iterator to point to the 3, and initializes an iterator to the reverse_iterator's base:

```
vector<int> v;
v.reserve(5);                         // see Item 14

for (int i = 1; i <= 5; ++i) {        // put 1-5 in the vector
  v.push_back(i);
}

vector<int>::reverse_iterator ri =    // make ri point to the 3
  find(v.rbegin(), v.rend(), 3);

vector<int>::iterator i(ri.base());   // make i the same as ri's base
```

After executing this code, things can be thought of as looking like this:

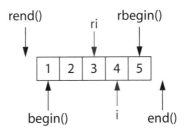

This picture is nice, displaying the characteristic offset of a reverse_iterator and its corresponding base iterator that mimics the offset of rbegin() and rend() with respect to begin() and end(), but it doesn't tell you everything you need to know. In particular, it doesn't explain how to use i to perform operations you'd like to perform on ri.

As Item 26 explains, some container member functions accept only iterators as iterator parameters, so if you want to, say, insert a new element at the location identified by ri, you can't do it directly; vector's insert function won't take reverse_iterators. You'd have a similar problem if you wanted to erase the element pointed to by ri. The erase member functions reject reverse_iterators, insisting instead on iterators. To perform insertions or erasures, you must convert reverse_iterators into iterators via base, then use the iterators to get the jobs done.

So let's suppose you *do* want to insert a new element into v at the position indicated by ri. In particular, let's assume you want to insert the value 99. Bearing in mind that ri is part of a traversal from right to left in the picture above and that insertion takes place in *front* of the element indicated by the iterator used to specify the insertion position, we'd expect the 99 to end up in front of the 3 with respect to a reverse traversal. After the insertion, then, v would look like this:

| 1 | 2 | 3 | 99 | 4 | 5 |

Of course, we can't use ri to indicate where to insert something, because it's not an iterator. We must use i instead. As noted above, when ri points at 3, i (which is ri.base()) points at 4. That's exactly where i needs to point for an insertion if the inserted value is to end up where it would have had we been able to use ri to specify the insertion location. Conclusion?

- To emulate insertion at a position specified by a reverse_iterator ri, insert at the position ri.base() instead. For purposes of insertion, ri and ri.base() are equivalent, and ri.base() is truly the iterator *corresponding* to ri.

Let us now consider erasing an element. Look again at the relationship between ri and i in the original vector (i.e., prior to the insertion of 99):

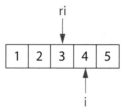

If we want to erase the element pointed to by ri, we can't just use i, because i doesn't point to the same element as ri. Instead, we must erase the element *preceding* i. Hence,

- To emulate erasure at a position specified by a reverse_iterator ri, erase at the position *preceding* ri.base() instead. For purposes of erasure, ri and ri.base() are *not* equivalent, and ri.base() is *not* the iterator corresponding to ri.

It's worth looking at the code to perform such an erasure, because it holds a surprise.

```
vector<int> v;

...                                   // as above, put 1-5 in v
vector<int>::reverse_iterator ri =    // as above, make ri point to the 3
    find(v.rbegin(), v.rend(), 3);
v.erase(--ri.base());                 // attempt to erase at the position
                                      // preceding ri.base(); for a vector,
                                      // this will typically not compile
```

There's nothing wrong with this design. The expression --ri.base() correctly specifies the element we'd like to erase. Furthermore, this code will work with every standard container except vector and string. It might work with vector and string, too, but for many vector and string implementations, it won't compile. In such implementations, iterators (and const_iterators) are implemented as built-in pointers, so the result of ri.base() is a pointer.

Both C and C++ dictate that pointers returned from functions shall not be modified, so for STL platforms where string and vector iterators are pointers, expressions like --ri.base() won't compile. To portably erase something at a position specified by a reverse_iterator, then, you must take pains to avoid modifying base's return value. No problem. If you can't decrement the result of calling base, just increment the reverse_iterator and *then* call base!

```
...                                   // as above
v.erase((++ri).base());               // erase the element pointed to by
                                      // ri; this should always compile
```

Because this approach works with every standard container, it is the preferred technique for erasing an element pointed to by a reverse_iterator.

It should now be clear that it's not accurate to say that a reverse_iterator's base member function returns the "corresponding" iterator. For insertion purposes, it does, but for erasure purposes, it does not. When converting reverse_iterators to iterators, it's important that you know what you plan to do with the resulting iterator, because only then can you determine whether the iterator you have is the one you need.

Item 29: Consider istreambuf_iterators for character-by-character input.

Let's suppose you'd like to copy a text file into a string object. This seems like a pretty reasonable way to do it:

```
ifstream inputFile("interestingData.txt");

string fileData((istream_iterator<char>(inputFile)),   // read inputFile into
                istream_iterator<char>());              // fileData; see below
                                                        // for why this isn't
                                                        // quite right, and see
                                                        // Item 6 for a warning
                                                        // about this syntax
```

It wouldn't take long before you'd notice that this approach fails to copy whitespace in the file into the string. That's because istream_iterators use operator<< functions to do the actual reading, and, by default, operator<< functions skip whitespace.

Assuming you'd like to retain the whitespace, all you need to do is override the default. Just clear the skipws flag for the input stream:

```
ifstream inputFile("interestingData.txt");

inputFile.unsetf(ios::skipws);                   // disable the skipping of
                                                 // whitespace in inputFile

string fileData((istream_iterator<char>(inputFile)),
                istream_iterator<char>());
```

Now all the characters in inputFile are copied into fileData.

Alas, you may discover that they aren't copied as quickly as you'd like. The operator<< functions on which istream_iterators depend perform formatted input, and that means they must undertake a fair amount of work on your behalf each time you call one. They have to create and destroy sentry objects (special iostream objects that perform setup and cleanup activities for each call to operator<<), they have to check stream flags that might affect their behavior (e.g., skipws), they have to perform comprehensive checking for read errors, and, if they encounter a problem, they have to check the stream's exception mask to determine whether an exception should be thrown. Those are all important activities if you're performing formatted input, but if all you want to do is grab the next character from the input stream, it's overkill.

A more efficient approach is to use one of the STL's best kept secrets: istreambuf_iterators. You use istreambuf_iterators like istream_iterators, but where istream_iterator<char> objects use operator<< to read individual characters from an input stream, istreambuf_iterator<char> objects go straight to the stream's buffer and read the next character directly. (More specifically, an istreambuf_iterator<char> object reading from an istream s will call s.rdbuf()->sgetc() to read s's next character.)

Modifying our file-reading code to use istreambuf_iterators is so easy, most Visual Basic programmers need no more than two tries to get it right:

```
ifstream inputFile("interestingData.txt");
string fileData((istreambuf_iterator<char>(inputFile)),
                 istreambuf_iterator<char>());
```

Notice how there's no need to "unset" the skipws flag here. istreambuf_iterators never skip any characters. Whatever's next in the stream buffer, that's what they grab.

Compared to istream_iterators, they grab it quickly — up to 40% faster in the simple benchmarks I performed, though don't be surprised if your mileage varies. Don't be surprised if the speed advantage increases over time, too, because istreambuf_iterators inhabit a seldom-visited corner of the STL where implementers haven't yet spent a lot of time on optimizations. For example, in one implementation I used, istreambuf_iterators were only about 5% faster than istream_iterators on my primitive tests. Such implementations clearly have lots of room to streamline their istreambuf_iterator implementations.

If you need to read the characters in a stream one by one, you don't need the power of formatted input, and you care about how long it takes to read the stream, typing three extra characters per iterator is a small price to pay for what is often a significant increase in performance. For unformatted character-by-character input, you should always consider istreambuf_iterators.

While you're at it, you should also consider ostreambuf_iterators for the corresponding unformatted character-by-character output operations. They avoid the overhead (and flexibility) of their ostream_iterator cousins, so they generally outperform them, too.

5 Algorithms

I noted at the beginning of Chapter 1 that containers get the lion's share of the STL acclaim. In a sense, that's understandable. The containers are remarkable accomplishments, and they make life easier for legions of C++ programmers on a daily basis. Still, the STL algorithms are significant in their own right, equally capable of lightening a developer's burden. In fact, given that there are over 100 algorithms, it's easy to argue that they offer programmers a more finely honed tool set than the containers (a mere eight strong) could ever hope to match. Perhaps their number is part of the problem. Making sense of eight distinct container types is surely less work than remembering 70 algorithm names and trying to keep track of which does what.

I have two primary goals in this chapter. First, I want to introduce you to some lesser-known algorithms by showing you how they can make your life easier. Rest assured that I'm not going to punish you with lists of names to memorize. The algorithms I show you are in this chapter because they solve common problems, like performing case-insensitive string comparisons, efficiently finding the n most desirable objects in a container, summarizing the characteristics of all the objects in a range, and implementing the behavior of copy_if (an algorithm from the original HP STL that was dropped during standardization).

My second goal is to show you how to avoid common usage problems with the algorithms. You can't call remove, for example, or its cousins remove_if and unique unless you understand *exactly* what these algorithms do (and do *not* do). This is especially true when the range from which you're removeing something holds pointers. Similarly, a number of algorithms work only with sorted ranges, so you need to understand which ones they are and why they impose that constraint. Finally, one of the most common algorithm-related mistakes involves asking an algorithm to write its results to a place that doesn't exist, so I explain how this absurdity can come about and how to ensure that you're not afflicted.

By the end of the chapter, you may not hold algorithms in the same high regard you probably already accord containers, but I'm hopeful you'll be willing to let them share the limelight more often than you have in the past.

Item 30: Make sure destination ranges are big enough.

STL containers automatically expand themselves to hold new objects as they are added (via insert, push_front, push_back, etc.). This works so well, some programmers lull themselves into the belief that they never have to worry about making room for objects in containers, because the containers themselves take care of things. If only it were so!

The problems arise when programmers *think* about inserting objects into containers, but don't tell the STL what they're thinking. Here's a common way this can manifest itself:

```
int transmogrify(int x);                // this function produces
                                        // some new value from x

vector<int> values;

...                                     // put data into values

vector<int> results;                    // apply transmogrify to
transform( values.begin(), values.end(),  // each object in values,
          results.end(),                // appending the return
          transmogrify);                // values to results; this
                                        // code has a bug!
```

In this example, transform is told that the beginning of its destination range is results.end(), so that's where it starts writing the results of invoking transmogrify on every element of values. Like every algorithm that uses a destination range, transform writes its results by making assignments to the elements in the destination range. transform will thus apply transmogrify to values[0] and assign the result to *results.end(). It will then apply transmogrify to values[1] and assign the result to *(results.end()+1). This can lead only to disaster, because *there is no object* at *results.end(), much less at *(results.end()+1)! The call to transform is wrong, because it's asking for assignments to be made to objects that don't exist. (Item 50 explains how a debugging implementation of the STL can detect this problem at runtime.)

Programmers who make this kind of mistake almost always intend for the results of the algorithm they're calling to be inserted into the destination container. If that's what you want to happen, you have to say so. The STL is a library, not a psychic. In this example, the way to say "please put transform's results at the end of the container called results" is to call back_inserter to generate the iterator specifying the beginning of the destination range:

```
vector<int> results;              // apply transmogrify to
transform( values.begin(), values.end(),   // each object in values,
        back_inserter(results),   // inserting the return
        transmogrify);            // values at the end of
                                  // results
```

Internally, the iterator returned by back_inserter causes push_back to be called, so you may use back_inserter with any container offering push_back (i.e., any of the standard sequence containers: vector, string, deque, and list). If you'd prefer to have an algorithm insert things at the front of a container you can use front_inserter. Internally, front_inserter makes use of push_front, so front_inserter works only for the containers offering that member function (i.e, deque and list):

```
...                               // same as before

list<int> results;                // results is now a list

transform( values.begin(), values.end(),   // insert transform's
        front_inserter(results),  // results at the front of
        transmogrify);            // results in reverse order
```

Because front_inserter causes each object added to results to be push_fronted, the order of the objects in results will be the *reverse* of the order of the corresponding objects in values. This is one reason why front_inserter isn't used as often as back_inserter. Another reason is that vector doesn't offer push_front, so front_inserter can't be used with vectors.

If you want transform to put its output at the front of results, but you also want the output to be in the same order as the corresponding objects in values, just iterate over values in reverse order:

```
list<int> results;                // same as before

transform( values.rbegin(), values.rend(),   // insert transform's
        front_inserter(results),  // results at the front of
        transmogrify);            // results; preserve the
                                  // relative object ordering
```

Given that front_inserter lets you force algorithms to insert their results at the front of a container and back_inserter lets you tell them to put their results at the back of a container, it's little surprise that inserter allows you to force algorithms to insert their results into containers at arbitrary locations:

```
vector<int> values;               // as before
...
```

```
vector<int> results;                              // as before, except now
...                                               // results has some data
                                                  // in it prior to the call to
                                                  // transform

transform( values.begin(), values.end(),          // insert the
        inserter(results, results.begin() + results.size() / 2),  // results of
        transmogrify);                            // the trans-
                                                  // mogrifica-
                                                  // tions at
                                                  // the middle
                                                  // of results
```

Regardless of whether you use back_inserter, front_inserter, or inserter, each insertion into the destination range is done one object at a time. Item 5 explains that this can be expensive for contiguous-memory containers (vector, string, and deque), but Item 5's suggested solution (using range member functions) can't be applied when it's an algorithm doing the inserting. In this example, transform will write to its destination range one value at a time, and there's nothing you can do to change that.

When the container into which you're inserting is a vector or a string, you can minimize the expense by following the advice of Item 14 and calling reserve in advance. You'll still have to absorb the cost of shifting elements up each time an insertion takes place, but at least you'll avoid the need to reallocate the container's underlying memory:

```
vector<int> values;                               // as above
vector<int> results;
...

results.reserve(results.size() + values.size());  // ensure that results has
                                                  // the capacity for at least
                                                  // values.size() more
                                                  // elements

transform( values.begin(), values.end(),          // as above,
        inserter(results, results.begin() + results.size() / 2),  // but results
        transmogrify);                            // won't do
                                                  // any reallo-
                                                  // cations
```

When using reserve to improve the efficiency of a series of insertions, always remember that reserve increases only a container's *capacity*; the container's size remains unchanged. Even after calling reserve, you must use an insert iterator (e.g., one of the iterators returned from back_inserter, front_inserter, or inserter) with an algorithm when you want that algorithm to add new elements to a vector or string.

To make this absolutely clear, here is the *wrong* way to improve the efficiency of the example at the beginning of this Item (the one where we append to results the outcome of transmogrifying the data in values):

```
vector<int> values;                        // as above
vector<int> results;

...

results.reserve(results.size() + values.size());    // as above

transform( values.begin(), values.end(),   // write the results of
           results.end(),                  // the transmogrifications
           transmogrify);                  // to uninitialized memory;
                                           // behavior is undefined!
```

In this code, transform blithely attempts to make assignments to the raw, uninitialized memory at the end of results. In general, this will fail at runtime, because assignment is an operation that makes sense only between two objects, not between one object and a chunk of primordial bits. Even if this code happens to do what you want it to, results won't know about the new "objects" transform "created" in its unused capacity. As far as results would be aware, its size would be the same after the call to transform as it was before. Similarly, its end iterator would point to the same place it did prior to the call to transform. Conclusion? Using reserve without also using an insert iterator leads to undefined behavior inside algorithms as well as to corrupted containers.

The correct way to code this example uses both reserve *and* an insert iterator:

```
vector<int> values;                        // as above
vector<int> results;

...

results.reserve(results.size() + values.size());    // as above

transform( values.begin(), values.end(),   // write the results of
           back_inserter(results),         // the transmogrifications
           transmogrify);                  // to the end of results,
                                           // avoiding reallocations
                                           // during the process
```

So far, I've assumed that you want algorithms like transform to insert their results as new elements into a container. This is a common desire, but sometimes you want to overwrite the values of existing container elements instead of inserting new ones. When that's the case, you don't need an insert iterator, but you still need to follow the advice of this Item and make sure your destination range is big enough.

For example, suppose you want transform to overwrite results' elements. As long as results has at least as many elements as values does, that's easy. If it doesn't, you must either use resize to make sure it does,

```
vector<int> values;
vector<int> results;
...
if (results.size() < values.size()) {         // make sure results is at
   results.resize(values.size());             // least as big as values is
}
transform(values.begin(), values.end(),       // overwrite the first
          results.begin(),                     // values.size() elements of
          transmogrify);                       // results
```

or you can clear results and then use an insert iterator in the usual fashion:

```
...
results.clear();                              // destroy all elements in
                                               // results

results.reserve(values.size());              // reserve enough space

transform( values.begin(), values.end(),     // put transform's return
           back_inserter(results),            // values into results
           transmogrify);
```

This Item has demonstrated a number of variations on a theme, but I hope the underlying melody is what sticks in your mind. Whenever you use an algorithm requiring specification of a destination range, ensure that the destination range is big enough already or is increased in size as the algorithm runs. To increase the size as you go, use insert iterators, such as ostream_iterators or those returned by back_inserter, front_inserter, or inserter. That's all you need to remember.

Item 31: Know your sorting options.

How can I sort thee? Let me count the ways.

When many programmers think of ordering objects, only a single algorithm comes to mind: sort. (Some programmers think of qsort, but once they've read Item 46, they recant and replace thoughts of qsort with those of sort.)

Now, sort is a wonderful algorithm, but there's no point in squandering wonder where you don't need it. Sometimes you don't need a full sort. For example, if you have a vector of Widgets and you'd like to select the 20 highest-quality Widgets to send to your most loyal customers, you need to do only enough sorting to identify the 20 best Widgets; the remainder can remain unsorted. What you need is a partial sort, and there's an algorithm called partial_sort that does exactly what the name suggests:

```
bool qualityCompare(const Widget& lhs, const Widget& rhs)
{
    // return whether lhs's quality is greater than rhs's quality
}

...

partial_sort(widgets.begin(),                // put the best 20 elements
             widgets.begin() + 20,           // (in order) at the front of
             widgets.end(),                  // widgets
             qualityCompare);

...                                          // use widgets...
```

After the call to partial_sort, the first 20 elements of widgets are the best in the container and are in order, i.e., the highest-quality Widget is widgets[0], the next highest is widgets[1], etc. That makes it easy to send your best Widget to your best customer, the next best Widget to your next best customer, etc.

If all you care about is that the 20 best Widgets go to your 20 best customers, but you don't care which Widget goes to which customer, partial_sort gives you more than you need. In that case, all you need is the 20 best Widgets in *any* order. The STL has an algorithm that does exactly what you want, though the name isn't likely to spring to mind. It's called nth_element.

nth_element sorts a range so that the element at position n (which you specify) is the one that would be there if the range had been fully sorted. In addition, when nth_element returns, none of the elements in the positions up to n follow the element at position n in the sort order, and none of the elements in positions following n precede the element at position n in the sort order. If that sounds complicated, it's only because I have to select my words carefully. I'll explain why in a moment, but first let's look at how to use nth_element to make sure the best 20 Widgets are at the front of the widgets vector:

```
nth_element(widgets.begin(),                 // put the best 20 elements
            widgets.begin() + 20,            // at the front of widgets,
            widgets.end(),                   // but don't worry about
            qualityCompare);                 // their order
```

As you can see, the call to nth_element is essentially identical to the call to partial_sort. The only difference in their effect is that partial_sort sorts the elements in positions 1-20, while nth_element doesn't. Both algorithms, however, move the 20 highest-quality Widgets to the front of the vector.

That gives rise to an important question. What do these algorithms do when there are elements with the same level of quality? Suppose, for example, there are 12 elements with a quality rating of 1 (the best possible) and 15 elements with a quality rating of 2 (the next best). In that case, choosing the 20 best Widgets involves choosing the 12 with a rating of 1 and 8 of the 15 with a rating of 2. How should partial_sort and nth_element determine which of the 15 to put in the top 20? For that matter, how should sort figure out which order to put elements in when multiple elements have equivalent values?

partial_sort and nth_element order elements with equivalent values any way they want to, and you can't control this aspect of their behavior. (See Item 19 for what it means for two values to be equivalent.) In our example, when faced with the need to choose Widgets with a quality rating of 2 to put into the last 8 spots in the vector's top 20, they'd choose whichever ones they wanted. That's not unreasonable. If you ask for the 20 best Widgets and some Widgets are equally good, you're in no position to complain as long as the 20 you get back are at least as good as the ones you didn't.

For a full sort, you have slightly more control. Some sorting algorithms are *stable*. In a stable sort, if two elements in a range have equivalent values, their relative positions are unchanged after sorting. Hence, if Widget A precedes Widget B in the (unsorted) widgets vector and both have the same quality rating, a stable sorting algorithm will guarantee that after the vector is sorted, Widget A still precedes Widget B. An algorithm that is not stable would not make this guarantee.

partial_sort is not stable. Neither is nth_element. sort, too, fails to offer stability, but there is an algorithm, stable_sort, that does what its name suggests. If you need stability when you sort, you'll probably want to use stable_sort. The STL does not contain stable versions of partial_sort or nth_element.

Speaking of nth_element, this curiously named algorithm is remarkably versatile. In addition to letting you find the top n elements of a range, it can also be used to find the median value in a range or to find the value at a particular percentile:

```
vector<Widget>::iterator begin(widgets.begin());   // convenience vars
vector<Widget>::iterator end(widgets.end());       // for widgets' begin
                                                   // and end iterators

vector<Widget>::iterator goalPosition;             // iter indicating where
                                                   // the widget of interest
                                                   // is located

// The following code finds the Widget with
// the median level of quality

goalPosition = begin + widgets.size() / 2;         // the widget of interest
                                                   // would be in the middle
                                                   // of the sorted vector

nth_element(begin, goalPosition, end,              // find the median quality
            qualityCompare);                       // value in widgets

...                                                // goalPosition now points
                                                   // to the Widget with a
                                                   // median level of quality


// The following code finds the Widget with
// a level of quality at the 75th percentile

vector<Widget>::size_type goalOffset =             // figure out how far from
    0.25 * widgets.size();                         // the beginning the
                                                   // Widget of interest is

nth_element(begin, begin + goalOffset, end,        // find the quality value at
            qualityCompare);                       // the 75th percentile

...                                                // begin+goalOffset now
                                                   // points to the Widget
                                                   // with the 75th percentile
                                                   // level of quality
```

sort, stable_sort, and partial_sort are great if you really need to put things in order, and nth_element fills the bill when you need to identify the top *n* elements or the element at a particular position, but sometimes you need something similar to nth_element, but not quite the same. Suppose, for example, you didn't need to identify the 20 highest-quality Widgets. Instead, you needed to identify all the Widgets with a quality rating of 1 or 2. You could, of course, sort the vector by quality and then search for the first one with a quality rating worse than 2. That would identify the beginning of a range of poor-quality Widgets.

A full sort can be a lot of work, however, and that much work is not necessary for this job. A better strategy is to use the partition algorithm, which reorders element in a range so that all elements satisfying a particular criterion are at the beginning of the range.

For example, to move all the Widgets with a quality rating of 2 or better to the front of widgets, we define a function that identifies which Widgets make the grade,

```
bool hasAcceptableQuality(const Widget& w)
{
    // return whether w has a quality rating of 2 or better;
}
```

then pass that function to partition:

```
vector<Widget>::iterator goodEnd =          // move all widgets satisfying
    partition( widgets.begin(),             // hasAcceptableQuality to
        widgets.end(),                      // the front of widgets, and
        hasAcceptableQuality);              // return an iterator to the first
                                            // widget that isn't satisfactory
```

After this call, the range from widgets.begin() to goodEnd holds all the Widgets with a quality of 1 or 2, and the range from goodEnd to widgets.end() contains all the Widgets with lower quality ratings. If it were important to maintain the relative positions of Widgets with equivalent quality levels during the partitioning, we'd naturally reach for stable_partition instead of partition.

The algorithms sort, stable_sort, partial_sort, and nth_element require random access iterators, so they may be applied only to vectors, strings, deques, and arrays. It makes no sense to sort elements in standard associative containers, because such containers use their comparison functions to remain sorted at all times. The only container where we might like to use sort, stable_sort, partial_sort, or nth_element, but can't, is list, and list compensates somewhat by offering its sort member function. (Interestingly, list::sort performs a stable sort.) If you want to sort a list, then, you can, but if you want to use partial_sort, or nth_element on the objects in a list, you have to do it indirectly. One indirect approach is to copy the elements into a container with random access iterators, then apply the desired algorithm to that. Another is to create a container of list::iterators, use the algorithm on that container, then access the list elements via the iterators. A third is to use the information in an ordered container of iterators to iteratively splice the list's elements into the positions you'd like them to be in. As you can see, there are lots of options.

partition and stable_partition differ from sort, stable_sort, partial_sort, and nth_element in requiring only bidirectional iterators. You can therefore use partition and stable_partition with any of the standard sequence containers.

Let's summarize your sorting options.

- If you need to perform a full sort on a vector, string, deque, or array, you can use sort or stable_sort.

- If you have a vector, string, deque, or array and you need to put only the top *n* elements in order, partial_sort is available.

- If you have a vector, string, deque, or array and you need to identify the element at position *n* or you need to identify the top *n* elements without putting them in order, nth_element is at your beck and call.

- If you need to separate the elements of a standard sequence container or an array into those that do and do not satisfy some criterion, you're probably looking for partition or stable_partition.

- If your data is in a list, you can use partition and stable_partition directly, and you can use list::sort in place of sort and stable_sort. If you need the effects offered by partial_sort or nth_element, you'll have to approach the task indirectly, but there are a number of options, as I sketched above.

In addition, you can keep things sorted at all times by storing your data in a standard associative container. You might also consider the standard non-STL container priority_queue, which also keeps its elements ordered all the time. (priority_queue is traditionally considered part of the STL, but, as I noted in the Introduction, my definition of "the STL" requires that STL containers support iterators, and priority_queue doesn't do iterators.)

"But what about performance?", you wonder. Excellent question. Broadly speaking, algorithms that do more work take longer to do it, and algorithms that must sort stably take longer than algorithms that can ignore stability. We can order the algorithms we've discussed in this Item as follows, with algorithms that tend to use fewer resources (time and space) listed before those that require more:

1. partition	4. partial_sort
2. stable_partition	5. sort
3. nth_element	6. stable_sort

My advice on choosing among the sorting algorithms is to make your selection based on what you need to accomplish, not on performance considerations. If you choose an algorithm that does only what you need to do (e.g., a partition instead of a full sort), you're likely to end up with code that's not only the clearest expression of what you want to do, it's also the most efficient way to accomplish it using the STL.

Item 32: Follow remove-like algorithms by erase if you really want to remove something.

I begin this Item with a review of remove, because remove is the most confusing algorithm in the STL. Misunderstanding remove is easy, and it's important to dispel all doubt about what remove does, why it does it, and how it goes about doing it.

Here is the declaration for remove:

```
template<class ForwardIterator, class T>
ForwardIterator remove(ForwardIterator first, ForwardIterator last,
                       const T& value);
```

Like all algorithms, remove receives a pair of iterators identifying the range of elements over which it should operate. It does not receive a container, so remove doesn't know which container holds the elements it's looking at. Furthermore, it's not possible for remove to discover that container, because there is no way to go from an iterator to the container corresponding to that iterator.

Think for a moment about how one eliminates elements from a container. The only way to do it is to call a member function on that container, almost always some form of erase. (list has a couple of member functions that eliminate elements and are not named erase, but they're still member functions.) Because the only way to eliminate an element from a container is to invoke a member function on that container, and because remove cannot know the container holding the elements on which it is operating, *it is not possible for remove to eliminate elements from a container.* That explains the otherwise baffling observation that removeing elements from a container never changes the number of elements in the container:

```
vector<int> v;                    // create a vector<int> and fill it with
v.reserve(10);                    // the values 1-10. (See Item 14 for an
for (int i = 1; i <= 10; ++i) {   // explanation of the reserve call.)
  v.push_back(i);
}

cout << v.size();                 // prints 10

v[3] = v[5] = v[9] = 99;          // set 3 elements to 99

remove(v.begin(), v.end(), 99);   // remove all elements with value 99

cout << v.size();                 // still prints 10!
```

To make sense of this example, memorize the following:

remove doesn't "really" remove anything, because it can't.

Repetition is good for you:

> remove doesn't "really" remove anything, *because it can't.*

remove doesn't know the container it's supposed to remove things from, and without that container, there's no way for it to call the member functions that are necessary if one is to "really" remove something.

That explains what remove doesn't do, and it explains why it doesn't do it. What we need to review now is what remove *does* do.

Very briefly, remove moves elements in the range it's given until all the "unremoved" elements are at the front of the range (in the same relative order they were in originally). It returns an iterator pointing one past the last "unremoved" element. This return value is the "new logical end" of the range.

In terms of our example, this is what v looks like prior to calling remove,

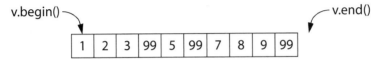

and if we store remove's return value in a new iterator called newEnd,

vector<int>::iterator newEnd(**remove**(v.begin(), v.end(), 99));

this is what v looks like after the call:

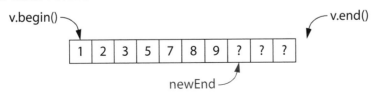

Here I've used question marks to indicate the values of elements that have been conceptually removed from v but continue to exist.

It seems logical that if the "unremoved" elements are in v between v.begin() and newEnd, the "removed" elements must be between new-End and v.end(). *This is not the case!* The "removed" values aren't necessarily in v any longer at all. remove doesn't change the order of the elements in a range so that all the "removed" ones are at the end, it arranges for all the "unremoved" values to be at the beginning. Though the Standard doesn't require it, the elements beyond the new logical end of the range typically *retain their old values*. After calling remove, v looks like this in every implementation I know:

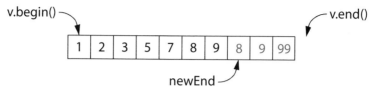

As you can see, two of the "99" values that used to exist in v are no longer there, while one "99" remains. In general, after calling remove, the values removed from the range may or may not continue to exist in the range. Most people find this surprising, but why? You asked remove to get rid of some values, so it did. You didn't ask it to put the removed values in a special place where you could get at them later, so it didn't. What's the problem? (If you don't want to lose any values, you should probably be calling partition instead of remove. partition is described in Item 31.)

remove's behavior sounds spiteful, but it's simply a fallout of the way the algorithm operates. Internally, remove walks down the range, over-writing values that are to be "removed" with later values that are to be retained. The overwriting is accomplished by making assignments to the elements holding the values to be overwritten.

You can think of remove as performing a kind of compaction, where the values to be removed play the role of holes that are filled during compaction. For our vector v, it plays out as follows.

1. remove examines v[0], sees that its value isn't supposed to be re-moved, and moves on to v[1]. It does the same for v[1] and v[2].

2. It sees that v[3] should be removed, so it notes that v[3]'s value may be overwritten, and it moves on to v[4]. This is akin to not-ing that v[3] is a "hole" that needs to be filled.

3. It sees that v[4]'s value should be retained, so it assigns v[4] to v[3], notes that v[4] may now be overwritten, and moves on to v[5]. Continuing the compaction analogy, it "fills" v[3] with v[4] and notes that v[4] is now a hole.

4. It finds that v[5] should be removed, so it ignores it and moves on to v[6]. It continues to remember that v[4] is a hole waiting to be filled.

5. It sees that v[6] is a value that should be kept, so it assigns v[6] to v[4], remembers that v[5] is now the next hole to be filled, and moves on to v[7].

6. In a manner analogous to the above, it examines v[7], v[8] and v[9]. It assigns v[7] to v[5] and v[8] to v[6], ignoring v[9], because the value at v[9] is to be removed.

7. It returns an iterator indicating the next element to be overwritten, in this case the element at v[7].

You can envision the values moving around in v as follows:

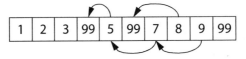

As Item 33 explains, the fact that remove overwrites some of the values it is removing has important repercussions when those values are pointers. For this Item, however, it's enough to understand that remove doesn't eliminate any elements from a container, because it can't. Only container member functions can eliminate container elements, and that's the whole point of this Item: You should follow remove by erase if you really want to remove something.

The elements you want to erase are easy to identify. They're the elements of the original range that start at the "new logical end" of the range and continue until the real end of the range. To get rid of these elements, all you need to do is call the range form of erase (see Item 5) with these two iterators. Because remove itself conveniently returns the iterator for the new logical end of the range, the call is straightforward:

```
vector<int> v;                            // as before
...

v.erase(remove(v.begin(), v.end(), 99), v.end());   // really remove all
                                          // elements with value 99

cout << v.size();                         // now returns 7
```

Passing remove's return value as the first argument to the range form of erase is so common, it's idiomatic. In fact, remove and erase are so closely allied, the two are merged in the list member function remove. This is the only function in the STL named remove that eliminates elements from a container:

```
list<int> li;                             // create a list
...                                        // put some values into it
li.remove(99);                            // eliminate all elements with value 99;
                                          // this really removes elements, so li's
                                          // size may change
```

Frankly, calling this function remove is an inconsistency in the STL. The analogous function in the associative containers is called erase, and list's remove should be called erase, too. It's not, however, so we all have to get used to it. The world in which we frolic may not be the best of all possible worlds, but it is the one we've got. (On the plus side, Item 44 points out that, for lists, calling the remove member function is more efficient than applying the erase-remove idiom.)

Once you understand that remove can't "really" remove things from a container, using it in conjunction with erase becomes second nature. The only other thing you need to bear in mind is that remove isn't the only algorithm for which this is the case. There are two other "remove-like" algorithms: remove_if and unique.

The similarity between remove and remove_if is so straightforward, I won't dwell on it, but unique also behaves like remove. It is asked to remove things (adjacent repeated values) from a range without having access to the container holding the range's elements. As a result, you must also pair calls to unique with calls to erase if you really want to remove elements from a container. unique is also analogous to remove in its interaction with list. Just as list::remove really removes things (and does so more efficiently than the erase-remove idiom), list::unique really removes adjacent duplicates (also with greater efficiency than would erase-unique).

Item 33: Be wary of remove-like algorithms on containers of pointers.

So you conjure up a bunch of dynamically allocated Widgets, each of which may be certified, and you store the resulting pointers in a vector:

```
class Widget {
public:
    ...
    bool isCertified() const;              // whether the Widget is certified
    ...
};
vector<Widget*> v;                         // create a vector and fill it with
    ...                                    // pointers to dynamically
v.push_back(new Widget);                   // allocated Widgets
    ...
```

After working with v for a while, you decide to get rid of the uncertified Widgets, because you don't need them any longer. Bearing in mind Item 43's admonition to prefer algorithm calls to explicit loops and having read Item 32's discourse on the relationship between remove and erase, your thoughts naturally turn to the erase-remove idiom, though in this case it's remove_if you employ:

```
v.erase( remove_if(v.begin(), v.end(),                    // erase ptrs to
                   not1(mem_fun(&Widget::isCertified))), // uncertified
        v.end());                                         // Widgets; see
                                                          // Item 41 for
                                                          // info on
                                                          // mem_fun
```

Suddenly you begin to worry about the call to erase, because you dimly recall Item 7's discussion of how destroying a pointer in a container fails to delete what the pointer points to. This is a legitimate worry, but in this case, it comes too late. By the time erase is called, there's an excellent chance you have already leaked resources. Worry about erase, yes, but first, worry about remove_if.

Let's assume that prior to the remove_if call, v looks like this, where I've indicated the uncertified Widgets.

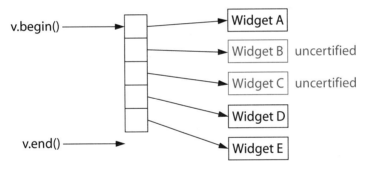

After the call to remove_if, v will typically look like this (including the iterator returned from remove_if):

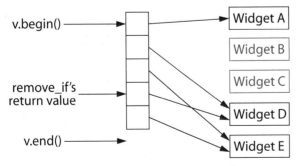

If this transformation makes no sense, kindly turn to Item 32, because it explains exactly what happens when remove — or, in this case, remove_if — is called.

The reason for the resource leak should now be apparent. The "removed" pointers to Widgets B and C have been overwritten by later "unremoved" pointers in the vector. Nothing points to the two uncertified Widgets, they can never be deleted, and their memory and other resources are leaked.

Once both remove_if and erase have returned, the situations looks as follows:

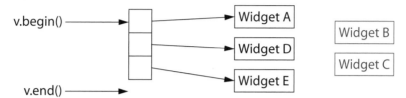

This makes the resource leak especially obvious, and it should now be clear why you should try to avoid using remove and similar algorithms (i.e., remove_if and unique) on containers of dynamically allocated pointers. In many cases, you'll find that the partition algorithm (see Item 31) is a reasonable alternative.

If you can't avoid using remove on such containers, one way to eliminate this problem is to delete the pointers and set them to null prior to applying the erase-remove idiom, then eliminate all the null pointers in the container:

```
void delAndNullifyUncertified(Widget*& pWidget)   // if *pWidget is an
{                                                 // uncertified Widget,
  if (!pWidget->isCertified()) {                  // delete the pointer
    delete pWidget;                               // and set it to null
    pWidget = 0;
  }
}

for_each( v.begin(), v.end(),                     // delete and set to
        delAndNullifyUncertified);                // null all ptrs to
                                                  // uncertified widgets

v.erase( remove(v.begin(), v.end(),               // eliminate null ptrs
              static_cast<Widget*>(0)),           // from v; 0 must be
          v.end());                               // cast to a ptr so C++
                                                  // correctly deduces
                                                  // the type of
                                                  // remove's 3rd param
```

Of course, this assumes that the vector doesn't hold any null pointers you'd like to retain. If it does, you'll probably have to write your own loop that erases pointers as you go. Erasing elements from a container as you traverse that container has some subtle aspects to it, so be sure to read Item 9 before considering that approach.

If you're willing to replace the container of pointers with a container of *smart* pointers that perform reference counting, the remove-related difficulties wash away, and you can use the erase-remove idiom directly:

```
template<typename T>              // RCSP = "Reference Counting
class RCSP { ... };               //           Smart Pointer"

typedef RCSP<Widget> RCSPW;       // RCSPW = "RCSP to Widget"

vector<RCSPW> v;                  // create a vector and fill it with
...                               // smart pointers to dynamically
v.push_back(RCSPW(new Widget));   // allocated Widgets
...

v.erase(remove_if(v.begin(), v.end(),                // erase the ptrs
            not1(mem_fun(&Widget::isCertified))),    // to uncertified
        v.end());                                    // Widgets; no
                                                     // resources are
                                                     // leaked
```

For this to work, it must be possible to implicitly convert your smart pointer type (e.g., RCSP<Widget>) to the corresponding built-in pointer type (e.g., Widget*). That's because the container holds smart pointers, but the member function being called (e.g., Widget::isCertified) insists on built-in pointers. If no implicit conversion exists, your compilers will squawk.

If you don't happen to have a reference counting smart pointer template in your programming toolbox, you owe it to yourself to check out the shared_ptr template in the Boost library. For an introduction to Boost, take a look at Item 50.

Regardless of how you choose to deal with containers of dynamically allocated pointers, be it by reference counting smart pointers, manual deletion and nullification of pointers prior to invoking a remove-like algorithm, or some technique of your own invention, the guidance of this Item remains the same: Be wary of remove-like algorithms on containers of pointers. Failure to heed this advice is just *asking* for resource leaks.

Item 34: Note which algorithms expect sorted ranges.

Not all algorithms are applicable to all ranges. For example, remove (see Items 32 and 33) requires forward iterators and the ability to make assignments through those iterators. As a result, it can't be applied to ranges demarcated by input iterators, nor to maps or multimaps, nor to some implementations of set and multiset (see Item 22). Similarly, many of the sorting algorithms (see Item 31) demand random access iterators, so it's not possible to invoke these algorithms on the elements of a list.

If you violate these kinds of rules, your code won't compile, an event likely to be heralded by lengthy and incomprehensible error messages (see Item 49). Other algorithm preconditions, however, are more subtle. Among these, perhaps the most common is that some algorithms require ranges of *sorted* values. It's important that you adhere to this requirement whenever it applies, because violating it leads not to compiler diagnostics, but to undefined runtime behavior.

A few algorithms can work with sorted or unsorted ranges, but they are most useful when they operate on sorted ranges. You should understand how these algorithms work, because that will explain why sorted ranges suit them best.

Some of you, I know, are into brute-force memorization, so here's a list of the algorithms that require the data on which they operate to be sorted:

binary_search	lower_bound
upper_bound	equal_range
set_union	set_intersection
set_difference	set_symmetric_difference
merge	inplace_merge
includes	

In addition, the following algorithms are typically used with sorted ranges, though they don't require them:

unique	unique_copy

We'll see shortly that the definition of "sorted" has an important constraint, but first, let me try to make sense of this collection of algorithms. It's easier to remember which algorithms work with sorted ranges if you understand why such ranges are needed.

The search algorithms binary_search, lower_bound, upper_bound, and equal_range (see Item 45) require sorted ranges, because they look for values using binary search. Like the C library's bsearch, these algorithms promise logarithmic-time lookups, but in exchange, you must give them values that have already been put into order.

Actually, it's not quite true that these algorithms promise logarithmic-time lookup. They guarantee such performance only when they are passed random access iterators. If they're given less powerful iterators (such as bidirectional iterators), they still perform only a logarithmic number of comparisons, but they run in linear time. That's because, lacking the ability to perform "iterator arithmetic," they need linear time to move from place to place in the range being searched.

The quartet of algorithms set_union, set_intersection, set_difference, and set_symmetric_difference offer linear-time performance of the set-theoretical operations their names suggest. Why do they demand sorted ranges? Because without them, they couldn't do their work in linear time. If you're beginning to detect a trend suggesting that algorithms requiring sorted ranges do so in order to offer better performance than they'd be able to guarantee for ranges that might not be sorted, you're right. Stay tuned. The trend will continue.

merge and inplace_merge perform what is in effect a single pass of the mergesort algorithm: they read two sorted ranges and produce a new sorted range containing all the elements from both source ranges. They run in linear time, something they couldn't do if they didn't know that the source ranges were already sorted.

The final algorithm that requires sorted source ranges is includes. It's used to determine whether all the objects in one range are also in another range. Because includes may assume that both its ranges are sorted, it promises linear-time performance. Without that guarantee, it would generally run slower.

Unlike the algorithms we've just discussed, unique and unique_copy offer well-defined behavior even on unsorted ranges. But look at how the Standard describes unique's behavior (the italics are mine):

> Eliminates all but the first element from every *consecutive* group of equal elements.

In other words, if you want unique to eliminate all duplicates from a range (i.e., to make all values in the range "unique"), you must first make sure that all duplicate values are next to one another. And guess what? That's one of the things sorting does. In practice, unique is usually employed to eliminate all duplicate values from a range, so you'll almost always want to make sure that the range you pass unique (or unique_copy) is sorted. (Unix developers will recognize a striking similarity between STL's unique and Unix's uniq, a similarity I suspect is anything but coincidental.)

Incidentally, unique eliminates elements from a range the same way remove does, which is to say that it only "sort of" eliminates them. If you aren't sure what this means, please turn to Items 32 and 33 immediately. It is not possible to overemphasize the importance of understanding what remove and remove-like algorithms (including unique) do. Having a basic comprehension is not sufficient. If you don't *know* what they do, you will get into trouble.

Which brings me to the fine print regarding what it means for a range to be sorted. Because the STL allows you to specify comparison functions to be used during sorting, different ranges may be sorted in different ways. Given two ranges of ints, for example, one might be sorted the default way (i.e., in ascending order) while the other is sorted using greater<int>, hence in descending order. Given two ranges of Widgets, one might be sorted by price and another might be sorted by age. With so many different ways to sort things, it's critical that you give the STL consistent sorting-related information to work with. If you pass a sorted range to an algorithm that also takes a comparison function, be sure that the comparison function you pass behaves the same as the one you used to sort the range.

Here's an example of what you do *not* want to do:

```
vector<int> v;                          // create a vector, put some
...                                     // data into it, sort it into
sort(v.begin(), v.end(), greater<int>()); // descending order

...                                     // work with the vector
                                        // (without changing it)

bool a5Exists =                         // search for a 5 in the vector,
   binary_search(v.begin(), v.end(), 5); // assuming it's sorted in
                                        // ascending order!
```

By default, binary_search assumes that the range it's searching is sorted by "<" (i.e., the values are in ascending order), but in this example, the vector is sorted in *descending* order. You should not be surprised to learn that you get undefined results when you invoke binary_search (or lower_bound, etc.) on a range of values that is sorted in a different order from what the algorithm expects.

To get the code to behave correctly, you must tell binary_search to use the same comparison function that sort did:

```
bool a5Exists =                                      // search for a 5
   binary_search(v.begin(), v.end(), 5, greater<int>()); // using greater as
                                                     // the comparison
                                                     // function
```

All the algorithms that require sorted ranges (i.e., all the algorithms in this Item except unique and unique_copy) determine whether two values are "the same" by using equivalence, just like the standard associative containers (which are themselves sorted). In contrast, the default way in which unique and unique_copy determine whether two objects are "the same" is by using equality, though you can override this default by passing these algorithms a predicate defining an alternative definition of "the same." For a detailed discussion of the difference between equivalence and equality, consult Item 19.

The eleven algorithms that require sorted ranges do so in order to offer greater efficiency than would otherwise be possible. As long as you remember to pass them only sorted ranges, and as long as you make sure that the comparison function used by the algorithms is consistent with the one used to do the sorting, you'll revel in trouble-free search, set, and merge operations, plus you'll find that unique and unique_copy eliminate *all* duplicate values, as you almost certainly want them to.

Item 35: Implement simple case-insensitive string comparisons via mismatch or lexicographical_compare.

One of the most frequently asked questions by STL newbies is "How do I use the STL to perform case-insensitive string comparisons?" This is a deceptively simple question. Case-insensitive string comparisons are either really easy or really hard, depending on how general you want to be. If you're willing to ignore internationalization issues and restrict your concern to the kinds of strings strcmp is designed for, the task is easy. If you want to be able to handle strings of characters in languages where strcmp wouldn't apply (i.e., strings holding text in just about any language except English) or where programs use a locale other than the default, the task is very hard.

In this Item, I'll tackle the easy version of the problem, because that suffices to demonstrate how the STL can be brought to bear. (A harder version of the problem involves no more of the STL. Rather, it involves locale-dependent issues you can read about in Appendix A.) To make the easy problem somewhat more challenging, I'll tackle it twice. Programmers desiring case-insensitive string comparisons often need two different calling interfaces, one similar to strcmp (which returns a negative number, zero, or a positive number), the other akin to operator< (which returns true or false). I'll therefore show how to implement both calling interfaces using STL algorithms.

First, however, we need a way to determine whether two characters are the same, except for their case. When internationalization issues are taken into account, this is a complicated problem. The following character-comparing function is a simplistic solution, but it's akin to the strcmp approach to string comparison, and since in this Item I consider only strings where a strcmp-like approach is appropriate, internationalization issues don't count, and this function will do:

```
int ciCharCompare(char c1, char c2)      // case-insensitively compare chars
{                                        // c1 and c2, returning -1 if c1 < c2,
                                         // 0 if c1==c2, and 1 if c1 > c2
   int lc1 = tolower(static_cast<unsigned char>(c1));      // see below for
   int lc2 = tolower(static_cast<unsigned char>(c2));      // info on these
                                                           // statements

   if (lc1 < lc2) return -1;

   if (lc1 > lc2) return 1;

   return 0;
}
```

This function follows the lead of strcmp in returning a negative number, zero, or a positive number, depending on the relationship between c1 and c2. Unlike strcmp, ciCharCompare converts both parameters to lower case before performing the comparison. That's what makes it a case-insensitive character comparison.

Like many functions in <cctype> (and hence <ctype.h>), tolower's parameter and return value is of type int, but unless that int is EOF, its value must be representable as an unsigned char. In both C and C++, char may or may not be signed (it's up to the implementation), and when char is signed, the only way to ensure that its value is representable as an unsigned char is to cast it to one before calling tolower. That explains the casts in the code above. (On implementations where char is already unsigned, the casts are no-ops.) It also explains the use of int instead of char to store tolower's return value.

Given ciCharCompare, it's easy to write the first of our two case-insensitive string comparison functions, the one offering a strcmp-like interface. This function, ciStringCompare, returns a negative number, zero, or a positive number, depending on the relationship between the strings being compared. It's built around the mismatch algorithm, because mismatch identifies the first position in two ranges where the corresponding values are not the same.

Before we can call mismatch, we have to satisfy its preconditions. In particular, we have to make sure that if one string is shorter than the other, the shorter string is the first range passed. We'll therefore farm the real work out to a function called ciStringCompareImpl and have ciStringCompare simply make sure the arguments are passed in the correct order, adjusting the return value if the arguments have to be swapped:

```
int ciStringCompareImpl(const string& s1,           // see below for
                        const string& s2);          // implementation

int ciStringCompare(const string& s1, const string& s2)
{
    if (s1.size() <= s2.size()) return ciStringCompareImpl(s1, s2);
    else return -ciStringCompareImpl(s2, s1);
}
```

In ciStringCompareImpl, the heavy lifting is performed by mismatch. It returns a pair of iterators indicating the locations in the ranges where corresponding characters first fail to match:

```
int ciStringCompareImpl(const string& s1, const string& s2)
{
    typedef pair<string::const_iterator,             // PSCI = "pair of
                 string::const_iterator> PSCI;       // string::const_iterator"

    PSCI p = mismatch(                               // see below for an
                s1.begin(), s1.end(),                // explanation of why
                s2.begin(),                          // we need not2; see
                not2(ptr_fun(ciCharCompare)));       // Item 41 for why we
                                                     // need ptr_fun

    if (p.first == s1.end()) {                       // if true, either s1 and
        if (p.second == s2.end()) return 0;          // s2 are equal or
        else return -1;                              // s1 is shorter than s2
    }

    return ciCharCompare(*p.first, *p.second);       // the relationship of the
}                                                    // strings is the same as
                                                     // that of the
                                                     // mismatched chars
```

With any luck, the comments make pretty clear what is going on. Fundamentally, once you know the first place where the strings differ, it's easy to determine which string, if either, precedes the other. The only thing that may seem odd is the predicate passed to mismatch, which is not2(ptr_fun(ciCharCompare)). This predicate is responsible for returning true when the characters match, because mismatch will stop when the predicate return false. We can't use ciCharCompare for this purpose, because it returns -1, 1, or 0, and *it returns 0 when the characters match*, just like strcmp. If we passed ciCharCompare as the predicate to mismatch, C++ would convert ciCharCompare's return type to bool, and of course the bool equivalent of zero is false, precisely the opposite of what we want! Similarly, when ciCharCompare returned 1 or –1, that would be interpreted as true, because, as in C, all nonzero integral values are considered true. Again, this would be the opposite of what we want. To fix this semantic inversion, we throw a not2 and a ptr_fun in front of ciCharCompare, and we all live happily ever after.

Our second approach to ciStringCompare yields a conventional STL predicate; such a function could be used as a comparison function in associative containers. The implementation is short and sweet, because all we have to do is modify ciCharCompare to give us a character-comparison function with a predicate interface, then turn the job of performing a string comparison over to the algorithm with the second-longest name in the STL, lexicographical_compare:

```
bool ciCharLess(char c1, char c2)            // return whether c1
{                                            // precedes c2 in a case-
  return                                     // insensitive comparison;
     tolower(static_cast<unsigned char>(c1)) <   // Item 46 explains why a
     tolower(static_cast<unsigned char>(c2));     // function object might
}                                            // be preferable to this
                                             // function

bool ciStringCompare(const string& s1, const string& s2)
{
  return lexicographical_compare(s1.begin(), s1.end(),   // see below for
                                 s2.begin(), s2.end(),   // a discussion of
                                 ciCharLess);            // this algorithm
}                                                        // call
```

No, I won't keep you in suspense any longer. The longest algorithm name is set_symmetric_difference.

If you're familiar with the behavior of lexicographical_compare, the code above is as clear as clear can be. If you're not, it's probably about as clear as concrete. Fortunately, it's not hard to replace the concrete with glass.

lexicographical_compare is a generalized version of strcmp. Where strcmp works only with character arrays, however, lexicographical_compare works with ranges of values of any type. Also, while strcmp always compares two characters to see if their relationship is equal, less than, or greater than one another, lexicographical_compare may be passed an arbitrary predicate that determines whether two values satisfy a user-defined criterion.

In the call above, lexicographical_compare is asked to find the first position where s1 and s2 differ, based on the results of calls to ciCharLess. If, using the characters at that position, ciCharLess returns true, so does lexicographical_compare: if, at the first position where the characters differ, the character from the first string precedes the corresponding character from the second string, the first string precedes the second one. Like strcmp, lexicographical_compare considers two ranges of equal values to be equal, hence it returns false for such ranges: the first range does *not* precede the second. Also like strcmp, if the first range ends before a difference in corresponding values is found, lexicographical_compare returns true: a prefix precedes any range for which it is a prefix.

Enough about mismatch and lexicographical_compare. Though I focus on portability in this book, I would be remiss if I failed to mention that case-insensitive string comparison functions are widely available as nonstandard extensions to the standard C library. They typically have names like stricmp or strcmpi, and they typically offer no more support for internationalization than the functions we've developed in this Item. If you're willing to sacrifice some portability, you know that your strings never contain embedded nulls, and you don't care about internationalization, you may find that the easiest way to implement a case-insensitive string comparison doesn't use the STL at all. Instead, it converts both strings to const char* pointers (see Item 16) and then uses stricmp or strcmpi on the pointers:

```
int ciStringCompare(const string& s1, const string& s2)
{
    return stricmp(s1.c_str(), s2.c_str());      // the function name on
}                                                // your system might
                                                 // not be stricmp
```

Some may call this a hack, but stricmp/strcmpi, being optimized to do exactly one thing, typically run *much* faster on long strings than do the general-purpose algorithms mismatch and lexicographical_compare. If that's an important consideration for you, you may not care that you're trading standard STL algorithms for nonstandard C functions. Sometimes the most effective way to use the STL is to realize that other approaches are superior.

Item 36: Understand the proper implementation of copy_if.

One of the more interesting aspects of the STL is that although there are 11 algorithms with "copy" in their names,

copy	copy_backward
replace_copy	reverse_copy
replace_copy_if	unique_copy
remove_copy	rotate_copy
remove_copy_if	partial_sort_copy
uninitialized_copy	

none of them is copy_if. That means you can replace_copy_if, you can remove_copy_if, you can both copy_backward and reverse_copy, but if you simply want to copy the elements of a range that satisfy a predicate, you're on your own.

For example, suppose you have a function to determine whether a Widget is defective:

```
bool isDefective(const Widget& w);
```

and you'd like to write all the defective Widgets in a vector to cerr. If copy_if existed, you could simply do this:

```
vector<Widget> widgets;

...

copy_if( widgets.begin(), widgets.end(),          // this won't compile;
         ostream_iterator<Widget>(cerr, "\n"),     // there is no copy_if
         isDefective);                             // in the STL
```

Ironically, copy_if was part of the original Hewlett Packard STL that formed the basis for the STL that is now part of the standard C++ library. In one of those quirks that occasionally makes history interesting, during the process of winnowing the HP STL into something of a size manageable for standardization, copy_if was one of the things that got left on the cutting room floor.

In *The C++ Programming Language* [7], Stroustrup remarks that it's trivial to write copy_if, and he's right, but that doesn't mean that it's necessarily easy to come up with the correct trivia. For example, here's a reasonable-looking copy_if that many people (including me) have been known to come up with:

```
template< typename InputIterator,              // a not-quite-right
          typename OutputIterator,              // implementation of
          typename Predicate>                   // copy_if
OutputIterator copy_if( InputIterator begin,
                        InputIterator end,
                        OutputIterator destBegin,
                        Predicate p)
{
   return remove_copy_if(begin, end, destBegin, not1(p));
}
```

This approach is based on the observation that although the STL doesn't let you say "copy everything where this predicate is true," it does let you say "copy everything except where this predicate is *not* true." To implement copy_if, then, it seems that all we need to do is throw a not1 in front of the predicate we'd like to pass to copy_if, then pass the resulting predicate to remove_copy_if. The result is the code above.

If the above reasoning were valid, we could write out our defective Widgets this way:

```
copy_if( widgets.begin(), widgets.end(),         // well-intentioned code
         ostream_iterator<Widget>(cerr, "\n"),   // that will not compile
         isDefective);
```

Your STL platforms will take a jaundiced view of this code, because it tries to apply not1 to isDefective. (The application takes place inside copy_if). As Item 41 tries to make clear, not1 can't be applied directly to a function pointer; the function pointer must first be passed through ptr_fun. To call this implementation of copy_if, you must pass not just a function object, but an *adaptable* function object. That's easy enough to do, but clients of a would-be STL algorithm shouldn't have to. Standard STL algorithms never require that their functors be adaptable, and neither should copy_if. The above implementation is decent, but it's not decent enough.

Here's the correct trivial implementation of copy_if:

```
template< typename InputIterator,         // a correct
          typename OutputIterator,        // implementation of
          typename Predicate>             // copy_if
OutputIterator copy_if( InputIterator begin,
                        InputIterator end,
                        OutputIterator destBegin,
                        Predicate p)
{
  while (begin != end) {
    if (p(*begin)) *destBegin++ = *begin;
    ++begin;
  }

  return destBegin;
}
```

Given how useful copy_if is, plus the fact that new STL programmers tend to expect it to exist anyway, there's a good case to be made for putting copy_if — the correct one! — into your local STL-related utility library and using it whenever it's appropriate.

Item 37: Use accumulate or for_each to summarize ranges.

Sometimes you need to boil an entire range down to a single number, or, more generally, a single object. For commonly needed information, special-purpose algorithms exist to do the jobs. count tells you how many elements are in a range, for example, while count_if tells you how many elements satisfy a predicate. The minimum and maximum values in a range are available via min_element and max_element.

At times, however, you need to summarize a range in some custom manner, and in those cases, you need something more flexible than count, count_if, min_element, or max_element. For example, you might want the sum of the lengths of the strings in a container. You might want the product of a range of numbers. You might want the average coordinates of a range of points. In each of these cases, you need to *summarize* a range, but you need to be able to define the summary you want. Not a problem. The STL has the algorithm for you. It's called accumulate. You might not be familiar with accumulate, because, unlike most algorithms, it doesn't live in <algorithm>. Instead, it's located with three other "numeric algorithms" in <numeric>. (The three others are inner_product, adjacent_difference, and partial_sum.)

Like many algorithms, accumulate exists in two forms. The form taking a pair of iterators and an initial value returns the initial value plus the sum of the values in the range demarcated by the iterators:

```
list<double> ld;                                    // create a list and put
...                                                 // some doubles into it
double sum = accumulate(ld.begin(), ld.end(), 0.0); // calculate their sum,
                                                    // starting at 0.0
```

In this example, note that the initial value is specified as 0.0, not simply 0. That's important. The type of 0.0 is double, so accumulate internally uses a variable of type double to store the sum it's computing. Had the call been written like this,

```
double sum = accumulate(ld.begin(), ld.end(), 0);   // calculate their sum,
                                                    // starting at 0; this
                                                    // is not correct!
```

the initial value would be the int 0, so accumulate would internally use an int to store the value it was computing. That int would ultimately become accumulate's return value, and it would be used to initialize the variable sum. The code would compile and run, but sum's value would be incorrect. Instead of holding the true sum of a list of doubles, it would hold the result of adding all the doubles together, but converting the result to an int after each addition.

accumulate requires only input iterators, so you can use it even with istream_iterators and istreambuf_iterators (see Item 29):

```
cout << "The sum of the ints on the standard input is "  // print the sum of
     << accumulate( istream_iterator<int>(cin),          // the ints in cin
                    istream_iterator<int>(),
                    0);
```

It is this default behavior of accumulate that causes it to be labeled a numeric algorithm. But when accumulate is used in its alternate form, one taking an initial summary value and an arbitrary summarization function, it becomes much more general.

As an example, consider how to use accumulate to calculate the sum of the lengths of the strings in a container. To compute the sum, accumulate needs to know two things. First, as above, it must know the starting sum. In our case, it is zero. Second, it must know how to update this sum each time a new string is seen. To do that, we write a function that takes the sum so far and the new string and returns the updated sum:

```
string::size_type                          // see below for info
stringLengthSum(string::size_type sumSoFar,  // on string::size_type
                const string& s)
{
   return sumSoFar + s.size();
}
```

The body of this function reveals that what is going on is trivial, but you may find yourself bogged down in the appearances of string::size_type. Don't let that happen. Every standard STL container has a typedef called size_type that is the container's type for counting things. This is the type returned by the container's size function, for example. For all the standard containers, size_type must be size_t, but, in theory, nonstandard STL-compatible containers might use a different type for size_type (though I have a hard time imagining why they'd want to). For standard containers, you can think of *Container*::size_type as a fancy way of writing size_t.

stringLengthSum is representative of the summarization functions accumulate works with. It takes a summary value for the range so far as well as the next element of the range, and it returns the new summary value. In general, that means the function will take parameters of different types. That's what it does here. The summary so far (the sum of the lengths of the strings already seen) is of type string::size_type, while the type of the elements being examined is string. As is typically the case, the return type here is the same as that of the function's first parameter, because it's the updated summary value (the one taking the latest element into account).

We can use stringLengthSum with accumulate like this:

```
set<string> ss;                            // create container of strings,
...                                        // and populate it
```

```
string::size_type lengthSum =          // set lengthSum to the result
    accumulate(ss.begin(), ss.end(),   // of calling stringLengthSum on
               0, stringLengthSum);    // each element in ss, using 0
                                       // as the initial summary value
```

Nifty, huh? Calculating the product of a range of numbers is even easier, because we don't have to write our own summation function. We
can use the standard multiplies functor class:

```
vector<float> vf;                      // create container of floats
...                                    // and populate it

float product =                        // set product to the result of
    accumulate(vf.begin(), vf.end(),   // calling multiplies<float> on
               1.0, multiplies<float>()); // each element in vf, using 1.0
                                       // as the initial summary value
```

The only tricky thing here is remembering to use one (as a floating
point numbers, not as an int!) as the initial summary value instead of
zero. If we used zero as the starting value, the result would always be
zero, because zero times anything is zero, right?

Our final example is a bit more ambitious. It involves finding the average of a range of points, where a point looks like this:

```
struct Point {
    Point(double initX, double initY): x(initX), y(initY) {}
    double x, y;
};
```

The summation function will be an object of a functor class called
PointAverage, but before we look at PointAverage, let's look at its use in
the call to accumulate:

```
list<Point> lp;
...

Point avg =                                    // average the points in lp
    accumulate( lp.begin(), lp.end(),
                Point(0, 0), PointAverage());
```

Simple and straightforward, the way we like it. In this case, the initial
summary value is a Point object located at the origin, and all we need
to remember is not to take that point into account when computing
the average of the range.

PointAverage works by keeping track of the number of points it has
seen, as well as the sum of their x and y components. Each time it is
called, it updates these values and returns the average coordinates of
the points so far examined. Because it is called exactly once for each
point in the range, it divides the x and y sums by the number of points

in the range; the initial point value passed to accumulate is ignored, as it should be:

```
class PointAverage:
  public binary_function<Point, Point, Point> {          // see Item 40
public:
  PointAverage(): xSum(0), ySum(0), numPoints(0) {}

  const Point operator()(const Point& avgSoFar, const Point& p)
  {
    ++numPoints;
    xSum += p.x;
    ySum += p.y;

    return Point(xSum/numPoints, ySum/numPoints);
  }
private:
  size_t numPoints;
  double xSum;
  double ySum;
};
```

This works fine, and it is only because I sometimes associate with an inordinately demented group of people (many of them on the Standardization Committee) that I can envision STL implementations where it could fail. Nevertheless, PointAverage runs afoul of paragraph 2 of section 26.4.1 of the Standard, which, as I'm sure you recall, forbids side effects in the function passed to accumulate. Modification of the member variables numPoints, xSum, and ySum constitutes a side effect, so, technically speaking, the code I've just shown you yields undefined results. In practice, it's hard to imagine it not working, but I'm surrounded by menacing language lawyers as I write this, so I've no choice but to spell out the fine print on this matter.

That's okay, because it gives me a chance to mention for_each, another algorithm that can be used to summarize ranges and one that isn't constrained by the restrictions imposed on accumulate. Like accumulate, for_each takes a range and a function (typically a function object) to invoke on each element of the range, but the function passed to for_each receives only a single argument (the current range element), and for_each returns its function when it's done. (Actually, it returns a *copy* of its function — see Item 38.) Significantly, the function passed to (and later returned from) for_each *may* have side effects.

Ignoring the side effects issue, for_each differs from accumulate in two primary ways. First, the name accumulate suggests an algorithm that produces a summary of a range. for_each sounds like you simply want to do something to every element of a range, and, of course, that is the algorithm's primary application. Using for_each to summarize a range is legitimate, but it's not as clear as accumulate.

Second, accumulate returns the summary we want directly, while for_each returns a function object, and we must extract the summary information we want from this object. In C++ terms, that means we must add a member function to the functor class to let us retrieve the summary information we're after.

Here's the last example again, this time using for_each instead of accumulate:

```
struct Point { ... };                                        // as before

class PointAverage:
  public unary_function<Point, void> {                       // see Item 40
public:
  PointAverage(): xSum(0), ySum(0), numPoints(0) {}

  void operator()(const Point& p)
  {
    ++numPoints;
    xSum += p.x;
    ySum += p.y;
  }

  Point result() const
  {
    return Point(xSum/numPoints, ySum/numPoints);
  }
private:
  size_t numPoints;
  double xSum;
  double ySum;
};

list<Point> lp;
...
Point avg = for_each(lp.begin(), lp.end(), PointAverage()).result();
```

Personally, I prefer accumulate for summarizing, because I think it most clearly expresses what is going on, but for_each works, too, and the issue of side effects doesn't dog for_each as it does accumulate. Both algorithms can be used to summarize ranges. Use the one that suits you best.

You may be wondering why for_each's function parameter is allowed to have side effects while accumulate's is not. This is a probing question, one that strikes at the heart of the STL. Alas, gentle reader, there are some mysteries meant to remain beyond our ken. Why the difference between accumulate and for_each? I've yet to hear a convincing explanation.

Functors, Functor Classes, Functions, etc.

Like it or not, functions and function-like objects — *functors* — pervade the STL. Associative containers use them to keep their elements in order, algorithms such as find_if use them to control their behavior, components like for_each and transform are meaningless without them, and adapters like not1 and bind2nd actively produce them.

Yes, everywhere you look in the STL, you see functors and functor classes. Including in your source code. It's not possible to make effective use of the STL without knowing how to write well-behaved functors. That being the case, most of this chapter is devoted to explaining how to make your functors behave the way the STL expects them to. One Item, however, is devoted to a different topic, one sure to appeal to those who've wondered about the need to litter their code with ptr_fun, mem_fun, and mem_fun_ref. Start with that Item (Item 41), if you like, but please don't stop there. Once you understand those functions, you'll need the information in the remaining Items to ensure that your functors work properly with them, as well as with the rest of the STL.

Item 38: Design functor classes for pass-by-value.

Neither C nor C++ allows you to truly pass functions as parameters to other functions. Instead, you must pass *pointers* to functions. For example, here's a declaration for the standard library function qsort:

```
void qsort( void *base, size_t nmemb, size_t size,
            int (*cmpfcn)(const void*, const void*));
```

Item 46 explains why the sort algorithm is typically a better choice than the qsort function, but that's not at issue here. What is at issue is the declaration for qsort's parameter cmpfcn. Once you've squinted past all the asterisks, it becomes clear that the argument passed as cmpfcn, which is a pointer to a function, is copied (i.e., passed by value) from the call site to qsort. This is representative of the rule followed by the standard libraries for both C and C++, namely, that function pointers are passed by value.

STL function objects are modeled after function pointers, so the convention in the STL is that function objects, too, are passed by value (i.e., copied) when passed to and from functions. This is perhaps best demonstrated by the Standard's declaration of for_each, an algorithm which both takes and returns a function object by value:

```
template<class InputIterator,
         class Function>
Function                          // note return-by-value
for_each( InputIterator first,
          InputIterator last,
          Function f);            // note pass-by-value
```

In truth, the pass-by-value case is not quite this iron-clad, because for_each's caller could explicitly specify the parameter types at the point of the call. For example, the following would cause for_each to pass and return its functor by reference:

```
class DoSomething:
  public unary_function<int, void> {    // Item 40 explains base class

  void operator()(int x) { ... }

  ...

};

typedef deque<int>::iterator DequeIntIter;   // convenience typedef

deque<int> di;
...

DoSomething d;                          // create a function object
...

for_each<DequeIntIter,                  // call for_each with type
         DoSomething&>(di.begin(),      // parameters of DequeIntIter
                       di.end(),        // and DoSomething&;
                       d);              // this forces d to be
                                        // passed and returned
                                        // by reference
```

Users of the STL almost never do this kind of thing, however, and some implementations of some STL algorithms won't even compile if function objects are passed by reference. For the remainder of this Item, I'm going to pretend that function objects are always passed by value. In practice, that's virtually always true.

Because function objects are passed and returned by value, the onus is on you to make sure that your function objects behave well when passed that way (i.e., copied). This implies two things. First, your function objects need to be small. Otherwise they will be too expensive to copy. Second, your function objects must be *monomorphic* (i.e., not polymorphic) — they must not use virtual functions. That's because derived class objects passed by value into parameters of base class type suffer from the slicing problem: during the copy, their derived parts are removed. (For another example of how the slicing problem affects your use of the STL, see Item 3.)

Efficiency is important, of course, and so is avoiding the slicing problem, but not all functors are small, and not all are monomorphic, either. One of the advantages of function objects over real functions is that functors can contain as much state as you need. Some function objects are naturally hefty, and it's important to be able to pass such functors to STL algorithms with the same ease as we pass their anorexic counterparts.

The prohibition on polymorphic functors is equally unrealistic. C++ supports inheritance hierarchies and dynamic binding, and these features are as useful when designing functor classes as anyplace else. Functor classes without inheritance would be like, well, like C++ without the "++". Surely there's a way to let function objects be big and/or polymorphic, yet still allow them to mesh with the pass-functors-by-value convention that pervades the STL.

There is. Take the data and/or the polymorphism you'd like to put in your functor class, and move it into a different class. Then give your functor class a pointer to this new class. For example, if you'd like to create a polymorphic functor class containing lots of data,

```
template<typename T>
class BPFC:                                // BPFC = " Big Polymorphic
  public                                   //              Functor Class"
    unary_function<T, void> {              // Item 40 explains this
                                           // base class

private:
  Widget w;                                // this class has lots of data,
  int x;                                   // so it would be inefficient
  ...                                      // to pass it by value
public:
  virtual void operator()(const T& val) const;  // this is a virtual function,
  ...                                           // so slicing would be bad
};
```

create a small, monomorphic class that contains a pointer to an implementation class, and put all the data and virtual functions in the implementation class:

```
template<typename T>                           // new implementation class
class BPFCImpl {                               // for modified BPFC
private:
  Widget w;                                    // all the data that used to
  int x;                                       // be in BPFC are now here
  ...
  virtual ~BPFCImpl();                         // polymorphic classes need
                                               // virtual destructors

  virtual void operator()(const T& val) const;
friend class BPFC<T>;                          // let BPFC access the data
};

template<typename T>
class BPFC:                                    // small, monomorphic
  public unary_function<T, void> {             // version of BPFC
private:
  BPFCImpl<T> *pImpl;                          // this is BPFC's only data

public:
  void operator()(const T& val) const          // this is now nonvirtual;
  {                                             // it forwards to BPFCImpl
    pImpl->operator()(val);
  }
  ...
};
```

The implementation of BPFC::operator() exemplifies how all BPFC would-be virtual functions are implemented: they call their truly virtual counterparts in BPFCImpl. The result is a functor class (BPFC) that's small and monomorphic, yet has access to a large amount of state and acts polymorphically.

I'm glossing over a fair number of details here, because the basic technique I've sketched is well known in C++ circles. *Effective C++* treats it in Item 34. In *Design Patterns* by Gamma *et al.* [6], this is called the "Bridge Pattern." Sutter calls this the "Pimpl Idiom" in his *Exceptional C++* [8].

From an STL point of view, the primary thing to keep in mind is that functor classes using this technique must support copying in a reasonable fashion. If you were the author of BPFC above, you'd have to make sure that its copy constructor did something reasonable about the BPFCImpl object it points to. Perhaps the simplest reasonable thing would be to reference count it, using something like Boost's shared_ptr, which you can read about in Item 50.

In fact, for purposes of this Item, the *only* thing you'd have to worry about would be the behavior of BPFC's copy constructor, because function objects are always copied — passed by value, remember? — when passed to or returned from functions in the STL. That means two things. Make them small, and make them monomorphic.

Item 39: Make predicates pure functions.

I hate to do this to you, but we have to start with a short vocabulary lesson.

- A *predicate* is a function that returns bool (or something that can be implicitly converted to bool). Predicates are widely used in the STL. The comparison functions for the standard associative containers are predicates, and predicate functions are commonly passed as parameters to algorithms like find_if and the various sorting algorithms. (For an overview of the sorting algorithms, turn to Item 31.)

- A *pure function* is a function whose return value depends only on its parameters. If f is a pure function and x and y are objects, the return value of f(x, y) can change only if the value of x or y changes.

  In C++, all data consulted by pure functions are either passed in as parameters or are constant for the life of the function. (Naturally, such constant data should be declared const.) If a pure function consulted data that might change between calls, invoking the function at different times with the same parameters might yield different results, and that would be contrary to the definition of a pure function.

That should be enough to make it clear what it means to make predicates pure functions. All I have to do now is convince you that the advice is well founded. To help me do that, I hope you'll forgive me for burdening you with one more term.

- A *predicate class* is a functor class whose operator() function is a predicate, i.e., its operator() returns true or false. As you might expect, any place the STL expects a predicate, it will accept either a real predicate or an object of a predicate class.

That's it, I promise! Now we're ready to study why this Item offers guidance worth following.

Item 38 explains that function objects are passed by value, so you should design function objects to be copied. For function objects that are predicates, there is another reason to design them to behave well when they are copied. Algorithms may make copies of functors and hold on to them a while before using them, and some algorithm implementations take advantage of this freedom. A critical repercussion of this observation is that *predicate functions must be pure functions.*

To appreciate why this is the case, let's suppose you were to violate this constraint. Consider the following (badly designed) predicate class. Regardless of the arguments that are passed, it returns true exactly once: the third time it is called. The rest of the time it returns false.

```cpp
class BadPredicate:                              // see Item 40 for info
  public unary_function<Widget, bool> {          // on the base class
public:
  BadPredicate(): timesCalled(0) {}              // init timesCalled to 0

  bool operator()(const Widget&)
  {
     return ++timesCalled == 3;
  }
private:
  size_t timesCalled;
};
```

Suppose we use this class to eliminate the third Widget from a vector<Widget>:

```cpp
vector<Widget> vw;                       // create vector and put some
...                                      // Widgets into it
vw.erase(remove_if( vw.begin(),          // eliminate the third Widget;
               vw.end(),                 // see Item 32 for info on how
               BadPredicate()),          // erase and remove_if relate
        vw.end());
```

This code looks quite reasonable, but with many STL implementations, it will eliminate not just the third element from vw, it will also eliminate the sixth!

To understand how this can happen, it's helpful to see how remove_if is often implemented. Bear in mind that remove_if does not *have* to be implemented this way.

```cpp
template <typename FwdIterator, typename Predicate>
FwdIterator remove_if(FwdIterator begin, FwdIterator end, Predicate p)
{
   begin = find_if(begin, end, p);

   if (begin == end) return begin;
   else {
     FwdIterator next = begin;
     return remove_copy_if(++next, end, begin, p);
   }
}
```

The details of this code are not important, but note that the predicate p is passed first to find_if, then later to remove_copy_if. In both cases, of course, p is passed by value — is *copied* — into those algorithms. (Technically, this need not be true, but practically, it *is* true. For details, see Item 38.)

The initial call to remove_if (the one in the client code that wants to eliminate the third element from vw) creates an anonymous BadPredicate object, one with its internal timesCalled member set to zero. This object (known as p inside remove_if) is then copied into find_if, so find_if also receives a BadPredicate object with a timesCalled value of 0. find_if "calls" that object until it returns true, so it calls it three times. find_if then returns control to remove_if. remove_if continues to execute and ultimately calls remove_copy_if, passing as a predicate another copy of p. But p's timesCalled member is still 0! find_if never called p, it called only a *copy* of p. As a result, the third time remove_copy_if calls its predicate, it, too, will return true. And that's why remove_if will ultimately remove two Widgets from vw instead of just one.

The easiest way to keep yourself from tumbling into this linguistic crevasse is to declare your operator() functions const in predicate classes. If you do that, your compilers won't let you change any class data members:

```
class BadPredicate:
  public unary_function<Widget, bool> {
public:
  bool operator()(const Widget&) const
  {
    return ++timesCalled == 3;        // error! can't change local data
  }                                   // in a const member function

  ...

};
```

Because this is such a straightforward way of preventing the problem we just examined, I very nearly entitled this Item "Make operator() const in predicate classes." But that doesn't go far enough. Even const member functions may access mutable data members, non-const local static objects, non-const class static objects, non-const objects at namespace scope, and non-const global objects. A well-designed predicate class ensures that its operator() functions are independent of those kinds of objects, too. Declaring operator() const in predicate classes is *necessary* for correct behavior, but it's not *sufficient*. A well-behaved operator() is certainly const, but it's more than that. It's also a pure function.

Earlier in this Item, I remarked that any place the STL expects a predicate function, it will accept either a real function or an object of a predicate class. That's true in both directions. Any place the STL will accept an object of a predicate class, a predicate function (possibly modified by ptr_fun — see Item 41) is equally welcome. We now understand that operator() functions in predicate classes should be pure functions, so this restriction extends to predicate functions, too. This function is as bad a predicate as the objects generated from the BadPredicate class:

```
bool anotherBadPredicate(const Widget&, const Widget&)
{
    static int timesCalled = 0;        // No! No! No! No! No! No! No!
    return ++timesCalled == 3;         // Predicates should be pure functions,
}                                      // and pure functions have no state
```

Regardless of how you write your predicates, they should always be pure functions.

Item 40: Make functor classes adaptable.

Suppose I have a list of Widget* pointers and a function to determine whether such a pointer identifies a Widget that is interesting:

```
list<Widget*> widgetPtrs;

bool isInteresting(const Widget *pw);
```

If I'd like to find the first pointer to an interesting Widget in the list, it'd be easy:

```
list<Widget*>::iterator i = find_if(widgetPtrs.begin(), widgetPtrs.end(),
                                    isInteresting);

if (i != widgetPtrs.end()) {
    ...                                   // process the first
}                                         // interesting
                                          // pointer-to-widget
```

If I'd like to find the first pointer to a Widget that is *not* interesting, however, the obvious approach fails to compile:

```
list<Widget*>::iterator i =
    find_if(widgetPtrs.begin(), widgetPtrs.end(),
            not1(isInteresting));          // error! won't compile
```

Instead, I must apply ptr_fun to isInteresting before applying not1:

```
list<Widget*>::iterator i =
    find_if(widgetPtrs.begin(), widgetPtrs.end(),
            not1(ptr_fun(isInteresting)));    // fine

if (i != widgetPtrs.end()) {
    ...                                   // process the first
}                                         // dull ptr-to-Widget
```

That leads to some questions. *Why* do I have to apply ptr_fun to isInteresting before applying not1? What does ptr_fun do for me, and how does it make the above work?

The answer is somewhat surprising. The only thing ptr_fun does is make some typedefs available. That's it. These typedefs are required by not1, and that's why applying not1 to ptr_fun works, but applying not1 to isInteresting directly doesn't work. Being a lowly function pointer, isInteresting lacks the typedefs that not1 demands.

not1 isn't the only component in the STL making such demands. Each of the four standard function adapters (not1, not2, bind1st, and bind2nd) requires the existence of certain typedefs, as do any non-standard STL-compatible adapters written by others (e.g., those available from SGI and Boost — see Item 50). Function objects that provide the necessary typedefs are said to be *adaptable*, while function objects lacking these typedefs are not adaptable. Adaptable function objects can be used in more contexts than can function objects that are not adaptable, so you should make your function objects adaptable whenever you can. It costs you nothing, and it may buy clients of your functor classes a world of convenience.

I know, I know, I'm being coy, constantly referring to "certain typedefs" without telling you what they are. The typedefs in question are argument_type, first_argument_type, second_argument_type, and result_type, but it's not quite that straightforward, because different kinds of functor classes are expected to provide different subsets of these names. In all honesty, unless you're writing your own adapters (a topic not covered in this book), you don't need to know anything about these typedefs. That's because the conventional way to provide them is to inherit them from a base class, or, more precisely, a base struct. For functor classes whose operator() takes one argument, the struct to inherit from is std::unary_function. For functor classes whose operator() takes two arguments, the struct to inherit from is std::binary_function.

Well, sort of. unary_function and binary_function are templates, so you can't inherit from them directly. Instead, you must inherit from structs they generate, and that requires that you specify some type arguments. For unary_function, you must specify the type of parameter taken by your functor class's operator(), as well as its return type. For binary_function, you specify three types: the types of your operator()'s first and second parameters, and your operator()'s return type.

Here are a couple of examples:

```
template<typename T>
class MeetsThreshold: public std::unary_function<Widget, bool> {
private:
   const T threshold;

public:
   MeetsThreshold(const T& threshold);

   bool operator()(const Widget&) const;

   ...

};

struct WidgetNameCompare:
   std::binary_function<Widget, Widget, bool> {

   bool operator()(const Widget& lhs, const Widget& rhs) const;

};
```

In both cases, notice how the types passed to unary_function or binary_function are the same as the types taken and returned by the functor class's operator(), though it is a bit of an oddity that operator()'s return type is passed as the last argument to unary_function or binary_function.

You may have noticed that MeetsThreshold is a class, while Widget-NameCompare is a struct. MeetsThreshold has internal state (its threshold data member), and a class is the logical way to encapsulate such information. WidgetNameCompare has no state, hence no need to make anything private. Authors of functor classes where everything is public often declare structs instead of classes, probably for no other reason than to avoid typing "public" in front of the base class and the operator() function. Whether to declare such functors as classes or structs is purely a matter of personal style. If you're still refining your personal style and would like to emulate the pros, note that stateless functor classes within the STL itself (e.g., less<T>, plus<T>, etc.) are generally written as structs.

Look again at WidgetNameCompare:

```
struct WidgetNameCompare:
   std::binary_function<Widget, Widget, bool> {

   bool operator()(const Widget& lhs, const Widget& rhs) const;

};
```

Even though operator()'s arguments are of type const Widget&, the type passed to binary_function is Widget. In general, non-pointer types passed to unary_function or binary_function have consts and references stripped off. (Don't ask why. The reasons are neither terribly good nor terribly interesting. If you're dying to know anyway, write some programs where you don't strip them off, then dissect the resulting compiler diagnostics. If, having done that, you're *still* interested in the matter, visit boost.org (see Item 50) and check out their work on call traits and function object adapters.)

The rules change when operator() takes pointer parameters. Here's a struct analogous to WidgetNameCompare, but this one works with Widget* pointers:

```
struct PtrWidgetNameCompare:
    std::binary_function<const Widget*, const Widget*, bool> {

    bool operator()(const Widget* lhs, const Widget* rhs) const;

};
```

Here, the types passed to binary_function are the *same* as the types taken by operator(). The general rule for functor classes taking or returning pointers is to pass to unary_function or binary_function whatever types operator() takes or returns.

Let's not forget the fundamental reason for all this unary_function and binary_function base class gobbledegook. These classes supply typedefs that are required by function object adapters, so inheritance from those classes yields adaptable function objects. That lets us do things like this:

```
list<Widget> widgets;

...

list<Widget>::reverse_iterator i1 =          // find the last widget
    find_if( widgets.rbegin(), widgets.rend(),   // that fails to meet the
        not1(MeetsThreshold<int>(10)));          // threshold of 10
                                                 // (whatever that means)

Widget w( constructor arguments );

list<Widget>::iterator i2 =                   // find the first widget
    find_if( widgets.begin(), widgets.end(),     // that precedes w in the
        bind2nd(WidgetNameCompare(), w));        // sort order defined by
                                                 // WidgetNameCompare
```

Had we failed to have our functor classes inherit from unary_function or binary_function, neither of these examples would compile, because not1 and bind2nd both work only with adaptable function objects.

STL function objects are modeled on C++ functions, and a C++ function has only one set of parameter types and one return type. As a result, the STL implicitly assumes that each functor class has only one operator() function, and it's the parameter and return types for this function that should be passed to unary_function or binary_function (in accord with the rules for reference and pointer types we just discussed). This means that, tempting though it might be, you shouldn't try to combine the functionality of WidgetNameCompare and PtrWidget-NameCompare by creating a single struct with two operator() functions. If you did, the functor would be adaptable with respect to at most one of its calling forms (whichever one you used when passing parameters to binary_function), and a functor that's adaptable only half the time might just as well not be adaptable at all.

Sometimes it makes sense to give a functor class multiple invocation forms (thereby abandoning adaptability), and Items 7, 20, 23, and 25 give examples of situations where that is the case. Such functor classes are the exception, however, not the rule. Adaptability is important, and you should strive to facilitate it each time you write a functor class.

Item 41: Understand the reasons for ptr_fun, mem_fun, and mem_fun_ref.

What *is* it with this ptr_fun/mem_fun/mem_fun_ref stuff? Sometimes you have to use these functions, sometimes you don't, and what do they do, anyway? They just seem to sit there, pointlessly hanging around function names like ill-fitting garments. They're unpleasant to type, annoying to read, and resistant to comprehension. Are these things additional examples of STL artifacts (such as the ones described in Items 10 and 18), or just some syntactic joke foisted on us by members of a Standardization Committee with too much free time and a twisted sense of humor?

Calm yourself. The names are less than inspired, but ptr_fun, mem_fun, and mem_fun_ref do important jobs, and as far as syntactic jokes go, one of the primary tasks of these functions is to paper over one of C++'s inherent syntactic inconsistencies.

If I have a function f and an object x, I wish to invoke f on x, and I'm outside x's member functions, C++ gives me three different syntaxes for making the call:

```
f(x);                        // Syntax #1: When f is a
                             // non-member function

x.f();                       // Syntax #2: When f is a member
                             // function and x is an object or
                             // a reference to an object

p->f();                      // Syntax #3: When f is a member
                             // function and p is a pointer to x
```

Now, suppose I have a function that can test Widgets,

```
void test(Widget& w);          // test w and mark it as "failed" if
                               // it doesn't pass the test
```

and I have a container of Widgets:

```
vector<Widget> vw;             // vw holds widgets
```

To test every Widget in vw, I can use for_each in the obvious manner:

```
for_each(vw.begin(), vw.end(), test);    // Call #1 (compiles)
```

But imagine that test is a member function of Widget instead of a non-member function, i.e., that Widget supports self-testing:

```
class Widget {
public:
   ...
   void test();                // perform a self-test; mark *this
   ...                         // as "failed" if it doesn't pass
};
```

In a perfect world, I'd also be able to use for_each to invoke Widget::test on each object in vw:

```
for_each( vw.begin(), vw.end(),
          &Widget::test);      // Call #2 (won't compile)
```

In fact, if the world were really perfect, I'd be able to use for_each to invoke Widget::test on a container of Widget* pointers, too:

```
list<Widget*> lpw;            // lpw holds pointers to widgets

for_each( lpw.begin(), lpw.end(),
          &Widget::test);      // Call #3 (also won't compile)
```

But think of what would have to happen in this perfect world. Inside the for_each function in Call #1, we'd be calling a non-member function with an object, so we'd have to use Syntax #1. Inside the for_each function in Call #2, we'd have to use Syntax #2, because we'd have an object and a member function. And inside the for_each function in Call #3, we'd need to use Syntax #3, because we'd be dealing with a member function and a pointer to an object. We'd therefore need three different versions of for_each, and how perfect would that world be?

In the world we do have, we possess only one version of for_each. It's not hard to envision an implementation:

```
template<typename InputIterator, typename Function>
Function for_each(InputIterator begin, InputIterator end, Function f)
{
   while (begin != end) f(*begin++);
}
```

Here I've highlighted the fact that for_each uses Syntax #1 when making the call. This is a universal convention in the STL: functions and function objects are always invoked using the syntactic form for non-member functions. This explains why Call #1 compiles while Calls #2 and #3 don't. It's because STL algorithms (including for_each) hardwire in Syntax #1, and only Call #1 is compatible with that syntax.

Perhaps it's now clear why mem_fun and mem_fun_ref exist. They arrange for member functions (which must ordinarily be called using Syntax #2 or #3) to be called using Syntax #1.

The way mem_fun and mem_fun_ref do this is simple, though it's a little clearer if you take a look at a declaration for one of these functions. They're really function templates, and several variants of the mem_fun and mem_fun_ref templates exist, corresponding to different numbers of parameters and the constness (or lack thereof) of the member functions they adapt. Seeing one declaration is enough to understand how things are put together:

```
template<typename R, typename C>     // declaration for mem_fun for
mem_fun_t<R,C>                        // non-const member functions
mem_fun(R (C::*pmf)());              // taking no parameters. C is the
                                     // class, R is the return type of the
                                     // pointed-to member function
```

mem_fun takes a pointer to a member function, pmf, and returns an object of type mem_fun_t. This is a functor class that holds the member function pointer and offers an operator() that invokes the pointed-to member function on the object passed to operator(). For example, in this code,

```
list<Widget*> lpw;                   // same as above

...

for_each(lpw.begin(), lpw.end(),
         mem_fun(&Widget::test));    // this will now compile
```

for_each receives an object of type mem_fun_t holding a pointer to Widget::test. For each Widget* pointer in lpw, for_each "calls" the mem_fun_t object using Syntax #1, and that object immediately invokes Widget::test on the Widget* pointer using Syntax #3.

Overall, mem_fun adapts Syntax #3, which is what Widget::test requires when used with a Widget* pointer, to Syntax #1, which is what for_each uses. It's thus no wonder that classes like mem_fun_t are known as *function object adapters*. It should not surprise you to learn that, completely analogously with the above, the mem_fun_ref functions adapt Syntax #2 to Syntax #1 and generate adapter objects of type mem_fun_ref_t.

The objects produced by mem_fun and mem_fun_ref do more than allow STL components to assume that all functions are called using a single syntax. They also provide important typedefs, just like the objects produced by ptr_fun. The story behind these typedefs is told in Item 40, so I won't repeat it here. However, this puts us in a position to understand why this call compiles,

```
for_each(vw.begin(), vw.end(), test);          // as above, Call #1;
                                               // this compiles
```

while these do not:

```
for_each(vw.begin(), vw.end(), &Widget::test);    // as above, Call #2;
                                                  // doesn't compile

for_each(lpw.begin(), lpw.end(), &Widget::test);  // as above, Call #3;
                                                  // doesn't compile
```

The first call (Call #1) passes a real function, so there's no need to adapt its calling syntax for use by for_each; the algorithm will inherently call it using the proper syntax. Furthermore, for_each makes no use of the typedefs that ptr_fun adds, so it's not necessary to use ptr_fun when passing test to for_each. On the other hand, adding the typedefs can't hurt anything, so this will do the same thing as the call above:

```
for_each(vw.begin(), vw.end(), ptr_fun(test));   // compiles and behaves
                                                 // like Call #1 above
```

If you get confused about when to use ptr_fun and when not to, consider using it every time you pass a function to an STL component. The STL won't care, and there is no runtime penalty. About the worst that can be said is that some people reading your code might raise an eyebrow when they see an unnecessary use of ptr_fun. How much that bothers you depends, I suppose, on your sensitivity to raised eyebrows.

An alternative strategy with respect to ptr_fun is to use it only when you're forced to. If you omit it when the typedefs are necessary, your compilers will balk at your code. Then you'll have go back and add it.

The situation with mem_fun and mem_fun_ref is fundamentally different. You must employ them whenever you pass a member function to an STL component, because, in addition to adding typedefs (which may or may not be necessary), they adapt the calling syntaxes from the ones normally used with member functions to the one used everywhere in the STL. If you don't use them when passing member function pointers, your code will never compile.

Which leaves just the names of the member function adapters, and here, finally, we have a genuine historical STL artifact. When the need for these kinds of adapters first became apparent, the people working on the STL focused on containers of pointers. (Given the drawbacks of such containers described in Items 7, 20, and 33, this might seem surprising, but remember that containers of pointers support polymorphism, while containers of objects do not.) They needed an adapter for member functions, so they chose mem_fun. Only later did they realize that they needed a different adapter for containers of objects, so they hacked up the name mem_fun_ref for that. No, it's not very elegant, but these things happen. Tell me *you've* never given any of your components a name that you later realized was, er, difficult to generalize... .

Item 42: Make sure less<T> means operator<.

As all Widget-savvy people are aware, Widgets have both a weight and a maximum speed:

```
class Widget {
public:
  ...
  size_t weight() const;
  size_t maxSpeed() const;

  ...
};
```

Also well known is that the natural way to sort Widgets is by weight. operator< for Widgets reflects this:

```
bool operator<(const Widget& lhs, const Widget& rhs)
{
  return lhs.weight() < rhs.weight();
}
```

But suppose we'd like to create a multiset<Widget> where the Widgets are sorted by maximum speed. We know that the default comparison function for multiset<Widget> is less<Widget>, and we know that less<Widget>, by default, does its work by calling operator< for Widgets. That being the case, it seems clear that one way to get a multiset<Widget> sorted by maximum speed is to sever the tie between less<Widget> and operator< by specializing less<Widget> to look only at a Widget's maximum speed:

```
template<>                              // This is a specialization
struct std::less<Widget>:               // of std::less for Widget;
  public                                // it's also a very bad idea
  std::binary_function<Widget,
                       Widget,          // See Item 40 for info
                       bool> {          // on this base class
  bool operator()(const Widget& lhs, const Widget& rhs) const
  {
    return lhs.maxSpeed() < rhs.maxSpeed();
  }

};
```

This both looks ill-advised and is ill-advised, but it may not be ill-advised for the reason you think. Does it surprise you that it compiles at all? Many programmers point out that the above isn't just a specialization of a template, it's a specialization of a template in the std namespace. "Isn't std supposed to be sacred, reserved for library implementers and beyond the reach of mere programmers?" they ask. "Shouldn't compilers reject this attempt to tamper with the workings of the C++ immortals?" they wonder.

As a general rule, trying to modify components in std is indeed forbidden (and doing so typically transports one to the realm of undefined behavior), but under some circumstances, tinkering is allowed. Specifically, programmers are allowed to specialize templates in std for user-defined types. Almost always, there are alternatives that are superior to specializing std templates, but on rare occasions, it's a reasonable thing to do. For instance, authors of smart pointer classes often want their classes to act like built-in pointers for sorting purposes, so it's not uncommon to see specializations of std::less for smart pointer types. The following, for example, is part of the Boost library's shared_ptr, a smart pointer you can read about in Items 7 and 50:

```
namespace std {

  template<typename T>                      // this is a spec. of std::less
  struct less< boost::shared_ptr<T> >:      // for boost::shared_ptr<T>
    public                                  // (boost is a namespace)
    binary_function<boost::shared_ptr<T>,
                    boost::shared_ptr<T>,   // this is the customary
                    bool> {                 // base class (see Item 40)
    bool operator()( const boost::shared_ptr<T>& a,
                     const boost::shared_ptr<T>& b) const
    {
      return less<T*>()(a.get(),b.get());   // shared_ptr::get returns
    }                                       // the built-in pointer that's
                                            // in the shared_ptr object
  };

}
```

This isn't unreasonable, and it certainly serves up no surprises, because this specialization of less merely ensures that sorting smart pointers behaves the same as sorting their built-in brethren. Alas, our tentative specialization of less for Widget *does* serve up surprises.

C++ programmers can be forgiven certain assumptions. They assume that copy constructors copy, for example. (As Item 8 attests, failure to adhere to this convention can lead to astonishing behavior.) They assume that taking the address of an object yields a pointer to that object. (Turn to Item 18 to read about what can happen when this isn't true.) They assume that adapters like bind1st and not2 may be applied to function objects. (Item 40 explains how things break when this isn't the case.) They assume that operator+ adds (except for strings, but there's a long history of using "+" to mean string concatenation), that operator– subtracts, that operator== compares. And they assume that using less is tantamount to using operator<.

operator< is more than just the default way to implement less, it's *what programmers expect less to do*. Having less do something other than call operator< is a gratuitous violation of programmers' expectations. It runs contrary to what has been called "the principle of least astonishment." It's callous. It's mean. It's bad. You shouldn't do it.

Especially when there's no reason to. There's not a place in the STL using less where you can't specify a different comparison type instead. Returning to our original example of a multiset<Widget> ordered by maximum speed, all we need to do to get what we want is create a functor class called almost anything *except* less that performs the comparison we're interested in. Why, here's one now:

```
struct MaxSpeedCompare:
  public binary_function<Widget, Widget, bool> {
  bool operator()(const Widget& lhs, const Widget& rhs) const
  {
    return lhs.maxSpeed() < rhs.maxSpeed();
  }
};
```

To create our multiset, we use MaxSpeedCompare as the comparison type, thus avoiding use of the default comparison type (which is, of course, less<Widget>):

```
multiset<Widget, MaxSpeedCompare> widgets;
```

This code says exactly what it means. It creates a multiset of Widgets sorted as defined by the functor class MaxSpeedCompare.

Contrast that with this:

```
multiset<Widget> widgets;
```

This says that widgets is a multiset of Widgets sorted in the default manner. Technically, that means it uses less<Widget>, but virtually everybody is going to assume that really means it's sorted by operator<.

Don't mislead all those programmers by playing games with the definition of less. If you use less (explicitly or implicitly), make sure it means operator<. If you want to sort objects using some other criterion, create a special functor class that's *not* called less. It's really as simple as that.

Programming with the STL

It's traditional to summarize the STL as consisting of containers, iterators, algorithms, and function objects, but *programming* with the STL is much more than that. Programming with the STL is knowing when to use loops, when to use algorithms, and when to use container member functions. It's knowing when equal_range is a better way to search than lower_bound, knowing when lower_bound is preferable to find, and knowing when find beats equal_range. It's knowing how to improve algorithm performance by substituting functors for functions that do the same thing. It's knowing how to avoid unportable or incomprehensible code. It's even knowing how to read compiler error messages that run to thousands of characters. And it's knowing about Internet resources for STL documentation, STL extensions, even complete STL implementations.

Yes, programming with the STL involves knowing many things. This chapter gives you much of the knowledge you need.

Item 43: Prefer algorithm calls to hand-written loops.

Every algorithm takes at least one pair of iterators that specify a range of objects over which to do something. min_element finds the smallest value in the range, for example, while accumulate summarizes some information about the range as a whole (see Item 37) and partition separates all the elements of a range into those that do and do not satisfy some criterion (see Item 31). For algorithms to do their work, they must examine every object in the range(s) they are passed, and they do this in the way you'd expect: they loop from the beginning of the range(s) to the end. Some algorithms, such as find and find_if, may return before they complete the traversal, but even these algorithms internally contain a loop. After all, even find and find_if must look at every element of a range before they can conclude that what they are looking for is *not* present.

Internally, then, algorithms are loops. Furthermore, the breadth of STL algorithms means that many tasks you might naturally code as loops could also be written using algorithms. For example, if you have a Widget class that supports redrawing,

```
class Widget {
public:
  ...
  void redraw() const;
  ...
};
```

and you'd like to redraw all the Widgets in a list, you could do it with a loop, like this,

```
list<Widget> lw;

...

for (list<Widget>::iterator i = lw.begin(); i != lw.end(); ++i) {
  i->redraw();
}
```

but you could also do it with the for_each algorithm:

```
for_each(lw.begin(), lw.end(),          // see Item 41 for info
         mem_fun_ref(&Widget::redraw));  // on mem_fun_ref
```

For many C++ programmers, writing the loop is more natural than calling the algorithm, and reading the loop is more comfortable than making sense of mem_fun_ref and the taking of Widget::redraw's address. Yet this Item argues that the algorithm call is preferable. In fact, this Item argues that calling an algorithm is usually preferable to *any* hand-written loop. Why?

There are three reasons:

- **Efficiency**: Algorithms are often more efficient than the loops programmers produce.

- **Correctness**: Writing loops is more subject to errors than is calling algorithms.

- **Maintainability**: Algorithm calls often yield code that is clearer and more straightforward than the corresponding explicit loops.

The remainder of this Item lays out the case for algorithms.

From an efficiency perspective, algorithms can beat explicit loops in three ways, two major, one minor. The minor way involves the elimination of redundant computations. Look again at the loop we just saw:

```
for (list<Widget>::iterator i = lw.begin(); i != lw.end(); ++i) {
  i->redraw();
}
```

I've highlighted the loop termination test to emphasize that each time around the loop, i will be checked against lw.end(). That means that each time around the loop, the function list::end will be invoked. But we don't need to call end more than once, because we're not modifying the list. A single call to end would suffice, and, if we look again at the algorithm invocation, we'll see that that's exactly how many times end is evaluated:

```
for_each( lw.begin(), lw.end(),              // this call evaluates
          mem_fun_ref(&Widget::redraw));     // lw.end() exactly once
```

To be fair, STL implementers understand that begin and end (and similar functions, such as size) are used frequently, so they're likely to design them for maximal efficiency. They'll almost certainly inline them and strive to code them so that most compilers will be able to avoid repeated computations by hoisting their results out of loops like the one above. Experience shows that implementers don't always succeed, however, and when they don't, the avoidance of repeated computations is enough to give the algorithm a performance edge over the hand-written loop.

But that's the minor efficiency argument. The first major argument is that library implementers can take advantage of their knowledge of container implementations to optimize traversals in a way that no library user ever could. For example, the objects in a deque are typically stored (internally) in one or more fixed-size arrays. Pointer-based traversals of these arrays are faster than iterator-based traversals, but only library implementers can use pointer-based traversals, because only they know the size of the internal arrays and how to move from one array to the next. Some STLs contain algorithm implementations that take their deque's internal data structures into account, and such implementations have been known to clock in at more than 20% faster than the "normal" implementations of the algorithms.

The point is not that STL implementations are optimized for deques (or any other specific container type), but that implementers know more about their implementations than you do, and they can take advantage of this knowledge in algorithm implementations. If you shun algorithm calls in favor of your own loops, you forgo the opportunity to benefit from any implementation-specific optimizations they may have provided.

The second major efficiency argument is that all but the most trivial STL algorithms use computer science algorithms that are more sophisticated — sometimes *much* more sophisticated — than anything the average C++ programmer will be able to come up with. It's next to impossible to beat sort or its kin (see Item 31); the search algorithms for sorted ranges (see Items 34 and 45) are equally good; and even such mundane tasks as eliminating some objects from contiguous-memory containers are more efficiently accomplished using the erase-remove idiom than the loops most programmers come up with (see Item 9).

If the efficiency argument for algorithms doesn't persuade you, perhaps you're more amenable to a plea based on correctness. One of the trickier things about writing your own loops is making sure you use only iterators that (a) are valid and (b) point where you want them to. For example, suppose you have an array (presumably due to a legacy C API — see Item 16), and you'd like to take each array element, add 41 to it, then insert it into the front of a deque. Writing your own loop, you might come up with this (which is a variant on an example from Item 16):

```
// C API: this function takes a pointer to an array of at most arraySize
// doubles and writes data to it. It returns the number of doubles written.
size_t fillArray(double *pArray, size_t arraySize);

double data[maxNumDoubles];              // create local array of
                                         // max possible size

deque<double> d;                         // create deque, put
...                                      // data into it

size_t numDoubles =
   fillArray(data, maxNumDoubles);       // get array data from API

for (size_t i = 0; i < numDoubles; ++i) {   // for each i in data,
   d.insert(d.begin(), data[i] + 41);       // insert data[i]+41 at the
}                                           // front of d; this code
                                            // has a bug!
```

This works, as long as you're happy with a result where the newly inserted elements are in the reverse order of the corresponding elements in data. Because each insertion location is d.begin(), the last element inserted will go at the front of the deque!

If that's not what you wanted (and admit it, it's not), you might think to fix it like this:

```
deque<double>::iterator insertLocation = d.begin();   // remember d's
                                                      // begin iterator

for (size_t i = 0; i < numDoubles; ++i) {   // insert data[i]+41
   d.insert(insertLocation++, data[i] + 41);   // at insertLocation, then
}                                              // increment
                                               // insertLocation; this
                                               // code is also buggy!
```

This looks like a double win, because it not only increments the iterator specifying the insertion position, it also eliminates the need to call begin each time around the loop; that eliminates the minor efficiency hit we discussed earlier. Alas, this approach runs into a different problem: it yields undefined results. Each time deque::insert is called, it invalidates all iterators into the deque, and that includes insertLocation. After the first call to insert, insertLocation is invalidated, and subsequent loop iterations are allowed to head straight to looneyland.

Once you puzzle this out (possibly with the aid of STLport's debug mode, which is described in Item 50), you might come up with the following:

```
deque<double>::iterator insertLocation =
    d.begin();                              // as before
for (size_t i = 0; i < numDoubles; ++i) {   // update insertLocation
    insertLocation =                        // each time insert is
        d.insert(insertLocation, data[i] + 41);  // called to keep the
    ++insertLocation;                       // iterator valid, then
}                                           // increment it
```

This code finally does what you want, but think about how much work it took to get here! Compare that to the following call to transform:

```
transform(data, data + numDoubles,       // copy all elements
        inserter(d, d.begin()),          // from data to the front
        bind2nd(plus<int>(), 41));       // of d, adding 41 to each
```

The "bind2nd(plus<int>(), 41)" might take you a couple of minutes to get right (especially if you don't use STL's binders very often), but the only iterator-related worries you have are specifying the beginning and end of the source range (which was never a problem) and being sure to use inserter as the beginning of the destination range (see Item 30). In practice, figuring out the correct initial iterators for source and destination ranges is usually easy, or at least a lot easier than making sure the body of a loop doesn't inadvertently invalidate an iterator you need to keep using.

This example is representative of a broad class of loops that are difficult to write correctly, because you have to be on constant alert for iterators that are incorrectly manipulated or are invalidated before you're done using them. To see a different example of how inadvertent iterator invalidation can lead to trouble, turn to Item 9, which describes the subtleties involved in writing loops that call erase.

Given that using invalidated iterators leads to undefined behavior, and given that undefined behavior has a nasty habit of failing to show itself during development and testing, why run the risk if you don't have to? Turn the iterators over to the algorithms, and let *them* worry about the vagaries of iterator manipulation.

I've explained why algorithms can be more efficient than hand-written loops, and I've described why such loops must navigate a thicket of iterator-related difficulties that algorithms avoid. With luck, you are now an algorithm believer. Yet luck is fickle, and I'd prefer a more secure conviction before I rest my case. Let us therefore move on to the issue of code clarity. In the long run, the best software is the clearest software, the software that is easiest to understand, the software that can most readily be enhanced, maintained, and molded to fit new circumstances. The familiarity of loops notwithstanding, algorithms have an advantage in this long-term competition.

The key to their edge is the power of a known vocabulary. There are 70 algorithm names in the STL — a total of over 100 different function templates, once overloading is taken into account. Each of those algorithms carries out some well-defined task, and *it is reasonable to expect professional C++ programmers to know (or be able to look up) what each does.* Thus, when a programmer sees a transform call, that programmer recognizes that some function is being applied to every object in a range, and the results of those calls are being written somewhere. When the programmer sees a call to replace_if, he or she knows that all the objects in a range that satisfy some predicate are being modified. When the programmer comes across an invocation of partition, she or he understands that the objects in a range are being moved around so that all the objects satisfying a predicate are grouped together (see Item 31). The names of STL algorithms convey a lot of semantic information, and that makes them clearer than any random loop can hope to be.

When you see a for, while, or do, all you know is that some kind of loop is coming up. To acquire even the faintest idea of what that loop does, you have to examine it. Not so with algorithms. Once you see a call to an algorithm, the name alone sketches the outline of what it does. To understand exactly what will happen, of course, you must inspect the arguments being passed to the algorithm, but that's often less work than trying to divine the intent of a general looping construct.

Simply put, algorithm names suggest what they do. "for," "while," and "do" don't. In fact, this is true of any component of the standard C or C++ library. Without doubt, you could write your own implementations of strlen, memset, or bsearch, if you wanted to, but you don't. Why not? Because (1) somebody has already written them, so there's no point in your doing it again; (2) the names are standard, so everybody knows what they do; and (3) you suspect that your library implementer knows some efficiency tricks you don't know, and you're unwilling to give up the possible optimizations a skilled library implementer might provide. Just as you don't write your own versions of strlen *et al.*, it makes no sense to write loops that duplicate functionality already present in STL algorithms.

I wish that were the end of the story, because I think it's a strong finish. Alas, this is a tale that refuses to go gentle into that good night.

Algorithm names are more meaningful than bare loops, it's true, but specifying what to do during an iteration can be clearer using a loop than using an algorithm. For example, suppose you'd like to identify the first element in a vector whose value is greater than some x and less than some y. Here's how you could do it using a loop:

```
vector<int> v;
int x, y;
...

vector<int>::iterator i = v.begin();    // iterate from v.begin() until an
for( ; i != v.end(); ++i) {             // appropriate value is found or
   if (*i > x && *i < y) break;         // v.end() is reached
}
...                                     // i now points to the value or is
                                        // the same as v.end()
```

It is possible to pass this same logic to find_if, but it requires that you use a nonstandard function object adapter like SGI's compose2 (see Item 50):

```
vector<int> iterator i =
   find_if( v.begin(), v.end(),                   // find the first value val
            compose2( logical_and<bool>(),        // where the "and" of
                      bind2nd(greater<int>(), x), // val > x and
                      bind2nd(less<int>(), y)));   // val < y
                                                   // is true
```

Even if this didn't use nonstandard components, many programmers would object that it's nowhere near as clear as the loop, and I have to admit to being sympathetic to that view (see Item 47).

The find_if call can be made less imposing by moving the test logic into a separate functor class,

```
template<typename T>
class BetweenValues:
   public unary_function<T, bool> {              // see Item 40
public:
   BetweenValues(const T& lowValue,
                 const T& highValue)             // have the ctor save the
     : lowVal(lowValue), highVal(highValue)      // values to be between
     {}

   bool operator()(const T& val) const           // return whether
   {                                             // val is between the
      return val > lowVal && val < highVal;      // saved values
   }

private:
   T lowVal;
   T highVal;
};

...

vector<int> iterator i = find_if(v.begin(), v.end(),
                        BetweenValues<int>(x, y));
```

but this has its own drawbacks. First, creating the BetweenValues template is a lot more work than writing the loop body. Just count the lines. Loop body: one; BetweenValues template: fourteen. Not a very good ratio. Second, the details of what find_if is looking for are now physically separate from the call. To really understand the call to find_if, one must look up the definition of BetweenValues, but Between-Values must be defined outside the function containing the call to find_if. If you try to declare BetweenValues *inside* the function containing the call to find_if, like this,

```
{                                          // beginning of function
   ...

   template <typename T>
   class BetweenValues: public unary_function<T, bool> { ... };

   vector<int>::iterator i = find_if(v.begin(), v.end(),
                            BetweenValues<int>(x, y));

   ...

}                                          // end of function
```

you'll discover that it won't compile, because templates can't be declared inside functions. If you try to avoid that restriction by making BetweenValues a class instead of a template,

```
{                                          // beginning of function
  ...
  class BetweenValues: public unary_function<int, bool> { ... };
  vector<int> iterator i = find_if( v.begin(), v.end(),
                            BetweenValues(x, y));

  ...
}                                          // end of function
```

you'll find that you're still out of luck, because classes defined inside functions are known as *local classes*, and local class types can't be bound to template type arguments (such as the type of the functor taken by find_if). Sad as it may seem, functor classes and functor class templates are not allowed to be defined inside functions, no matter how convenient it would be to be able to do it.

In the ongoing tussle between algorithm calls and hand-written loops, the bottom line on code clarity is that it all depends on what you need to do inside the loop. If you need to do something an algorithm already does, or if you need to do something very similar to what an algorithm does, the algorithm call is clearer. If you need a loop that does something fairly simple, but would require a confusing tangle of binders and adapters or would require a separate functor class if you were to use an algorithm, you're probably better off just writing the loop. Finally, if you need to do something fairly long and complex inside the loop, the scales tilt back toward algorithms, because long, complex computations should generally be moved into separate functions, anyway. Once you've moved the loop body into a separate function, you can almost certainly find a way to pass that function to an algorithm (often for_each) such that the resulting code is direct and straightforward.

If you agree with this Item that algorithm calls are generally preferable to hand-written loops, and if you also agree with Item 5 that range member functions are preferable to loops that iteratively invoke single-element member functions, an interesting conclusion emerges: well-crafted C++ programs using the STL contain far fewer loops than equivalent programs not using the STL. This is a good thing. Any time we can replace low-level words like for, while, and do with higher-level terms like insert, find, and for_each, we raise the level of abstraction in our software and thereby make it easier to write, document, enhance, and maintain.

Item 44: Prefer member functions to algorithms with the same names.

Some containers have member functions with the same names as STL algorithms. The associative containers offer count, find, lower_bound, upper_bound, and equal_range, while list offers remove, remove_if, unique, sort, merge, and reverse. Most of the time, you'll want to use the member functions instead of the algorithms. There are two reasons for this. First, the member functions are faster. Second, they integrate better with the containers (especially the associative containers) than do the algorithms. That's because algorithms and member functions that share the same name typically do *not* do exactly the same thing.

We'll begin with an examination of the associative containers. Suppose you have a set<int> holding a million values and you'd like to find the first occurrence of the value 727, if there is one. Here are the two most obvious ways to perform the search:

```
set<int> s;                                     // create set, put
...                                             // 1,000,000 values
                                                // into it

set<int>::iterator i = s.find(727);             // use find member
if (i != s.end()) ...                           // function

set<int>::iterator i = find(s.begin(), s.end(), 727);   // use find algorithm
if (i != s.end()) ...
```

The find member function runs in logarithmic time, so, regardless of whether 727 is in the set, set::find will perform no more than about 40 comparisons looking for it, and usually it will require only about 20. In contrast, the find algorithm runs in linear time, so it will have to perform 1,000,000 comparisons if 727 isn't in the set. Even if 727 is in the set, the find algorithm will perform, on average, 500,000 comparisons to locate it. The efficiency score is thus

Member find: About 40 (worst case) to about 20 (average case)
Algorithm find: 1,000,000 (worst case) to 500,000 (average case)

As in golf, the low score wins, and as you can see, this matchup is not much of a contest.

I have to be a little cagey about the number of comparisons required by member find, because it's partially dependent on the implementation used by the associative containers. Most implementations use red-black trees, a form of balanced tree that may be out of balance by up to a factor of two. In such implementations, the maximum number of comparisons needed to search a set of a million values is 38, but for the vast majority of searches, no more than 22 comparisons is required. An implementation based on perfectly balanced trees would never require more than 21 comparisons, but in practice, the overall performance of such perfectly balanced trees is inferior to that of red-black trees. That's why most STL implementations use red-black trees.

Efficiency isn't the only difference between member and algorithm find. As Item 19 explains, STL algorithms determine whether two objects have the same value by checking for equality, while associative containers use equivalence as their "sameness" test. Hence, the find algorithm searches for 727 using equality, while the find member function searches using equivalence. The difference between equality and equivalence can be the difference between a successful search and an unsuccessful search. For example, Item 19 shows how using the find algorithm to look for something in an associative container could fail even when the corresponding search using the find member function would succeed! You should therefore prefer the member form of find, count, lower_bound, etc., over their algorithm eponyms when you work with associative containers, because they offer behavior that is consistent with the other member functions of those containers. Due to the difference between equality and equivalence, algorithms don't offer such consistent behavior.

This difference is especially pronounced when working with maps and multimaps, because these containers hold pair objects, yet their member functions look only at the key part of each pair. Hence, the count member function counts only pairs with matching keys (a "match," naturally, is determined by testing for equivalence); the value part of each pair is ignored. The member functions find, lower_bound, upper_bound, and equal_range behave similarly. If you use the count algorithm, however, it will look for matches based on (a) equality and (b) both components of the pair; find, lower_bound, etc., do the same thing. To get the algorithms to look at only the key part of a pair, you have to jump through the hoops described in Item 23 (which would also allow you to replace equality testing with equivalence testing).

On the other hand, if you are really concerned with efficiency, you may decide that Item 23's gymnastics, in conjunction with the logarithmic-time lookup algorithms of Item 34, are a small price to pay for an increase in performance. Then again, if you're *really* concerned with efficiency, you'll want to consider the non-standard hashed containers described in Item 25, though there you'll again confront the difference between equality and equivalence.

For the standard associative containers, then, choosing member functions over algorithms with the same names offers several benefits.

First, you get logarithmic-time instead of linear-time performance. Second, you determine whether two values are "the same" using equivalence, which is the natural definition for associative containers. Third, when working with maps and multimaps, you automatically deal only with key values instead of with (key, value) pairs. This triumvirate makes the case for preferring member functions pretty iron-clad.

Let us therefore move on to list member functions that have the same names as STL algorithms. Here the story is almost completely about efficiency. Each of the algorithms that list specializes (remove, remove_if, unique, sort, merge, and reverse) copies objects, but list-specific versions copy nothing; they simply manipulate the pointers connecting list nodes. The algorithmic complexity of the algorithms and the member functions is the same, but, under the assumption that manipulating pointers is less expensive than copying objects, list's versions of these functions should offer better performance.

It's important to bear in mind that the list member functions often behave differently from their algorithm counterparts. As Item 32 explains, calls to the algorithms remove, remove_if, and unique must be followed by calls to erase if you really want to eliminate objects from a container, but list's remove, remove_if, and unique member functions honestly get rid of elements; no subsequent call to erase is necessary.

A significant difference between the sort algorithm and list's sort function is that the former can't be applied to lists. Being only bidirectional iterators, list's iterators can't be passed to sort. A gulf also exists between the behavior of the merge algorithm and list's merge. The algorithm isn't permitted to modify its source ranges, but list::merge *always* modifies the lists it works on.

So there you have it. When faced with a choice between an STL algorithm or a container member function with the same name, you should prefer the member function. It's almost certain to be more efficient, and it's likely to be better integrated with the container's usual behavior, too.

Item 45: **Distinguish among** count, find, binary_search, lower_bound, upper_bound, **and** equal_range.

So you want to look for something, and you have a container or you have iterators demarcating a range where you think it's located. How do you conduct the search? Your quiver is fairly bursting with arrows: count, count_if, find, find_if, binary_search, lower_bound, upper_bound, and equal_range. Decisions, decisions! How do you choose?

Easy. You reach for something that's fast and simple. The faster and simpler, the better.

For the time being, we'll assume that you have a pair of iterators specifying a range to be searched. Later, we'll consider the case where you have a container instead of a range.

In selecting a search strategy, much depends on whether your iterators define a sorted range. If they do, you can get speedy (usually logarithmic-time — see Item 34) lookups via binary_search, lower_bound, upper_bound, and equal_range. If the iterators don't demarcate a sorted range, you're limited to the linear-time algorithms count, count_if, find, and find_if. In what follows, I'll ignore the _if variants of count and find, just as I'll ignore the variants of binary_search, lower_ and upper_bound, and equal_range taking a predicate. Whether you rely on the default search predicate or you specify your own, the considerations for choosing a search algorithm are the same.

If you have an unsorted range, your choices are count or find. They answer slightly different questions, so it's worth taking a closer look at them. count answers the question, "Is the value there, and if so, how many copies are there?" while find answers the question, "Is it there, and if so, where is it?"

Suppose all you want to know is whether some special Widget value w is in a list. Using count, the code looks like this:

```
list<Widget> lw;              // list of Widgets
Widget w;                     // special Widget value

...
if (count(lw.begin(), lw.end(), w)) {
  ...                                       // w is in lw
} else {
  ...                                       // it's not
}
```

This demonstrates a common idiom: using count as an existence test. count returns either zero or a positive number, so we rely on the conversion of nonzero values to true and zero to false. It would arguably be clearer to be more explicit about what we are doing,

```
if (count(lw.begin(), lw.end(), w) != 0) ...
```

and some programmers do write it that way, but it's quite common to rely on the implicit conversion, as in the original example.

Compared to that original code, using find is slightly more complicated, because you have to test find's return value against the list's end iterator:

```
if (find(lw.begin(), lw.end(), w) != lw.end()) {
  ...
} else {
  ...
}
```

For existence testing, the idiomatic use of count is slightly simpler to code. At the same time, it's also less efficient when the search is successful, because find stops once it's found a match, while count must continue to the end of the range looking for additional matches. For most programmers, find's edge in efficiency is enough to justify the slight increase in usage complexity.

Often, knowing whether a value is in a range isn't enough. Instead, you'll want to know the first object in the range with the value. For example, you might want to print the object, you might want to insert something in front of it, or you might want to erase it (but see Item 9 for guidance on erasing while iterating). When you need to know not just whether a value exists but also which object (or objects) has that value, you need find:

```
list<Widget>::iterator i = find(lw.begin(), lw.end(), w);
if (i != lw.end()) {
  ...                                   // found it, i points to the first one
} else {
  ...                                   // didn't find it
}
```

For sorted ranges, you have other choices, and you'll definitely want to use them. count and find run in linear time, but the search algorithms for sorted ranges (binary_search, lower_bound, upper_bound, and equal_range) run in logarithmic time.

The shift from unsorted ranges to sorted ranges leads to another shift: from using equality to determine whether two values are the same to using equivalence. Item 19 comprises a discourse on equality versus equivalence, so I won't repeat it here. Instead, I'll simply note that the count and find algorithms both search using equality, while binary_search, lower_bound, upper_bound, and equal_range employ equivalence.

To test for the existence of a value in a sorted range, use binary_search. Unlike bsearch in the standard C library (and hence also in the standard C++ library), binary_search returns only a bool: whether the value was found. binary_search answers the question, "Is it there?," and its answer is either yes or no. If you need more information than that, you need a different algorithm.

Here's an example of binary_search applied to a sorted vector. (You can read about the virtues of sorted vectors in Item 23.)

```
vector<Widget> vw;                          // create vector, put
...                                          // data into it, sort the
sort(vw.begin(), vw.end());                 // data

Widget w;                                    // value to search for
...
if (binary_search(vw.begin(), vw.end(), w)) {
    ...                                      // w is in vw
} else {
    ...                                      // it's not
}
```

If you have a sorted range and your question is, "Is it there, and if so, where is it?" you want equal_range, but you may think you want lower_bound. We'll discuss equal_range shortly, but first, let's examine lower_bound as a way of locating values in a range.

When you ask lower_bound to look for a value, it returns an iterator pointing to either the first copy of that value (if it's found) or to the proper insertion location for that value (if it's not). lower_bound thus answers the question, "Is it there? If so, where is the first copy, and if it's not, where would it go?" As with find, the result of lower_bound must be tested to see if it's pointing to the value you're looking for. Unlike find, you can't just test lower_bound's return value against the end iterator. Instead, you must test the object lower_bound identifies to see if that's the value you want.

Many programers use lower_bound like this:

```
vector<Widget>::iterator i = lower_bound(vw.begin(), vw.end(), w);
if (i != vw.end() && *i == w) {             // make sure i points to an object;
                                            // make sure the object has the
                                            // correct value; this has a bug!

    ...                                      // found the value, i points to the
                                            // first object with that value
} else {
    ...                                      // not found
}
```

This works most of the time, but it's not really correct. Look again at the test to determine whether the desired value was found:

```
if (i != vw.end() && *i == w) ...
```

This is an *equality* test, but lower_bound searched using *equivalence*. Most of the time, tests for equivalence and equality yield the same results, but Item 19 demonstrates that it's not that hard to come up with situations where equality and equivalence are different. In such situations the code above is wrong.

To do things properly, you must check to see if the iterator returned from lower_bound points to an object with a value that is equivalent to the one you searched for. You could do that manually (Item 19 shows you how, and Item 24 provides an example of when it can be worthwhile), but it can get tricky, because you have to be sure to use the same comparison function that lower_bound used. In general, that could be an arbitrary function (or function object). If you passed a comparison function to lower_bound, you'd have to be sure to use the same comparison function in your hand-coded equivalence test. *That* would mean that if you changed the comparison function you passed to lower_bound, you'd have to make the corresponding change in your check for equivalence. Keeping the comparison functions in sync isn't rocket science, but it is another thing to remember, and I suspect you already have plenty you're expected to keep in mind.

There is an easier way: use equal_range. equal_range returns a *pair* of iterators, the first equal to the iterator lower_bound would return, the second equal to the one upper_bound would return (i.e., the one-past-the-end iterator for the range of values equivalent to the one searched for). equal_range, then, returns a pair of iterators that demarcate the range of values equivalent to the one you searched for. A well-named algorithm, no? (equivalent_range would be better, of course, but equal_range is still pretty good.)

There are two important observations about equal_range's return value. First, if the two iterators are the same, that means the range of objects is empty; the value wasn't found. That observation is the key to using equal_range to answer the question, "Is it there?" You use it like this:

```
vector<Widget> vw;
...
sort(vw.begin(), vw.end());

typedef vector<Widget>::iterator VWIter;    // convenience typedefs
typedef pair<VWIter, VWIter> VWIterPair;

VWIterPair p = equal_range(vw.begin(), vw.end(), w);

if (p.first != p.second) {                   // if equal_range didn't return
                                             // an empty range...

    ...                                      // found it, p.first points to the
                                             // first one and p.second
                                             // points to one past the last

} else {
```

```
    ...                                        // not found, both p.first and
                                               // p.second point to the
    }                                          // insertion location for
                                               // the value searched for
```

This code uses only equivalence, so it is always correct.

The second thing to note about equal_range's return value is that the distance between its iterators is equal to the number of objects in the range, i.e., the objects with a value equivalent to the one that was searched for. As a result, equal_range not only does the job of find for sorted ranges, it also replaces count. For example, to locate the Widgets in vw with a value equivalent to w and then print out how many such Widgets exist, you could do this:

```
    VWIterPair p = equal_range(vw.begin(), vw.end(), w);

    cout  << "There are " << distance(p.first, p.second)
          << " elements in vw equivalent to w.";
```

So far, our discussion has assumed we want to search for a value in a range, but sometimes we're more interested in finding a *location* in a range. For example, suppose we have a Timestamp class and a vector of Timestamps that's sorted so that older timestamps come first:

```
    class Timestamp { ... };

    bool operator<(const Timestamp& lhs,       // returns whether lhs
                   const Timestamp& rhs);       // precedes rhs in time

    vector<Timestamp> vt;                      // create vector, fill it with
    ...                                        // data, sort it so that older
    sort(vt.begin(), vt.end());                // times precede newer ones
```

Now suppose we have a special timestamp, ageLimit, and we want to remove from vt all the timestamps that are older than ageLimit. In this case, we don't want to search vt for a Timestamp equivalent to ageLimit, because there might not be any elements with that exact value. Instead, we need to find a *location* in vt: the first element that is no older than ageLimit. This is as easy as easy can be, because lower_bound will give us precisely what we need:

```
    Timestamp ageLimit;
    ...
    vt.erase(vt.begin(), lower_bound(vt.begin(),   // eliminate from vt all
                                     vt.end(),      // objects that precede
                                     ageLimit));    // ageLimit's value
```

If our requirements change slightly so that we want to eliminate all the timestamps that are at least as old as ageLimit, we need to find the location of the first timestamp that is *younger* than ageLimit. That's a job tailor-made for upper_bound:

```
vt.erase(vt.begin(), upper_bound(vt.begin(),    // eliminate from vt all
                                 vt.end(),      // objects that precede
                                 ageLimit));    // or are equivalent
                                                // to ageLimit's value
```

upper_bound is also useful if you want to insert things into a sorted range so that objects with equivalent values are stored in the order in which they were inserted. For example, we might have a sorted list of Person objects, where the objects are sorted by name:

```
class Person {
public:
   ...
   const string& name() const;
   ...
};

struct PersonNameLess:
   public binary_function<Person, Person, bool> {        // see Item 40

   bool operator()(const Person& lhs, const Person& rhs) const
   {
      return lhs.name() < rhs.name();
   }
};
list<Person> lp;
...

lp.sort(PersonNameLess());                               // sort lp using
                                                         // PersonNameLess
```

To keep the list sorted the way we desire (by name, with equivalent names stored in the order in which they are inserted), we can use upper_bound to specify the insertion location:

```
Person newPerson;

...

lp.insert( upper_bound(lp.begin(),          // insert newPerson after
                       lp.end(),            // the last object in lp
                       newPerson,           // that precedes or is
                       PersonNameLess()),   // equivalent to
           newPerson);                      // newPerson
```

This works fine and is quite convenient, but it's important not to be misled by this use of upper_bound into thinking that we're magically looking up an insertion location in a list in logarithmic time. We're not. Item 34 explains that because we're working with a list, the lookup takes linear time, but it performs only a logarithmic number of comparisons.

Up to this point, we have considered only the case where you have a pair of iterators defining a range to be searched. Often you have a container, not a range. In that case, you must distinguish between the sequence and associative containers. For the standard sequence containers (vector, string, deque, and list), you follow the advice we've outlined in this Item, using the containers' begin and end iterators to demarcate the range.

The situation is different for the standard associative containers (set, multiset, map, and multimap), because they offer member functions for searching that are generally better choices than the STL algorithms. Item 44 goes into the details of why they are better choices, but briefly, it's because they're faster and they behave more naturally. Fortunately, the member functions usually have the same names as the corresponding algorithms, so where the foregoing discussion recommends you choose algorithms named count, find, equal_range, lower_bound, or upper_bound, you simply select the same-named member functions when searching associative containers. binary_search calls for a different strategy, because there is no member function analogue to this algorithm. To test for the existence of a value in a set or map, use count in its idiomatic role as a test for membership:

```
set<Widget> s;                    // create set, put data into it
...
Widget w;                         // w still holds the value to search for
...
if (s.count(w)) {
   ...                            // a value equivalent to w exists
} else {
   ...                            // no such value exists
}
```

To test for the existence of a value in a multiset or multimap, find is generally superior to count, because find can stop once it's found a single object with the desired value, while count, in the worst case, must examine every object in the container.

However, count's role for counting things in associative containers is secure. In particular, it's a better choice than calling equal_range and applying distance to the resulting iterators. For one thing, it's clearer: count means "count." For another, it's easier; there's no need to create a pair and pass its components to distance. For a third, it's probably a little faster.

Given everything we've considered in this Item, where do we stand? The following table says it all.

What You Want to Know	Algorithm to Use		Member Function to Use	
	On an Unsorted Range	On a Sorted Range	With a set or map	With a multiset or multimap
Does the desired value exist?	find	binary_search	count	find
Does the desired value exist? If so, where is the first object with that value?	find	equal_range	find	find or lower_bound (see below)
Where is the first object with a value not preceding the desired value?	find_if	lower_bound	lower_bound	lower_bound
Where is the first object with a value succeeding the desired value?	find_if	upper_bound	upper_bound	upper_bound
How many objects have the desired value?	count	equal_range	count	count
Where are all the objects with the desired value?	find (iteratively)	equal_range	equal_range	equal_range

In the column summarizing how to work with sorted ranges, the frequency with which equal_range occurs may be surprising. That frequency arises from the importance of testing for equivalence when searching. With lower_bound and upper_bound, it's too easy to fall back on equality tests, but with equal_range, testing only for equivalence is the natural thing to do. In the second row for sorted ranges, equal_range beats out find for an additional reason: equal_range runs in logarithmic time, while find takes linear time.

For multisets and multimaps, the table lists both find and lower_bound as candidates when you're looking for the first object with a particular value. find is the usual choice for this job, and you may have noticed that it's the one listed in the table for sets and maps. For the multi containers, however, find is not guaranteed to identify the *first* element in the container with a given value if more than one is present; its charter is only to identify *one* of those elements. If you really need to find the *first* object with a given value, you'll want to employ lower_bound, and you'll have to manually perform the second half of the equivalence test described in Item 19 to confirm that you've found the value you were looking for. (You could avoid the manual equivalence test by using equal_range, but calling equal_range is more expensive than calling lower_bound.)

Selecting among count, find, binary_search, lower_bound, upper_bound, and equal_range is easy. Choose the algorithm or member function that offers you the behavior and performance you need and that requires the least amount of work when you call it. Follow that advice (or consult the table), and you should never get confused.

Item 46: Consider function objects instead of functions as algorithm parameters.

One of the complaints about programming in high-level languages is that as the level of abstraction gets higher, the efficiency of the generated code gets lower. In fact, Alexander Stepanov (the inventor of the STL) once produced a small benchmark suite that tried to measure the "abstraction penalty" of C++ vis-à-vis C. Among other things, the results of that benchmark revealed that it's nearly universal for the code generated for manipulating a class containing a double to be less efficient than the corresponding code for manipulating a double directly. It may thus come as a surprise to learn that passing STL function objects — objects masquerading as functions — to algorithms typically yields code that is *more* efficient than passing real functions.

For example, suppose you need to sort a vector of doubles in descending order. The straightforward STL way to do it is via the sort algorithm and a function object of type greater<double>:

```
vector<double> v;

...

sort(v.begin(), v.end(), greater<double>());
```

If you're wary of the abstraction penalty, you might decide to eschew the function object in favor of a real function, a function that's not only real, it's inline:

```
inline
bool doubleGreater(double d1, double d2)
{
  return d1 > d2;
}

...

sort(v.begin(), v.end(), doubleGreater);
```

Interestingly, if you were to compare the performance of the two calls to sort (one using greater<double>, one using doubleGreater), you'd almost certainly find that the one using greater<double> was faster. For instance, I timed the two calls to sort on a vector of a million doubles using four different STL platforms, each set to optimize for speed, and the version using greater<double> was faster every time. At worst, it was 50% faster, at best it was 160% faster. So much for the abstraction penalty.

The explanation for this behavior is simple: inlining. If a function object's operator() function has been declared inline (either explicitly via inline or implicitly by defining it in its class definition), the body of that function is available to compilers, and most compilers will happily inline that function during template instantiation of the called algorithm. In the example above, greater<double>::operator() is an inline function, so compilers inline-expand it during instantiation of sort. As a result, sort contains zero function calls, and compilers are able to perform optimizations on this call-free code that are otherwise not usually attempted. (For a discussion of the interaction between inlining and compiler optimization, see Item 33 of *Effective C++* and chapters 8–10 of Bulka and Mayhew's *Efficient C++* [10].)

The situation is different for the call to sort using doubleGreater. To see how it's different, we must recall that there's no such thing as passing a function as a parameter to another function. When we try to pass a function as a parameter, compilers silently convert the function into a *pointer* to that function, and it's the pointer we actually pass. Hence, the call

```
sort(v.begin(), v.end(), doubleGreater);
```

doesn't pass doubleGreater to sort, it passes a pointer to doubleGreater. When the sort template is instantiated, this is the declaration for the function that is generated:

```
void sort( vector<double>::iterator first,        // beginning of range
           vector<double>::iterator last,         // end of range
           bool (*comp)(double, double));         // comparison function
```

Because comp is a pointer to a function, each time it's used inside sort, compilers make an indirect function call — a call through a pointer. Most compilers won't try to inline calls to functions that are invoked through function pointers, even if, as in this example, such functions have been declared inline and the optimization appears to be straightforward. Why not? Probably because compiler vendors have never felt that it was worthwhile to implement the optimization. You have to have a little sympathy for compiler vendors. They have lots of demands on their time, and they can't do everything. Not that this should stop you from asking them for it.

The fact that function pointer parameters inhibit inlining explains an observation that long-time C programmers often find hard to believe: C++'s sort virtually always embarrasses C's qsort when it comes to speed. Sure, C++ has function and class templates to instantiate and funny-looking operator() functions to invoke while C makes a simple function call, but all that C++ "overhead" is absorbed during compilation. At runtime, sort makes inline calls to its comparison function (assuming the comparison function has been declared inline and its body is available during compilation) while qsort calls its comparison function through a pointer. The end result is that sort runs faster. In my tests on a vector of a million doubles, it ran up to 670% faster, but don't take my word for it, try it yourself. It's easy to verify that when comparing function objects and real functions as algorithm parameters, there's an abstraction *bonus*.

There's another reason to prefer function objects to functions as algorithm parameters, and it has nothing to do with efficiency. It has to do with getting your programs to compile. For whatever reason, it's not uncommon for STL platforms to reject perfectly valid code, either through shortcomings in the compiler or the library or both. For example, one widely used STL platform rejects the following (valid) code to print to cout the length of each string in a set:

```
set<string> s;

...

transform( s.begin(), s.end(),
           ostream_iterator<string::size_type>(cout, "\n"),
           mem_fun_ref(&string::size));
```

The cause of the problem is that this particular STL platform has a bug in its handling of const member functions (such as string::size). A workaround is to use a function object instead:

```
struct StringSize:
  public unary_function<string, string::size_type> {          // see Item 40

  string::size_type operator()(const string& s) const
  {
    return s.size();
  }
};
transform(s.begin(), s.end(),
          ostream_iterator<string::size_type>(cout, "\n"),
          StringSize());
```

There are other workarounds for this problem, but this one does more than just compile on every STL platform I know. It also facilitates inlining the call to string::size, something that would almost certainly not take place in the code above where mem_fun_ref(&string::size) is passed to transform. In other words, creation of the functor class StringSize does more than sidestep compiler conformance problems, it's also likely to lead to an increase in performance.

Another reason to prefer function objects to functions is that they can help you avoid subtle language pitfalls. Occasionally, source code that looks reasonable is rejected by compilers for legitimate, but obscure, reasons. There are situations, for example, when the name of an instantiation of a function template is not equivalent to the name of a function. Here's one such situation:

```
template<typename FPType>                        // return the average
FPType average(FPType val1, FPType val2)         // of 2 floating point
{                                                // numbers
  return (val1 + val2) / 2;
}

template< typename InputIter1,
          typename InputIter2>
void writeAverages( InputIter1 begin1,           // write the pairwise
                    InputIter1 end1,             // averages of 2
                    InputIter2 begin2,           // sequences to a
                    ostream& s)                  // stream
{
  transform(
    begin1, end1, begin2,
    ostream_iterator<typename iterator_traits<InputIter1>::value_type>(s, "\n"),
```

```
        average<typename iterator_traits<InputIter1>::value_type>   // error?
      );
    }
```

Many compilers accept this code, but the C++ Standard appears to forbid it. The reasoning is that there could, in theory, be another function template named average that takes a single type parameter. If there were, the expression average<typename iterator_traits<InputIter1>:: value_type> would be ambiguous, because it would not be clear which template to instantiate. In this particular example, no ambiguity is present, but some compilers reject the code anyway, and they are allowed to do that. No matter. The solution to the problem is to fall back on a function object:

```
    template<typename FPType>
    struct Average:
      public binary_function<FPType, FPType, FPType> {          // see Item 40
      FPType operator()(FPType val1, FPType val2) const
      {
        return average(val1, val2);
      }
    };
    template<typename InputIter1, typename InputIter2>
    void writeAverages(InputIter1 begin1, InputIter1 end1,
                       InputIter2 begin2, ostream& s)
    {
      transform(
        begin1, end1, begin2,
        ostream_iterator<typename iterator_traits<InputIter1>::value_type>(s, "\n"),
        Average<typename iterator_traits<InputIter1>::value_type>()
      );
    }
```

Every compiler should accept this revised code. Furthermore, calls to Average::operator() inside transform are eligible for inlining, something that would not be true for an instantiation of average above, because average is a template for functions, not function *objects*.

Function objects as parameters to algorithms thus offer more than greater efficiency. They're also more robust when it comes to getting your code to compile. Real functions are useful, of course, but when it comes to effective STL programing, function objects are frequently more useful.

Item 47: Avoid producing write-only code.

Suppose you have a vector<int>, and you'd like to get rid of all the elements in the vector whose value is less than x, except that elements preceding the last occurrence of a value at least as big as y should be retained. Does the following instantly spring to mind?

```
vector<int> v;
int x, y;

...

v.erase(
  remove_if(find_if(v.rbegin(), v.rend(),
                      bind2nd(greater_equal<int>(), y)).base(),
              v.end(),
              bind2nd(less<int>(), x)),
    v.end());
```

One statement, and the job is done. Clear and straightforward. No problem. Right?

Well, let's step back for a moment. Does this strike you as reasonable, maintainable code? "No!" shriek most C++ programmers, fear and loathing in their voices. "Yes!" squeal a few, delight evident in theirs. And therein lies the problem. One programmer's vision of expressive purity is another programmer's demonic missive from Hell.

As I see it, there are two causes for concern in the code above. First, it's a rat's nest of function calls. To see what I mean, here is the same statement, but with all the function names replaced by f*n*, each *n* corresponding to one of the functions:

```
v.f1(f2(f3(v.f4(), v.f5(), f6(f7(), y)).f8(), v.f9(), f6(f10(), x)), v.f9());
```

This looks unnaturally complicated, because I've removed the indentation present in the original example, but I think it's safe to say that any statement involving twelve function calls to ten different functions would be considered excessive by most C++ software developers. Programmers weaned on functional languages such as Scheme might feel differently, however, and my experience has been that the majority of programmers who view the original code without raising an eyebrow have a strong functional programming background. Most C++ programmers lack this background, so unless your colleagues are versed in the ways of deeply nested function calls, code like the erase call above is almost sure to confound the next person who is forced to make sense of what you have written.

The second drawback of the code is the significant STL background needed to understand it. It uses the less common _if forms of find and remove, it uses reverse iterators (see Item 26), it converts reverse_iterators to iterators (see Item 28), it uses bind2nd, it creates anonymous function objects, and it employs the erase-remove idiom (see Item 32). Experienced STL programmers can swallow that combination without difficulty, but far more C++ developers will have their eyes glaze over before they've taken so much as a bite. If your colleagues are well-steeped in the ways of the STL, using erase, remove_if, find_if, base, and bind2nd in a single statement may be fine, but if you want your code to be comprehensible by C++ programmers with a more mainstream background, I encourage you to break it down into more easily digestible chunks.

Here's one way you could do it. (The comments aren't just for this book. I'd put them in the code, too.)

```
typedef vector<int>::iterator VecIntIter;
// initialize rangeBegin to the first element in v that's greater than
// or equal to the last occurrence of y. If no such element exists,
// initialize rangeBegin to v.begin()
VecIntIter rangeBegin = find_if(v.rbegin(), v.rend(),
                           bind2nd(greater_equal<int>(), y)).base();
// from rangeBegin to v.end(), erase everything with a value less than x
v.erase(remove_if(rangeBegin, v.end(), bind2nd(less<int>(), x)), v.end());
```

This is still likely to confuse some people, because it relies on an understanding of the erase-remove idiom, but between the comments in the code and a good STL reference (e.g., Josuttis' *The C++ Standard Library* [3] or SGI's STL web site [21]), every C++ programmer should be able to figure out what's going on without too much difficulty.

When transforming the code, it's important to note that I didn't abandon algorithms and try to write my own loops. Item 43 explains why that's generally an inferior option, and its arguments apply here. When writing source code, the goal is to come up with code that is meaningful to both compilers and humans and that offers acceptable performance. Algorithms are almost always the best way to achieve that goal. However, Item 43 also explains how the increased use of algorithms naturally leads to an increased tendency to nest function calls and to throw in binders and other functor adapters. Look again at the problem specification that opened this Item:

Suppose you have a vector<int>, and you'd like to get rid of all the elements in the vector whose value is less than x, except that elements preceding the last occurrence of a value at least as big as y should be retained.

The outline of a solution *does* spring to mind:

- Finding the last occurrence of a value in a vector calls for some application of find or find_if with reverse iterators.

- Getting rid of elements calls for either erase or the erase-remove idiom.

Put those two ideas together, and you get this pseudocode, where "something" indicates a placeholder for code that hasn't yet been fleshed out:

```
v.erase(remove_if(find_if(v.rbegin(), v.rend(), something).base(),
                  v.end(),
                  something)),
        v.end());
```

Once you've got that, figuring out the *something*s isn't terribly difficult, and the next thing you know, you have the code in the original example. That's why this kind of statement is often known as "write-only" code. As you write the code, it seems straightforward, because it's a natural outgrowth of some basic ideas (e.g., the erase-remove idiom plus the notion of using find with reverse iterators). *Readers*, however, have great difficulty in decomposing the final product back into the ideas on which it is based. That's the calling card of write-only code: it's easy to write, but it's hard to read and understand.

Whether code is write-only depends on who's reading it. As I noted, some C++ programmers think nothing of the code in this Item. If that's typical in the environment in which you work and you expect it to be typical in the future, feel free to unleash your most advanced STL programming inclinations. However, if your colleagues are less comfortable with a functional programming style and are less experienced with the STL, scale back your ambitions and write something more along the lines of the two-statement alternative I showed earlier.

It's a software engineering truism that code is read more often than it is written. Equally well established is that software spends far more time in maintenance than it does in development. Software that cannot be read and understood cannot be maintained, and software that cannot be maintained is hardly worth having. The more you work with the STL, the more comfortable you'll become with it, and the more you'll feel the pull to nest function calls and create function objects on the fly. There's nothing wrong with that, but always bear in mind that the code you write today will be read by somebody — possibly you — someday in the future. Prepare for that day.

Use the STL, yes. Use it well. Use it effectively. But avoid producing write-only code. In the long run, such code is anything *but* effective.

Item 48: Always #include **the proper headers.**

Among the minor frustrations of STL programming is that it is easy to create software that compiles on one platform, yet requires additional #include directives on others. This annoyance stems from the fact that the Standard for C++ (unlike the Standard for C) fails to dictate which standard headers must or may be #included by other standard headers. Given such flexibility, different implementers have chosen to do different things.

To give you some idea of what this means in practice, I sat down one day with five STL platforms (let's call them A, B, C, D, and E), and I spent a little time throwing toy programs at them to see which standard headers I could omit and still get a successful compilation. This indirectly told me which headers #include other headers. This is what I found:

- With A and C, <vector> #includes <string>.

- With C, <algorithm> #includes <string>.

- With C and D, <iostream> #includes <iterator>.

- With D, <iostream> #includes <string> and <vector>.

- With D and E, <string> #includes <algorithm>.

- With all five implementations, <set> #includes <functional>.

Except for the case of <set> #includeing <functional>, I didn't find a way to get a program with a missing header past implementation B. According to Murphy's Law, then, you will always develop under a platform like A, C, D, or E and you will always be porting to a platform like B, especially when the pressure for the port is greatest and the time to accomplish it is least. Naturally.

But don't blame your compilers or library implementations for your porting woes. It's your fault if you're missing required headers. Any time you refer to elements of namespace std, you are responsible for having #included the appropriate headers. If you omit them, your code might compile anyway, but you'll still be missing necessary headers, and other STL platforms may justly reject your code.

To help you remember what's required when, here's a quick summary of what's in each standard STL-related header:

- Almost all the containers are declared in headers of the same name, i.e., vector is declared in <vector>, list is declared in <list>, etc. The exceptions are <set> and <map>. <set> declares both set and multiset, and <map> declares both map and multimap.

- All but four algorithms are declared in <algorithm>. The exceptions are accumulate (see Item 37), inner_product, adjacent_difference, and partial_sum. Those algorithms are declared in <numeric>.

- Special kinds of iterators, including istream_iterators and istreambuf_iterators (see Item 29), are declared in <iterator>.

- Standard functors (e.g., less<T>) and functor adapters (e.g., not1, bind2nd) are declared in <functional>.

Any time you use any of the components in a header, be sure to provide the corresponding #include directive, even if your development platform lets you get away without it. Your diligence will pay off in reduced stress when you find yourself porting to a different platform.

Item 49: Learn to decipher STL-related compiler diagnostics.

It's perfectly legal to define a vector with a particular size,

```
vector<int> v(10);              // create a vector of size 10
```

and strings act a lot like vectors, so you might expect to be able to do this:

```
string s(10);                   // attempt to create a string of size 10
```

This won't compile. There is no string constructor taking an int argument. One of my STL platforms tells me that like this:

> example.cpp(20) : error C2664: '__thiscall std::basic_string<char,struct std::char_traits<char>,class std::allocator<char> >::std::basic_string<char,struct std::char_traits<char>,class std::allocator<char> >(const class std::allocator<char> &)' : cannot convert parameter 1 from 'const int' to 'const class std::allocator<char> &'

> Reason: cannot convert from 'const int' to 'const class std::allocator<char>'

> No constructor could take the source type, or constructor overload resolution was ambiguous

Isn't that wonderful? The first part of the message looks as if a cat walked across the keyboard, the second part mysteriously refers to an allocator never mentioned in the source code, and the third part says the constructor call is bad. The third part is accurate, of course, but let's first focus our attention on the result of the purported feline stroll, because it's representative of diagnostics you'll frequently see when using strings.

string isn't a class, it's a typedef. In particular, it's a typedef for this:

```
basic_string<char, char_traits<char>, allocator<char> >
```

That's because the C++ notion of a string has been generalized to
mean sequences of arbitrary character types with arbitrary character
characteristics ("traits") and stored in memory allocated by arbitrary
allocators. All string-like objects in C++ are really instantiations of the
template basic_string, and that's why most compilers refer to the type
basic_string when they issue diagnostics about programs making erro-
neous use of strings. (A few compilers are kind enough to use the
name string in diagnostics, but most aren't.) Often, such diagnostics
will explicitly note that basic_string (and the attendant helper templates char_traits and allocator) are in the std namespace, so it's not
uncommon to see errors involving strings yield diagnostics that mention this type:

```
std::basic_string<char, std::char_traits<char>, std::allocator<char> >
```

This is quite close to what's used in the compiler diagnostic above, but
different compilers use variations on the theme. Another STL platform
I uses refers to strings this way,

```
basic_string<char,string_char_traits<char>,__default_alloc_template<false,0> >
```

The names string_char_traits and __default_alloc_template are nonstandard, but that's life. Some STL implementations deviate from the standard. If you don't like the deviations in your current STL
implementation, consider replacing it with a different one. Item 50
gives examples of places you can go for alternative implementations.

Regardless of how a compiler diagnostic refers to the string type, the
technique for reducing the diagnostic to something meaningful is the
same: globally replace the basic_string gobbledegook with the text
"string". If you're using a command-line compiler, it's usually easy to
do this is with a program like sed or a scripting language like perl,
python, or ruby. (You'll find an example of such a script in Zolman's
article, "An STL Error Message Decryptor for Visual C++" [26].) In the
case of the diagnostic above, we globally replace

```
std::basic_string<char,struct std::char_traits<char>,class std::allocator<char> >
```

with string and we end up with this:

```
example.cpp(20) : error C2664: '__thiscall string::string(const class
std::allocator<char> &)' : cannot convert parameter 1 from 'const int' to
'const class std::allocator<char> &'
```

This makes clear (or at least clearer) that the problem is in the type of
the parameter passed to the string constructor, and even though the
mysterious reference to allocator<char> remains, it should be easy to

look up the constructor forms for string to see that none exists taking only a size.

By the way, the reason for the mysterious reference to an allocator is that each standard container has a constructor taking only an allocator. In the case of string, it's one of three constructors that can be called with one argument, but for some reason, this compiler figures that the one taking an allocator is the one you're trying to call. The compiler figures wrong, and the diagnostic is misleading. Oh well.

As for the constructor taking only an allocator, please don't use it. That constructor makes it easy to end up with containers of the same type but with inequivalent allocators. In general, that's bad. Very bad. To find out why, turn to Item 11.

Now let's tackle a more challenging diagnostic. Suppose you're implementing an email program that allows users to refer to people by nicknames instead of by email addresses. For example, such a program would make it possible to use "The Big Cheese" as a synonym for the email address of the President of the United States (which happens to be president@whitehouse.gov). Such a program might use a map from nicknames to email addresses, and it might offer a member function showEmailAddress that displays the email address associated with a given nickname:

```
class NiftyEmailProgram {
private:
    typedef map<string, string> NicknameMap;

    NicknameMap nicknames;          // map from nicknames to
                                    // email addresses
public:
    ...
    void showEmailAddress(const string& nickname) const;
};
```

Inside showEmailAddress, you'll need to find the map entry associated with a particular nickname, so you might write this:

```
void NiftyEmailProgram::showEmailAddress(const string& nickname) const
{
    ...
    NicknameMap::iterator i = nicknames.find(nickname);
    if (i != nicknames.end()) ...
    ...
}
```

Compilers don't like this, and with good reason, but the reason isn't obvious. To help you figure it out, here's what one STL platform helpfully emits:

example.cpp(17) : error C2440: 'initializing' : cannot convert from 'class std::_Tree<class
std::basic_string<char,struct std::char_traits<char>,class std::allocator<char> >,struct
std::pair<class std::basic_string<char,struct std::char_traits<char>,class
std::allocator<char> > const ,class std::basic_string<char,struct
std::char_traits<char>,class std::allocator<char> > >,struct std::map<class
std::basic_string<char,struct std::char_traits<char>,class std::allocator<char> >,class
std::basic_string<char,struct std::char_traits<char>,class std::allocator<char> >,struct
std::less<class std::basic_string<char,struct std::char_traits<char>,class
std::allocator<char> > >,class std::allocator<class std::basic_string<char,struct
std::char_traits<char>,class std::allocator<char> > > >::_Kfn,struct std::less<class
std::basic_string<char,struct std::char_traits<char>,class std::allocator<char> > >,class
std::allocator<class std::basic_string<char,struct std::char_traits<char>,class
std::allocator<char> > > >::const_iterator' to 'class std::_Tree<class
std::basic_string<char,struct std::char_traits<char>,class std::allocator<char> >,struct
std::pair<class std::basic_string<char,struct std::char_traits<char>,class
std::allocator<char> > const ,class std::basic_string<char,struct
std::char_traits<char>,class std::allocator<char> > >,struct std::map<class
std::basic_string<char,struct std::char_traits<char>,class std::allocator<char> >,class
std::basic_string<char,struct std::char_traits<char>,class std::allocator<char> >,struct
std::less<class std::basic_string<char,struct std::char_traits<char>,class
std::allocator<char> > >,class std::allocator<class std::basic_string<char,struct
std::char_traits<char>,class std::allocator<char> > > >::_Kfn,struct std::less<class
std::basic_string<char,struct std::char_traits<char>,class std::allocator<char> > >,class
std::allocator<class std::basic_string<char,struct std::char_traits<char>,class
std::allocator<char> > > >::iterator'

No constructor could take the source type, or constructor overload resolution was
ambiguous

At 2095 characters long, this message looks fairly gruesome, but I've
seen worse. One of my favorite STL platforms produces a diagnostic of
4812 characters for this example. As you might guess, features other
than its error messages are what have engendered my fondness for it.

Let's reduce this mess to something manageable. We begin with the
replacement of the basic_string gibberish with string. That yields this:

example.cpp(17) : error C2440: 'initializing' : cannot convert from 'class
std::_Tree<class string,struct std::pair<class string const ,class string
>,struct std::map<class string,class string,struct std::less<class string
>,class std::allocator<class string > >::_Kfn,struct std::less<class string
>,class std::allocator<class string > >::const_iterator' to 'class
std::_Tree<class string,struct std::pair<class string const ,class string
>,struct std::map<class string,class string,struct std::less<class string
>,class std::allocator<class string > >::_Kfn,struct std::less<class string
>,class std::allocator<class string > >::iterator'

No constructor could take the source type, or constructor overload
resolution was ambiguous

Much better. Now a svelte 745 characters long, we can start to actually look at the message. One of the things that is likely to catch our
eye is the mention of the template std::_Tree. The Standard says nothing about a template called _Tree, but the leading underscore in the
name followed by a capital letter jogs our memory that such names

are reserved for implementers. This is an internal template used to implement some part of the STL.

In fact, almost all STL implementations use some kind of underlying template to implement the standard associative containers (set, multiset, map, and multimap). In the same way that source code using string typically leads to diagnostics mentioning basic_string, source code using a standard associative container often leads to diagnostics mentioning some underlying tree template. In this case, it's called _Tree, but other implementations I know use __tree or __rb_tree, the latter reflecting the use of red-black trees, the most common type of balanced tree used in STL implementations.

Setting _Tree aside for a moment, the message above mentions a type we should recognize: std::map<class string,class string,struct std::less<class string >,class std::allocator<class string > >. This is precisely the type of map we are using, except that the comparison and allocator types (which we chose not to specify when we defined the map) are shown. The error message will be easier to understand if we replace that type with our typedef for it, NicknameMap. That leads to this:

```
example.cpp(17) : error C2440: 'initializing' : cannot convert from 'class
std::_Tree<class string,struct std::pair<class string const ,class string
>,struct NicknameMap::_Kfn,struct std::less<class string >,class
std::allocator<class string > >::const_iterator' to 'class std::_Tree<class
string,struct std::pair<class string const ,class string >,struct
NicknameMap::_Kfn,struct std::less<class string >,class std::allocator<class
string > >::iterator'
```

No constructor could take the source type, or constructor overload resolution was ambiguous

This message is shorter, but not much clearer. We need to do something with _Tree. Because _Tree is an implementation-specific template, the only way to know the meaning of its template parameters is to read the source code, and there's no reason to go rummaging through implementation-specific source code if we don't have to. Let's try simply replacing all the stuff passed to _Tree with SOMETHING to see what we get. This is the result:

```
example.cpp(17) : error C2440: 'initializing' : cannot convert from 'class
std::_Tree<SOMETHING>::const_iterator' to 'class
std::_Tree<SOMETHING>::iterator'
```

No constructor could take the source type, or constructor overload resolution was ambiguous

This is something we can work with. The compiler is complaining that we're trying to convert some kind of const_iterator into an iterator, a clear violation of const correctness. Let's look again at the offending code, where I've highlighted the line raising the compiler's ire:

```
class NiftyEmailProgram {
private:
  typedef map<string, string> NicknameMap;

  NicknameMap nicknames;

public:

  ...
  void showEmailAddress(const string& nickname) const;
};

void NiftyEmailProgram::showEmailAddress(const string& nickname) const
{
  ...
  NicknameMap::iterator i = nicknames.find(nickname);
  if (i != nicknames.end()) ...
  ...
}
```

The only interpretation that makes any sense is that we're trying to initialize i (which is an iterator) with a const_iterator returned from map::find. That seems odd, because we're calling find on nicknames, and nicknames is a non-const object. find should thus return a non-const iterator.

Look again. Yes, nicknames is declared as a non-const map, but show-EmailAddress is a *const* member function, and inside a const member function, all non-static data members of the class become const! Inside showEmailAddress, nicknames *is* a const map. Suddenly the error message makes sense. We're trying to generate an iterator into a map we've promised not to modify. To fix the problem, we must either make i a const_iterator or we must make showEmailAddress a non-const member function. Both solutions are probably less challenging than ferreting out the meaning of the error message.

In this Item, I've shown textual substitutions to reduce the complexity of error messages, but once you've practiced a little, you'll be able to perform the substitutions in your head most of the time. I'm no musician (I have trouble turning on the radio), but I'm told that good musicians can sight-read several bars at a glance; they don't need to look at individual notes. Experienced STL programmers develop a similar skill. They can internally translate things like std::basic_string<char,struct std::char_traits<char>,class std::allocator<char> > into string without thinking about it. You, too, will develop this skill, but until you do, remember that you can almost always reduce compiler diagnostics to something comprehensible by replacing lengthy template-based type names with shorter mnemonics. In many cases, all you have to do is replace typedef expansions with typedef names you're already using. That's what we did when we replaced std::map<class string,class string,struct std::less<class string >,class std::allocator<class string > > with NicknameMap.

Here are a few other hints that should help you make sense of STL-related compiler messages:

- For vector and string, iterators are usually pointers, so compiler diagnostics will likely refer to pointer types if you've made a mistake with an iterator. For example, if your source code refers to vector<double>::iterators, compiler messages will almost certainly mention double* pointers. (An exception is when you're using the STL implementation from STLport and you're running in debug mode. In that case, vector and string iterators are not pointers. For more on STLport and its debug mode, turn to Item 50.)

- Messages mentioning back_insert_iterator, front_insert_iterator, or insert_iterator almost always mean you've made a mistake calling back_inserter, front_inserter, or inserter, respectively. (back_inserter returns an object of type back_insert_iterator, front_inserter returns an object of type front_insert_iterator, and inserter returns an object of type insert_iterator. For information on the use of these inserters, consult Item 30.) If you didn't call these functions, some function you called (directly or indirectly) did.

- Similarly, if you get a message mentioning binder1st or binder2nd, you've probably made a mistake using bind1st or bind2nd. (bind1st returns an object of type binder1st, and bind2nd returns an object of type binder2nd.)

- Output iterators (e.g., ostream_iterators, ostreambuf_iterators (see Item 29), and the iterators returned from back_inserter, front_inserter, and inserter) do their outputting or inserting work inside assignment operators, so if you've made a mistake with one of these iterator types, you're likely to get a message complaining about something inside an assignment operator you've never heard of. To see what I mean, try compiling this code:

```
vector<string*> v;                          // try to print a container
copy(v.begin(), v.end(),                    // of string* pointers as
    ostream_iterator<string>(cout, "\n"));  // string objects
```

- If you get an error message originating from inside the implementation of an STL algorithm (i.e., the source code giving rise to the error is in <algorithm>), there's probably something wrong with the types you're trying to use with that algorithm. For example, you may be passing iterators of the wrong category. To see how such usage errors are reported, edify (and amuse!) yourself by feeding this to your compilers:

```
list<int>::iterator i1, i2;          // pass bidirectional iterators to
sort(i1, i2);                        // an algorithm requiring random
                                     // access iterators
```

- If you're using a common STL component like vector, string, or the for_each algorithm, and a compiler says it has no idea what you're talking about, you've probably failed to #include a required header file. As Item 48 explains, this problem can befall code that has been compiling smoothly for quite some time if you port it to a new platform.

Item 50: Familiarize yourself with STL-related web sites.

The Internet is rife with STL information. Ask your favorite search engine to look for "STL", and it's sure to return hundreds of links, some of which may actually be relevant. For most STL programmers, however, no searching is necessary. The following sites are likely to rise to the top of almost everybody's most-frequently-used list:

- **The SGI STL site**, http://www.sgi.com/tech/stl/.
- **The STLport site**, http://www.stlport.org/.
- **The Boost site**, http://www.boost.org/.

What follows are brief descriptions of why these sites are worth book-marking.

The SGI STL Web Site

SGI's STL web site tops the list, and for good reason. It offers comprehensive documentation on every component of the STL. For many programmers, this site is their on-line reference manual, regardless of which STL platform they are using. (The reference documentation was put together by Matt Austern, who later extended and polished it for his *Generic Programming and the STL* [4].) The material here covers more than just the STL components themselves. *Effective STL*'s discussion of thread safety in STL containers (see Item 12), for example, is based on the treatment of the topic at the SGI STL web site.

The SGI site offers something else for STL programmers: a freely downloadable implementation of the STL. This implementation has been ported to only a handful of compilers, but the SGI distribution is also the basis for the widely ported STLport distribution, about which I write more in a moment. Furthermore, the SGI implementation of the STL offers a number of nonstandard components that can make STL programming even more powerful, flexible, and fun. Foremost among these are the following:

- The **hashed associative containers** hash_set, hash_multiset, hash_map, and hash_multimap. For more information about these containers, turn to Item 25.

- A **singly linked list container**, slist. This is implemented as you'd imagine, and iterators point to the list nodes you'd expect them to point to. Unfortunately, this makes it expensive to implement the insert and erase member functions, because both require adjustment of the next pointer of the node *preceding* the node pointed to by the iterator. In a doubly linked list (such as the standard list container), this isn't a problem, but in a singly linked list, going "back" one node is a linear-time operation. For SGI's slist, insert and erase take linear instead of constant time, a considerable drawback. SGI addresses the problem through the nonstandard (but constant-time) member functions insert_after and erase_after. Notes SGI,

  > If you find that insert_after and erase_after aren't adequate for your needs and that you often need to use insert and erase in the middle of the list, you should probably use list instead of slist.

  Dinkumware also offers a singly linked list container called slist, but it uses a different iterator implementation that preserves the constant-time performance of insert and erase. For more information on Dinkumware, consult Appendix B.

- A **string-like container for very large strings**. The container is called rope, because a rope is a heavy-duty string, don't you see? SGI describes ropes this way:

  > Ropes are a scalable string implementation: they are designed for efficient operations that involve the string as a whole. Operations such as assignment, concatenation, and substring take time that is nearly independent of the length of the string. Unlike C strings, ropes are a reasonable representation for very long strings, such as edit buffers or mail messages.

  Under the hood, ropes are implemented as trees of reference-counted substrings, and each substring is stored as a char array. One interesting aspect of the rope interface is that the begin and

end member functions always return const_iterators. This is to dis-
courage clients from performing operations that change individual
characters. Such operations are expensive. ropes are optimized for
actions that involve entire strings (e.g., assignment, concatenation, and taking substrings, as mentioned above); single-character
operations perform poorly.

- A variety of **nonstandard function objects and adapters**. The
original HP STL implementation included more functor classes
than made it into standard C++. Two of the more widely missed by
old-time STL hackers are select1st and select2nd, because they are
so useful for working with maps and multimaps. Given a pair,
select1st returns its first component and select2nd returns its second. These nonstandard functor class templates can be used as
follows:

```
map<int, string> m;

...

// write all the map keys to cout
transform(m.begin(), m.end(),
          ostream_iterator<int>(cout, "\n"),
          select1st<map<int, string>::value_type>());

// create a vector and copy all the values in the map into it
vector<string> v;
transform(m.begin(), m.end(), back_inserter(v),
          select2nd<map<int, string>::value_type>());
```

As you can see, select1st and select2nd make it easy to use algorithm calls in places where you might otherwise have to write your
own loops (see Item 43), but, if you use these functors, the fact
that they are nonstandard leaves you open to the charge that you
are writing unportable and unmaintainable code (see Item 47).
Diehard STL aficionados don't care. They consider it an injustice
that select1st and select2nd didn't make it into the Standard in the
first place.

Other nonstandard function objects that are part of the SGI implementation include identity, project1st, project2nd, compose1 and
compose2. To find out what these do, you'll have to visit the web
site, though you'll find an example use of compose2 on page 187 of
this book. By now, I hope it's clear that visiting the SGI web site
will certainly be rewarding.

SGI's library implementation goes beyond the STL. Their goal is the
development of a complete implementation of the standard C++
library, except for the parts inherited from C. (SGI assumes you

already have a standard C library at your disposal.) As a result, another noteworthy download available from SGI is an implementation of the C++ iostreams library. As you might expect, this implementation integrates well with SGI's implementation of the STL, but it also features performance that's superior to that of many iostream implementations that ship with C++ compilers.

The STLport Web Site

STLport's primary selling point is that it offers a modified version of SGI's STL implementation (including iostreams, etc.) that's been ported to more than 20 compilers. Like SGI's library, STLport's is available for free download. If you're writing code that has to work on multiple platforms, you may be able to save yourself a wheelbarrow of grief by standardizing on the STLport implementation and using it with all your compilers.

Most of STLport's modifications to SGI's code base focus on improved portability, but STLport's STL is also the only implementation I know that offers a "debug mode" to help detect improper use of the STL — uses that compile but lead to undefined runtime behavior. For example, Item 30 uses this example in its discussion of the common mistake of writing beyond the end of a container:

```
int transmogrify(int x);                // this function produces
                                         // some new value from x

vector<int> values;

...                                      // put data into values

vector<int> results;
transform( values.begin(), values.end(),     // this will attempt to
           results.end(),                     // write beyond the
           transmogrify);                     // end of results!
```

This will compile, but when run, it yields undefined results. If you're lucky, something horrible will happen inside the call to transform, and debugging the problem will be relatively straightforward. If you're not lucky, the call to transform will trash data somewhere in your address space, but you won't discover that until later. At that point, determining the cause of the memory corruption will be — shall we say? — *challenging*.

STLport's debug mode all but eliminates the challenge. When the above call to transform is executed, the following message is generated (assuming STLport is installed in the directory C:\STLport):

```
C:\STLport\stlport\stl\debug\_iterator.h:265 STL assertion failure :
_Dereferenceable(*this)
```

The program then stops, because STLport debug mode calls abort if it encounters a usage error. If you'd prefer to have an exception thrown instead, you can configure STLport to do things your way.

Admittedly, the above error message isn't as clear as it might be, and it's unfortunate that the reported file and line correspond to the location of the internal STL assertion instead of the line calling transform, but this is still a lot better than running past the call to transform, then trying to figure out why your data structures are corrupt. With STLport's debug mode, all you need to do fire up your debugger and walk the call stack back into the code you wrote, then determine what you did wrong. Finding the offending source line is generally not a problem.

STLport's debug mode detects a variety of common errors, including passing invalid ranges to algorithms, attempting to read from an empty container, using an iterator from one container as the argument to a second container's member function, etc. It accomplishes this magic by having iterators and their containers track one another. Given two iterators, it's thus possible to check to see if they come from the same container, and when a container is modified, it's possible to invalidate the appropriate set of iterators.

Because STLport uses special iterator implementations in debug mode, iterators for vector and string are class objects instead of raw pointers. Hence, using STLport and compiling in debug mode is a good way to make sure that nobody is getting sloppy about the difference between pointers and iterators for these container types. That alone may be reason enough to give STLport's debug mode a try.

The Boost Web Site

In 1997, when the closing bell rang on the process that led to the International Standard for C++, some people were disappointed that library features they'd advocated hadn't made the cut. Some of these people were members of the Committee itself, so they set out to lay the foundation for additions to the standard library during the second round of standardization. The result is Boost, a web site whose mission is to "provide free, peer-reviewed, C++ libraries. The emphasis is on portable libraries which work well with the C++ Standard Library." Behind the mission is a motive:

> To the extent a library becomes "existing practice", the likelihood increases that someone will propose it for future standardization. Submitting a library to Boost.org is one way to establish existing practice... .

In other words, Boost offers itself as a vetting mechanism to help separate the sheep from the goats when it comes to potential additions to the standard C++ library. This is a worthy service, and we should all be grateful.

Another reason to be grateful is the collection of libraries you'll find at Boost. I won't attempt to describe them all here, not least because new ones will doubtless have been added by the time you read these words. For STL users, however, two kinds of libraries are particularly relevant. The first is the smart pointer library featuring shared_ptr, the template for reference-counted smart pointers that, unlike the standard library's auto_ptr, may safely be stored in STL containers (see Item 8). Boost's smart pointer library also offers shared_array, a reference-counted smart pointer for dynamically allocated arrays, but Item 13 argues that dynamically allocated arrays are inferior to vectors and strings, and I hope you find its argument persuasive.

Boost's second attraction for STL fans is its bevy of STL-related function objects and associated facilities. These libraries comprise a fundamental redesign and reimplementation of the ideas behind STL function objects and adapters, and the results eliminate a host of restrictions that artificially limit the utility of the standard functors. As an example of such a restriction, you'll find that if you try to use bind2nd with mem_fun or mem_fun_ref (see Item 41) to bind an object to a member function's parameter and that member function takes its parameter by reference, your code is unlikely to compile. You'll find the same if you try to use not1 or not2 with ptr_fun and a function declaring a by-reference parameter. The cause in both cases is that during template instantiation, most STL platforms generate a reference to a reference, and references to references are not legal in C++. (The Standardization Committee is mulling over a change in the Standard to address this matter.) Here's an example of what has become known as "the reference-to-reference problem:"

```
class Widget {
public:
  ...
  int readStream(istream& stream);            // readStream takes
  ...                                          // its parameter by
};                                             // reference
vector<Widget*> vw;

...
```

```
for_each(                                        // most STL platforms
    vw.begin(), vw.end(),                        // try to generate a
    bind2nd(mem_fun(&Widget::readStream), cin)   // reference to a
);                                               // reference in this
                                                 // call; such code
                                                 // won't compile
```

Boost's function objects avoid this and other issues, plus they expand the expressiveness of function objects considerably.

If you're intrigued by the potential of STL function objects and you want to explore it further, hurry over to Boost right away. If you abhor function objects and think they exist only to pacify a vocal minority of Lisp apologists turned C++ programmers, hurry over to Boost anyway. Boost's function object libraries are important, but they make up only a small part of what you'll find at the site.

Bibliography

Most of the publications below are cited in this book, though many citations occur only in the Acknowledgments. Uncited publications are bulleted instead of having a number.

Given the instability of Internet URLs, I hesitated before including them in this bibliography. In the end, I decided that even if a URL is broken by the time you try it, knowing where a document used to reside should help you find it at a different URL.

Things I Wrote

[1] Scott Meyers, *Effective C++: 50 Specific Ways to Improve Your Programs and Designs* (second edition), Addison-Wesley, 1998, ISBN 0-201-92488-9. Also available on *Effective C++ CD* (see below).

[2] Scott Meyers, *More Effective C++: 35 New Ways to Improve Your Programs and Designs*, Addison-Wesley, 1996, ISBN 0-201-63371-X. Also available on *Effective C++ CD* (see below).

- Scott Meyers, *Effective C++ CD: 85 Specific Ways to Improve Your Programs and Designs*, Addison-Wesley, 1999, ISBN 0-201-31015-5. Contains both books above, several related magazine articles, and several electronic publishing innovations. To experiment with the CD, visit http://meyerscd.awl.com/. To read about its innovations, check out http://zing.ncsl.nist.gov/hf-web/proceedings/meyers-jones/ and http://www.microsoft.com/Mind/1099/browsing/browsing.htm.

Things I Didn't Write (But Wish I Had)

[3] Nicolai M. Josuttis, *The C++ Standard Library: A Tutorial and Reference*, Addison-Wesley, 1999, ISBN 0-201-37926-0. An indispensable book. Every C++ programmer should have ready access to a copy.

[4]   Matthew H. Austern, *Generic Programming and the STL*, Addison-Wesley, 1999, ISBN 0-201-30956-4. This book is essentially a printed version of the material at the SGI STL Web Site, http://www.sgi.com/tech/stl/.

[5]   ISO/IEC, *International Standard, Programming Languages — C++*, Reference Number ISO/IEC 14882:1998(E), 1998. The official document describing C++. Available in PDF for US$18 from ANSI at http://webstore.ansi.org/ansidocstore/default.asp.

[6]   Erich Gamma, Richard Helm, Ralph Johnson, and John Vlissides, *Design Patterns: Elements of Reusable Object-Oriented Software*, Addison-Wesley, 1995, ISBN 0-201-63361-2. Also available as *Design Patterns CD*, Addison-Wesley, 1998, ISBN 0-201-63498-8. The definitive book on design patterns. Every practicing C++ programmer should be familiar with the patterns described here and should have easy access to the book or the CD.

[7]   Bjarne Stroustrup, *The C++ Programming Language* (third edition), Addison-Wesley, 1997, ISBN 0-201-88954-4. The "resource acquisition is initialization" idiom I mention in Item 12 is discussed in section 14.4.1 of this book, and the code I refer to in Item 36 is on page 530.

[8]   Herb Sutter, *Exceptional C++: 47 Engineering Puzzles, Programming Problems, and Solutions*, Addison-Wesley, 2000, ISBN 0-201-61562-2. An exemplary complement to my *Effective* books, I'd laud this even if Herb hadn't asked me to write the Foreword for it.

[9]   Herb Sutter, *More Exceptional C++: 40 More Engineering Puzzles, Programming Problems, and Solutions*, Addison-Wesley, scheduled for publication in 2001, tentative ISBN 0-201-70434-X. Based on the draft I've seen, this looks to be every bit as good as its predecessor [8].

[10] Dov Bulka and David Mayhew, *Efficient C++: Performance Programming Techniques*, Addison-Wesley, 2000, ISBN 0-201-37950-3. The only book devoted to efficiency in C++, hence the best.

[11] Matt Austern, "How to Do Case-Insensitive String Comparison," *C++ Report*, May 2000. This article is so useful, it's reproduced as Appendix A of this book.

[12]   Herb Sutter, "When Is a Container Not a Container?," *C++ Report*, May 1999. Available at http://www.gotw.ca/publications/mill09.htm. Revised and updated as Item 6 in *More Exceptional C++* [9].

[13]   Herb Sutter, "Standard Library News: sets and maps," *C++ Report*, October 1999. Available at http://www.gotw.ca/publications/mill11.htm. Revised and updated as Item 8 in *More Exceptional C++* [9].

[14]   Nicolai M. Josuttis, "Predicates vs. Function Objects," *C++ Report*, June 2000.

[15]   Matt Austern, "Why You Shouldn't Use set — and What to Use Instead," *C++ Report*, April 2000.

[16]   P. J. Plauger, "Hash Tables," *C/C++ Users Journal*, November 1998. Describes the Dinkumware approach to hashed containers (discussed in Item 25) and how it differs from competing designs.

[17]   Jack Reeves, "STL Gotcha's," *C++ Report*, January 1997. Available at http://www.bleading-edge.com/Publications/C++Report/v9701/abstract.htm.

[18]   Jack Reeves, "Using Standard string in the Real World, Part 2," *C++ Report*, January 1999. Available at http://www.bleading-edge.com/Publications/C++Report/v9901/abstract.htm.

[19]   Andrei Alexandrescu, "Traits: The else-if-then of Types," *C++ Report*, April 2000. Available at http://www.creport.com/html/from_pages/view_recent_articles_c.cfm?ArticleID=402.

[20]   Herb Sutter, "Optimizations That Aren't (In a Multithreaded World)," *C/C++ Users Journal*, June 1999. Available at http://www.gotw.ca/publications/optimizations.htm. Revised and updated as Item 16 in *More Exceptional C++* [9].

[21]   The SGI STL web site, http://www.sgi.com/tech/stl/. Item 50 summarizes the material at this important site. The page on thread safety in STL containers (which motivated Item 12) is at http://www.sgi.com/tech/stl/thread_safety.html.

[22]   The Boost web site, http://www.boost.org/. Item 50 summarizes the material at this important site.

[23]   Nicolai M. Josuttis, "User-Defined Allocator," http://www.josuttis.com/cppcode/allocator.html. This page is part of the web site for Josuttis' excellent book on C++'s standard library [3].

[24] Matt Austern, "The Standard Librarian: What Are Allocators Good For?," *C/C++ Users Journal*'s C++ Experts Forum (an on-line extension to the magazine), November 2000, http://www.cuj.com/experts/1812/austern.htm. Good information on allocators is hard to come by. This column complements the material in Items 10 and 11. It also includes a sample allocator implementation.

[25] Klaus Kreft and Angelika Langer, "A Sophisticated Implementation of User-Defined Inserters and Extractors," *C++ Report*, February 2000.

[26] Leor Zolman, "An STL Error Message Decryptor for Visual C++," *C/C++ Users Journal*, July 2001. This article and the software it describes are available at http://www.bdsoft.com/tools/stlfilt.html.

[27] Bjarne Stroustrup, "Sixteen Ways to Stack a Cat," *C++ Report*, October 1990. Available at http://www.csdn.net/dev/C&C++/Document/Stackcat.pdf.

- Herb Sutter, "Guru of the Week #74: Uses and Abuses of vector," September 2000, http://www.gotw.ca/gotw/074.htm. This quiz (and accompanying solution) does a good job of making you think about such vector-related issues as size vs. capacity (see Item 14), but it also discusses why algorithm calls are often superior to hand-written loops (see Item 43).

- Matt Austern, "The Standard Librarian: Bitsets and Bit Vectors?," *C/C++ Users Journal*'s C++ Experts Forum (an on-line extension to the magazine), May 2001, http://www.cuj.com/experts/1905/austern.htm. This article provides information on bitsets and how they compare to vector<bool>, topics I briefly examine in Item 18.

Things I Had To Write (But Wish I Hadn't)

- The *Effective C++* Errata List, http://www.aristeia.com/BookErrata/ec++2e-errata.html.

[28] The *More Effective C++* Errata List, http://www.aristeia.com/BookErrata/mec++-errata.html.

- The *Effective C++ CD* Errata List, http://www.aristeia.com/BookErrata/cd1e-errata.html.

[29] The *More Effective C++* auto_ptr Update page, http://www.awl.com/cseng/titles/0-201-63371-X/auto_ptr.html.

Locales and Case-Insensitive String Comparisons

Item 35 explains how to use mismatch and lexicographical_compare to implement case-insensitive string comparisons, but it also points out that a truly general solution to the problem must take locales into account. This book is about the STL, not internationalization, so I have next to nothing to say about locales. However, Matt Austern, author of *Generic Programming and the STL* [4], addressed the locale aspects of case-insensitive string comparison in a column in the May 2000 *C++ Report* [11]. In the interest of telling the whole story on this important topic, I am pleased to reprint his column here, and I am grateful to Matt and to 101communications for granting me permission to do so.

How to Do Case-Insensitive String Comparison

by Matt Austern

If you've ever written a program that uses strings (and who hasn't?), chances are you've sometimes needed to treat two strings that differ only by case as if they were identical. That is, you've needed comparisons — equality, less than, substring matches, sorting — to disregard case. And, indeed, one of the most frequently asked questions about the Standard C++ Library is how to make strings case insensitive. This question has been answered many times. Many of the answers are wrong.

First of all, let's dispose of the idea that you should be looking for a way to write a case-insensitive string class. Yes, it's technically possible, more or less. The Standard Library type std::string is really just an alias for the template std::basic_string<char, std::char_traits<char>, std::allocator<char> >. It uses the traits parameter for all comparisons, so, by providing a traits parameter with equality and less than redefined appropriately, you can instantiate basic_string in such a way so that the < and == operators are case insensitive. You can do it, but it isn't worth the trouble.

- *You won't be able to do I/O*, at least not without a lot of pain. The I/O classes in the Standard Library, like std::basic_istream and std::basic_ostream, are templatized on character type and traits just like std::basic_string is. (Again, std::ostream is just an alias for std::basic_ostream<char, char_traits<char> >.) The traits parameters have to match. If you're using std::basic_string<char, my_traits_class> for your strings, you'll have to use std::basic_ostream<char, my_traits_class> for your stream output. You won't be able to use ordinary stream objects like cin and cout.

- *Case insensitivity isn't about an object, it's about how you use an object.* You might very well need to treat a string as case-sensitive in some contexts and case-insensitive in others. (Perhaps depending on a user-controlled option.) Defining separate types for those two uses puts an artificial barrier between them.

- *It doesn't quite fit.* Like all traits classes,[†] char_traits is small, simple, and stateless. As we'll see later in this column, proper case-insensitive comparisons are none of those things.

- *It isn't enough.* Even if all of basic_string's own member functions were case insensitive, that still wouldn't help when you need to use nonmember generic algorithms like std::search and std::find_end. It also wouldn't help if you decided, for reasons of efficiency, to change from a container of basic_string objects to a string table.

A better solution, one that fits more naturally into the design of the Standard Library, is to ask for case-insensitive comparison when that's what you need. Don't bother with member functions like string::find_first_of and string::rfind; all of them duplicate functionality that's already there in nonmember generic algorithms. The generic algorithms, meanwhile, are flexible enough to accommodate case-insensitive strings. If you need to sort a collection of strings in case-insensitive order, for example, all you have to do is provide the appropriate comparison function object:

```
std::sort(C.begin(), C.end(), compare_without_case);
```

The remainder of this column will be about how to write that function object.

A first attempt

There's more than one way to alphabetize words. The next time you're in a bookstore, check how the authors' names are arranged: does

---

† See Andrei Alexandrescu's column in the April 2000 *C++ Report* [19].

Mary McCarthy come before Bernard Malamud, or after? (It's a matter of convention, and I've seen it done both ways.) The simplest kind of string comparison, though, is the one we all learned in elementary school: lexicographic or "dictionary order" comparison, where we build up string comparison from character-by-character comparison.

Lexicographic comparison may not be suitable for specialized applications (no single method is; a library might well sort personal names and place names differently), but it's suitable much of the time and it's what string comparison means in C++ by default. Strings are sequences of characters, and if x and y are of type std::string, the expression x < y is equivalent to the expression

```
std::lexicographical_compare(x.begin(), x.end(), y.begin(), y.end()).
```

In this expression, lexicographical_compare compares individual characters using operator<, but there's also a version of lexicographical_compare that lets you choose your own method of comparing characters. That other version takes five arguments, not four; the last argument is a function object, a Binary Predicate that determines which of two characters should precede the other. All we need in order to use lexicographical_compare for case-insensitive string comparison, then, is to combine it with a function object that compares characters without regard to case.

The general idea behind case-insensitive comparison of characters is to convert both characters to upper-case and compare the results. Here's the obvious translation of that idea into a C++ function object, using a well known function from the standard C library:

```
struct lt_nocase
  : public std::binary_function<char, char, bool> {

  bool operator()(char x, char y) const {
    return std::toupper(static_cast<unsigned char>(x)) <
           std::toupper(static_cast<unsigned char>(y));
  }
};
```

"For every complex problem there is a solution that is simple, neat, and wrong." People who write books about C++ are fond of this class, because it makes a nice, simple example. I'm as guilty as anyone else; I use it in my book a half dozen times. It's almost right, but that's not good enough. The problem is subtle.

Here's one example where you can begin to see the problem:

```
int main()
{
  const char* s1 = "GEW\334RZTRAMINER";
  const char* s2 = "gew\374rztraminer";
  printf("s1 = %s, s2 = %s\n", s1, s2);

  printf("s1 < s2: %s\n",
         std::lexicographical_compare(s1, s1 + 14, s2, s2 + 14, lt_nocase())
         ? "true" : "false");
}
```

You should try this out on your system. On my system (a Silicon Graphics O2 running IRIX 6.5), here's the output:

```
s1 = GEWÜRZTRAMINER, s2 = gewürztraminer
s1 < s2: true
```

Hm, how odd. If you're doing a case-insensitive comparison, shouldn't "gewürztraminer" and "GEWÜRZTRAMINER" be the same? And now a slight variation: if you insert the line

```
setlocale(LC_ALL, "de");
```

just before the printf statement, suddenly the output changes:

```
s1 = GEWÜRZTRAMINER, s2 = gewürztraminer
s1 < s2: false
```

Case-insensitive string comparison is more complicated than it looks. This seemingly innocent program depends crucially on something most of us would prefer to ignore: locales.

Locales

A char is really nothing more than a small integer. We can choose to interpret a small integer as a character, but there's nothing universal about that interpretation. Should some particular number be interpreted as a letter, a punctuation mark, or a nonprinting control character?

There's no single right answer, and it doesn't even make a difference as far as the core C and C++ languages are concerned. A few library functions need to make those distinctions: isalpha, for example, which determines whether a character is a letter, and toupper, which converts lowercase letters to uppercase and does nothing to uppercase letters or to characters that aren't letters. All of that depends on local cultural and linguistic conventions: distinguishing between letters and nonletters means one thing in English, another thing in Swedish. Conversion from lower to upper case means something different in the Roman alphabet than in the Cyrillic, and means nothing at all in Hebrew.

By default the character manipulation functions work with a character set that's appropriate for simple English text. The character '\374' isn't affected by toupper because it isn't a letter; it may look like ü when it's printed on some systems, but that's irrelevant for a C library routine that's operating on English text. There is no ü character in the ASCII character set. The line

```
setlocale(LC_ALL, "de");
```

tells the C library to start operating in accordance with German conventions. (At least it does on IRIX. Locale names are not standardized.) There is a character ü in German, so toupper changes ü to Ü.

If this doesn't make you nervous, it should. While toupper may look like a simple function that takes one argument, it also depends on a global variable—worse, a hidden global variable. This causes all of the usual difficulties: a function that uses toupper potentially depends on every other function in the entire program.

This can be disastrous if you're using toupper for case-insensitive string comparison. What happens if you've got an algorithm that depends on a list being sorted (binary_search, say), and then a new locale causes the sort order to change out from under it? Code like this isn't reusable; it's barely usable. You can't use it in libraries—libraries get used in all sorts of programs, not just programs that never call setlocale. You might be able to get away with using it in a large program, but you'll have a maintenance problem: maybe you can prove that no other module ever calls setlocale, but can you prove that no other module in next year's version of the program will call setlocale?

There's no good solution to this problem in C. The C library has a single global locale, and that's that. There is a solution in C++.

Locales in C++

A locale in the C++ Standard Library isn't global data buried deep within the library implementation. It's an object of type std::locale, and you can create it and pass it to functions just like any other object. You can create a locale object that represents the usual locale, for example, by writing

```
std::locale L = std::locale::classic();,
```

or you can create a German locale by writing

```
std::locale L("de");.
```

(As in the C library, names of locales aren't standardized. Check your implementation's documentation to find out what named locales are available.)

Locales in C++ are divided into *facets*, each of which handles a different aspect of internationalization, and the function std::use_facet extracts a specific facet from a locale object.[†] The ctype facet handles character classification, including case conversion. Finally, then, if c1 and c2 are of type char, this fragment will compare them in a case-insensitive manner that's appropriate to the locale L.

```
const std::ctype<char>& ct = std::use_facet<std::ctype<char> >(L);
bool result = ct.toupper(c1) < ct.toupper(c2);
```

There's also a special abbreviation: you can write

```
std::toupper(c, L),
```

which (if c is of type char) means the same thing as

```
std::use_facet<std::ctype<char> >(L).toupper(c).
```

It's worth minimizing the number of times you call use_facet, though, because it can be fairly expensive.

Just as lexicographical comparison isn't appropriate for all applications, so character-by-character case conversion isn't always appropriate. (In German, for example, the lowercase letter "ß" corresponds to the uppercase sequence "SS".) Unfortunately, however, character-by-character case conversion is all we've got. Neither the C nor the C++ standard library provides any form of case conversion that works with anything more than one character at a time. If this restriction is unacceptable for your purposes, then you're outside the scope of the standard library.

A digression: another facet

If you're already familiar with locales in C++, you may have thought of another way to perform string comparisons: The collate facet exists precisely to encapsulate details of sorting, and it has a member function with an interface much like that of the C library function strcmp. There's even a little convenience feature: if L is a locale object, you can compare two strings by writing L(x, y) instead of going through the nuisance of calling use_facet and then invoking a collate member function.

The "classic" locale has a collate facet that performs lexicographical comparison, just like string's operator< does, but other locales perform

---

[†] Warning: use_facet is a function template whose template parameter appears only in the return type, not in any of the arguments. Calling it uses a language feature called *explicit template argument specification*, and some C++ compilers don't support that feature yet. If you're using a compiler that doesn't support it, your library implementor may have provided a workaround so that you can call use_facet some other way.

whatever kind of comparison is appropriate. If your system happens to come with a locale that performs case-insensitive comparisons for whatever languages you're interested in, you can just use it. That locale might even do something more intelligent than character-by-character comparisons!

Unfortunately, this piece of advice, true as it may be, isn't much help for those of us who don't have such systems. Perhaps someday a set of such locales may be standardized, but right now they aren't. If someone hasn't already written a case-insensitive comparison function for you, you'll have to write it yourself.

Case-insensitive string comparison

Using ctype, it's straightforward to build case-insensitive string comparison out of case-insensitive character comparison. This version isn't optimal, but at least it's correct. It uses essentially the same technique as before: compare two strings using lexicographical_compare, and compare two characters by converting both of them to uppercase. The time, though, we're being careful to use a locale object instead of a global variable. (As an aside, converting both characters to uppercase might not always give the same results as converting both characters to lowercase: There's no guarantee that the operations are inverses. In French, for example, it's customary to omit accent marks on uppercase characters. In a French locale it might be reasonable for toupper to be a lossy conversion; it might convert both 'é' and 'e' to the same uppercase character, 'E'. In such a locale, then, a case-insensitive comparison using toupper will say that 'é' and 'E' are equivalent characters while a case-insensitive comparison using tolower will say that they aren't. Which is the right answer? Probably the former, but it depends on the language, on local customs, and on your application.)

```
struct lt_str_1
  : public std::binary_function<std::string, std::string, bool> {
  struct lt_char {
    const std::ctype<char>& ct;
    lt_char(const std::ctype<char>& c) : ct(c) {}
    bool operator()(char x, char y) const {
      return ct.toupper(x) < ct.toupper(y);
    }
  };
  std::locale loc;
  const std::ctype<char>& ct;
```

```
        lt_str_1(const std::locale& L = std::locale::classic())
          : loc(L), ct(std::use_facet<std::ctype<char> >(loc)) {}

        bool operator()(const std::string& x, const std::string& y) const {
          return std::lexicographical_compare(x.begin(), x.end(),
                                              y.begin(), y.end(),
                                              lt_char(ct));
        }
    };
```

This isn't quite optimal yet; it's slower than it ought to be. The problem is annoying and technical: we're calling toupper in a loop, and the C++ standard requires toupper to make a virtual function call. Some optimizers may be smart enough to move the virtual function overhead out of the loop, but most aren't. Virtual function calls in loops should be avoided.

In this case, avoiding it isn't completely straightforward. It's tempting to think that the right answer is another one of ctype's member functions,

```
        const char* ctype<char>::toupper(char* f, char* l) const,
```

which changes the case of the characters in the range [f, l). Unfortunately, this isn't quite the right interface for our purpose. Using it to compare two strings would require copying both strings to buffers and then converting the buffers to uppercase. Where do those buffers come from? They can't be fixed size arrays (how large is large enough?), but dynamic arrays would require an expensive memory allocation.

An alternative solution is to do the case conversion once for every character, and cache the result. This isn't a fully general solution—it would be completely unworkable, for example, if you were working with 32-bit UCS-4 characters. If you're working with char, though (8 bits on most systems), it's not so unreasonable to maintain 256 bytes of case conversion information in the comparison function object.

```
        struct lt_str_2 :
          public std::binary_function<std::string, std::string, bool> {

          struct lt_char {
            const char* tab;

            lt_char(const char* t) : tab(t) {}

            bool operator()(char x, char y) const {
              return tab[x - CHAR_MIN] < tab[y - CHAR_MIN];
            }
          };

          char tab[CHAR_MAX - CHAR_MIN + 1];
```

```
lt_str_2(const std::locale& L = std::locale::classic()) {
  const std::ctype<char>& ct = std::use_facet<std::ctype<char> >(L);

  for (int i = CHAR_MIN; i <= CHAR_MAX; ++i)
    tab[i - CHAR_MIN] = (char) i;

  ct.toupper(tab, tab + (CHAR_MAX - CHAR_MIN + 1));
}

bool operator()(const std::string& x, const std::string& y) const {
  return std::lexicographical_compare(x.begin(), x.end(),
                                      y.begin(), y.end(),
                                      lt_char(tab));
}

};
```

As you can see, lt_str_1 and lt_str_2 aren't very different. The former
has a character-comparison function object that uses a ctype facet directly, and the latter a character-comparison function object that
uses a table of precomputed uppercase conversions. This might be
slower if you're creating an lt_str_2 function object, using it to compare
a few short strings, and then throwing it away. For any substantial
use, though, lt_str_2 will be noticeably faster than lt_str_1. On my system the difference was more than a factor of two: it took 0.86 seconds
to sort a list of 23,791 words with lt_str_1, and 0.4 with lt_str_2.

What have we learned from all of this?

- A case-insensitive string class is the wrong level of abstraction.
  Generic algorithms in the C++ standard library are parameterized
  by policy, and you should exploit that fact.

- Lexicographical string comparisons are built out of character comparisons. Once you've got a case-insensitive character comparison
  function object, the problem is solved. (And you can reuse that
  function object for comparisons of other kinds of character sequences, like vector<char>, or string tables, or ordinary C strings.)

- Case-insensitive character comparison is harder than it looks. It's
  meaningless except in the context of a particular locale, so a character comparison function object needs to store locale information. If speed is a concern, you should write the function object to
  avoid repeated calls of expensive facet operations.

Correct case-insensitive comparison takes a fair amount of machin-
ery, but you only have to write it once. You probably don't want to
think about locales; most people don't. (Who wanted to think about
Y2K bugs in 1990?) You stand a better chance of being able to ignore
locales if you get locale-dependent code right, though, than if you
write code that glosses over the dependencies.

Remarks on Microsoft's STL Platforms

In the opening pages of this book, I introduced the term *STL platform* to refer to the combination of a particular compiler and a particular implementation of the Standard Template Library. If you are using version 6 or earlier of a Microsoft Visual C++ compiler (i.e., a compiler that ships with version 6 or earlier of Microsoft's Visual Studio), the distinction between a compiler and a library is particularly important, because the compiler is sometimes more capable than the accompanying STL implementation suggests. In this appendix, I describe an important shortcoming of older Microsoft STL platforms and I offer workarounds that can significantly improve your STL experience.

The information that follows is for developers using Microsoft Visual C++ (MSVC) versions 4–6. If you're using Visual C++ .NET, your STL platform doesn't have the problems described below, and you may ignore this appendix.

Member Function Templates in the STL

Suppose you have two vectors of Widgets and you'd like to copy the Widgets in one vector to the end of another. That's easy. Just use vector's range insert function (see Item 5):

```
vector<Widget> vw1, vw2;

...

vw1.insert(vw1.end(), vw2.begin(), vw2.end());        // append to vw1 a copy
                                                      // of the Widgets in vw2
```

If you have a vector and a deque, you do the same thing:

```
vector<Widget> vw;
deque<Widget> dw;

...

vw.insert(vw.end(), dw.begin(), dw.end());            // append to vw a copy
                                                      // of the Widgets in dw
```

In fact, you can do this no matter what the type of the container holding the objects to be copied. Even custom containers work:

```
vector<Widget> vw;
...
list<Widget> lw;
...
vw.insert(vw.begin(), lw.begin(), lw.end());        // prepend to vw a copy
                                                    // of the Widgets in lw

set<Widget> sw;
...
vw.insert(vw.begin(), sw.begin(), sw.end());        // prepend to vw a copy
                                                    // of the Widgets in sw

template<typename T,                                // template for a custom
         typename Allocator = allocator<T> >        // STL-compatible
class SpecialContainer { ... };                     // container

SpecialContainer<Widget> scw;
...
vw.insert(vw.end(), scw.begin(), scw.end());        // append to vw a copy
                                                    // of the Widgets in scw
```

This flexibility is possible because vector's range insert function isn't a function at all. Rather, it's a *member function template* that can be instantiated with *any iterator type* to generate a specific range insert function. For vector, the Standard declares the insert template like this:

```
template <class T, class Allocator = allocator<T> >
class vector {
public:

  ...

  template <class InputIterator>
  void insert(iterator position, InputIterator first, InputIterator last);

  ...

};
```

Each standard container is required to offer this templatized range insert. Similar member function templates are required for the containers' range constructors and for the range form of assign (both of which are discussed in Item 5).

MSVC Versions 4–6

Unfortunately, the STL implementation that ships with MSVC versions 4–6 declares no member function templates. This library was originally developed for MSVC version 4, and that compiler, like most compilers of its day, lacked member function template capabilities. Between MSVC4 and MSVC6, the compiler added support for these templates, but, due to legal proceedings that affected Microsoft without directly involving them, the library remained essentially frozen.

Because the STL implementation shipping with MSVC4–6 was designed for a compiler lacking member function templates, the library's authors approximated the functionality of such templates by replacing each template with a specific function, one that accepted only iterators from the same container type. For insert, for example, the member function template was replaced with this:

```
void insert( iterator position,          // "iterator" is the
             iterator first, iterator last);   // container's iterator type
```

This restricted form of range member functions makes it possible to perform a range insert from a vector<Widget> to a vector<Widget> or from a list<int> to a list<int>, but not from a vector<Widget> to a list<Widget> or from a set<int> to a deque<int>. It's not even possible to do a range insert (or assign or construction) from a vector<long> to a vector<int>, because vector<long>::iterator is not the same type as a vector<int>::iterator. As a result, the following perfectly valid code fails to compile using MSVC4–6:

```
istream_iterator<Widget> begin(cin), end;     // create begin and end
                                              // iterators for reading
                                              // Widgets from cin
                                              // (see Item 6)

vector<Widget> vw(begin, end);                // read cin's Widgets into vw
                                              // (again, see Item 6); won't
                                              // compile with MSVC4-6

list<Widget> lw;
...
lw.assign(vw.rbegin(), vw.rend());            // assign vw's contents to lw
                                              // (in reverse order); won't
                                              // compile with MSVC4-6

SpecialContainer<Widget> scw;
...
scw.insert(scw.end(), lw.begin(), lw.end());  // insert at the end of scw a
                                              // copy of the Widgets in lw;
                                              // won't compile with MSVC4-6
```

So what do you do if you must use MSVC4–6? That depends on the MSVC version you are using and whether you are forced to use the STL implementation that comes with the compiler.

A Workaround for MSVC4–5

Look again at the valid code examples that fail to compile with the STL that accompanies MSVC4–6:

```
vector<Widget> vw(begin, end);          // rejected by the MSVC4-6
                                        // STL implementation

list<Widget> lw;
...
lw.assign(vw.rbegin(), vw.rend());      //also rejected

SpecialContainer<Widget> scw;
...
scw.insert(scw.end(), lw.begin(), lw.end());    // ditto
```

These calls look rather different, but they all fail for the same reason: missing member function templates in the STL implementation. There's a single cure for all of them: use copy and an insert iterator (see Item 30) instead. Here, for example, are the workarounds for the examples above:

```
istream_iterator<Widget> begin(cin), end;

vector<Widget> vw;                      // default-construct vw;
copy(begin, end, back_inserter(vw));    // then copy the
                                        // Widgets in cin into it


list<Widget> lw;
...
lw.clear();                             // eliminate lw's old
copy(vw.rbegin(), vw.rend(), back_inserter(lw));  // Widgets; copy over
                                        // vw's Widgets (in
                                        // reverse order)

SpecialContainer<Widget> scw;
...
copy(lw.begin(), lw.end(),              // copy lw's Widgets to
        inserter(scw, scw.end()));      // the end of scw
```

I encourage you to use these copy-based workarounds with the library that ships with MSVC4–5, but beware! Don't fall into the trap of becoming so comfortable with the workarounds, you forget that they are *workarounds*. As Item 5 explains, using the copy algorithm is almost always inferior to using a range member function, so as soon as you have a chance to upgrade your STL platform to one that supports member function templates, stop using copy in places where range member functions are the proper approach.

An Additional Workaround for MSVC6

You can use the MSVC4–5 workaround with MSVC6, too, but for MSVC6 there is another option. The compilers that are part of MSVC4–5 offer no meaningful support for member function templates, so the fact that the STL implementation lacks them is immaterial. The situation is different with MSVC6, because MSVC6's compiler does support member function templates. It thus becomes reasonable to consider replacing the STL that ships with MSVC6 with an implementation that provides the member function templates the Standard prescribes.

Item 50 explains that both SGI and STLport offer freely downloadable STL implementations, and both of those implementations count the MSVC6 compiler as one with which they'll work. You can also purchase the latest MSVC-compatible STL implementation from Dinkumware. Each option has advantages and disadvantages.

SGI's and STLport's implementations are free, and I suspect you know what that means as regards official support for the software: there isn't any. Furthermore, because SGI and STLport design their libraries to work with a variety of compilers, you will probably have to manually configure their implementations to get the most out of MSVC6. In particular, you may have to explicitly enable support for member function templates, because, working with many compilers as they do, SGI and/or STLport may not enable that by default. You may also have to worry about linking with other MSVC6 libraries (especially DLLs), including things like making sure you use the appropriate builds for threading and debugging, etc.

If that kind of thing scares you, or if you've been known to grumble that you can't afford free software, you may want to look into Dinkumware's replacement library for MSVC6. It's designed to be drop-in compatible with the native MSVC6 STL and to maximize MSVC6's adherence to the Standard as an STL platform. Since Dinkumware authored the STL that ships with MSVC6, there's a decent chance their latest STL implementation really *is* a drop-in replacement. To learn more about Dinkumware STL implementations, visit the company's web site: http://www.dinkumware.com/.

Regardless of whether you choose SGI's, STLport's, or Dinkumware's implementation as an STL replacement, you'll do more than gain an STL with member function templates. You'll also bypass conformance problems in other areas of the library, such as string failing to declare push_back. Furthermore, you'll gain access to useful STL extensions, including hashed containers (see Item 25) and singly linked lists (slists).

SGI's and STLport's implementations also offer a variety of nonstandard functor classes, such as select1st and select2nd (see Item 50).

Even if you're trapped with the STL implementation that ships with MSVC6, it's probably worth your while to visit the Dinkumware web site. That site lists known bugs in the MSVC6 library implementation and explains how to modify your copy of the library to reduce its shortcomings. Needless to say, editing your library headers is something you do at your own risk. If you run into trouble, don't blame me.

Index

The example classes and class templates declared or defined in this book are indexed under *example classes/templates*. The example functions and function templates are indexed under *example functions/templates*.

STL overview in xi
URL for auto_ptr update page for 228
URL for errata list for 228
More Exceptional C++
bibliography entry for 226
multimap
constness of elements 95
find vs. count in 199
find vs. lower_bound in 201
indeterminate traversal order in 87
iterator invalidation in, see iterators,
invalidation
key, casting away constness 99
value_type typedef 108
multiple deletes 64
multiplies 159
multiset
constness of elements 95
corrupting via element modification 97
find vs. count in 199
find vs. lower_bound in 201
indeterminate traversal order in 87
iterator invalidation in, see iterators,
invalidation
keys, modifying 95–100
multithreading
allocators and 54
containers and 58–62
reference counting and 64–65
string and 64–65

N

Naran, Siemel xvi
newsgroups xv
comp.lang.c++.moderated xv
comp.std.c++ xv
microsoft.public.vc.stl xv
node-based containers
see also standard associative containers, list, slist, hashed containers
allocators and 52
clustering in 103
definition of 13
nonstandard containers
see hashed containers, slist, rope
not1 155, 156, 169, 170, 172, 210, 222
adaptability and 170
not2 152, 222
adaptability and 170
nth_element 133–138
nulls, embedded 75, 154
<numeric> 157

O

objects
copying, in containers 20–22
for locking 60
slicing 21–22, 164
temporary, created via casts 98
One True Editor, the, see Emacs
operator new, interface,
vs.allocator::allocate 51
operator() 5
declaring const 168
functor class and 5
inlining and 202
overloading
adaptability and 173
in functor classes 114
operator++, side effects in 45
operator--, forward iterators and 5
operator. ("operator dot") 49
operator<, less and 177–180
operator<<
istream_iterators and 126
sentry objects and 126
whitespace and 126
operator[], vs. insert in map 106–111
optimizations
algorithms and 183
function pointers and 203
inlining and 202
istreambuf_iterators and 127
range insertions and 31
reference counting and 64
small strings and 71
stricmp/strcmpi and 154
to reduce default allocator size 70
ostream, relation to basic_ostream 230
ostream_iterators 216
ostreambuf_iterators 216
efficiency and 127
output iterator, definition of 5
overloading, operator() in functor
classes 114

P

page faults 102, 103
pair, comparison functions for 104
parameters
function objects vs. functions 201–205
pointers to functions 34
type, local classes and 189
parentheses
ignored, around parameter names 33
to distinguish function and object
declarations 35